H. D. THOREAU: A WRITER'S JOURNAL

Selected and Edited with an Introduction

by

LAURENCE STAPLETON

Mary E. Garrett Professor of English, Bryn Mawr College

DOVER PUBLICATIONS, INC.
NEW YORK

Published in Canada by General Publishing Company, Ltd.,
30 Lesmill Road, Don Mills, Toronto, Ontario.

H. D. Thoreau: A Writer's Journal is a new work
published for the first time in 1960 by Dover
Publications, Inc.

The work comprises an Introduction and selections by Laurence Stapleton from the "Walden"
edition of the *Journal of Henry D. Thoreau* published
in 1906 as volumes VII through XX of *The
Writings of Henry David Thoreau.*

International Standard Book Number: 0-486-20678-5
Library of Congress Catalog Card Number: 60-52316

Manufactured in the United States of America

DOVER PUBLICATIONS, INC.
180 Varick Street
New York, N. Y. 10014

FOREWORD

This selection from *The Journal of Henry D. Thoreau* is made on a new principle, growing out of the conviction that it is primarily in his work as a writer that Thoreau attained unity of imagination. I have included many of the longer sequences, hitherto available only in the complete 14-volume edition. In particular, the account of an all-day walk and of an all-night walk show Thoreau experimenting with continuity of observation.

In the latter volumes of the journal, Thoreau is preparing the mood of his intended book on Concord. As many as possible of the passages that suggest the nature of that book have been included here. Finally, the selections demonstrate and in my Introduction I have discussed the resemblances between Thoreau's work and some themes of modern writing. The selections are unified by these major themes and make as nearly as can be a book by Thoreau hitherto unpublished.

The standard or "Walden" edition of the journal was edited by Bradford Torrey and Francis H. Allen, and occupies volumes VII through XX of *The Writings of Henry David Thoreau*, Boston: Houghton Mifflin Company, 1906. I am grateful to the publishers for permission to use the text of this edition. I have given dates of the entries, when available, to facilitate comparison with the complete text. Where entries are undated by Thoreau, I have followed the practice of Mr. Torrey and Mr. Allen in grouping them by the period of years to which the notebooks apparently belong. Where there are omissions in the middle of a passage, they are indicated by an ellipsis. The punctuation of the text follows that of the Walden edition, except that the use of italics to indicate dates and time of day has been made uniform.

L. S.

Bryn Mawr, Pa.
May, 1959

CONTENTS

INTRODUCTION		ix
SELECTED BIBLIOGRAPHY		xxxi
I	SIMPLY SEEING	1
II	WALKING BY NIGHT	41
III	STANDING AT A DISTANCE	81
IV	GOODWIN AND CO.	120
V	DISCOVERING SOMETHING OLD	172
VI	THE MUSQUASH HUNTERS	195
INDEX		229

INTRODUCTION

"Says I to myself"[1]: this, Thoreau resolved, should be the motto of his journal. And he understood that the journal must, therefore, excel in some respects his other writing. By it the sap ascended; in it he grew newness of thought and feeling, and shook off inspiration ill-disposed.

Thoreau's life was an intuitive speaking, a testimony such as we have witnessed in Gandhi or in Schweitzer. How such men live instructs us, even that another individual could not repeat their choices. But while Thoreau could make a simple action suggest a parable, he knew that his calling was that of a writer. To make the discipline of the writer not only a theme but a celebration: for this he kept his journal.

The journal is Thoreau's principal, if not his greatest work. It provided the motif and much of the substance of his books. Yet we must prefer *A Week on the Concord and the Merrimack*, and *Walden*, to any section of the journal with which they may be compared. The significance of the journal is that in it Thoreau practiced: practiced his ways of observing, his laments, his methods of composition, and his sentences.

To be fully aware of the unique worth of the journal we must read it slowly, over a period of time, and read consecutively. A true selection will induce the thoughtful and responsive reader to proceed to an acquaintance with the whole. To learn from Thoreau as a writer, to hear his prophecy—neither identical with nor in conflict with his art—we must be in his company as often as he permits. Thus we may obtain his thought even on those walks when he would allow no companion.

It is time to emancipate Thoreau from transcendentalism and from the concerns he shared with his contemporaries—whether

---

[1]Bradford Torrey and Francis H. Allen (ed.), *The Journal of Henry D. Thoreau* (Boston: Houghton Mifflin Company, 1906), III, 107. Hereafter only the volume and page number will be cited.

with Emerson, the younger Channing, Alcott, or John Brown. The co-existence of these men speaks to us powerfully and we benefit because their association made a difference to the outcome of their lives. But Thoreau has, in addition to these, other affiliations, which connect him with writers since his time—with Virginia Woolf, for instance, or Gerard Manley Hopkins. And the nature of his commitment to his art, the resolve that he would speak first to himself, stands to the modern writer an incorruptible revelation.

Few have so sharply considered the economy of the writer. By the economy of the writer, I mean not merely how he gets a living, but what he decides about the uses of his time when he is not writing. Thoreau perceived early that there were certain uses of his time that he could not afford—either for the sake of money or of being more affable with his neighbors. "In my experience nothing is so opposed to poetry—not crime—as business" (IV, 162). He often wryly commented on the seemingly industrious villagers who thought his sauntering by the river margins or through the woodlots an idle thing. For in these "true paths to perception and enjoyment" (X, 146) his highest energy was employed. "How much, what infinite leisure it requires . . . to appreciate a single phenomenon. You must camp down beside it as if for life, . . . and give yourself wholly to it" (IV, 433). Both the day's excursion and his recording of it braced his mind to overcome the dissipation of attention caused by trivial persons and events (III, 5) of whom there were, and always will be many. He walked "to return to his senses" (II, 110).

Thoreau lived in the way that enabled him to write what he was best fitted to write. The force of his example lies not in the specific solution he achieved for himself, but in the manner of his deciding. Every true writer has both to learn his own discipline, and to learn to live with what he lacks of it. Thoreau was entitled to say to himself, "By poverty I am crystallized" (IX, 246); yet with as much nobility, Emerson could have witnessed, "I am improved by some prosperity." It is not the being poor, or prosperous, that diminishes creative power, but the irrelevant choice or incongruous necessity of either.

Thoreau had chosen relevantly and had no need to doubt. He was not unaware of the cost of having been, "by the want of pecuniary wealth, . . . nailed down to [his] native region so long and steadily" (V, 496-97). He did not conceal his disappointment that his townsmen placed a higher value on what was second-best in him—his surveyor's skill—than on his prophetic teaching. They showed little desire to hear him at the Lyceum. Although he would not have written in order to earn his living as a writer, he would have preferred to have had more manuscripts accepted, to have had sold more than 200 copies of the small edition of his first book. But although he understood, as well as anyone ever can, that the activities of getting a living, so consecrated in our present society, must be secondary to the purpose of a whole human life, he neither failed to support himself nor overlooked the indubitable value to the writer of some task other than writing.

Of the occupations to which at various times he set himself— teaching, handyman extraordinary, pencil manufacturer—that of surveyor proved best. It kept him outdoors where he meant to be. If it compelled him to abandon his lean diet, and eat coarse meals in the usually unrewarding company of farmers, it brought him across the trail of hunters, fishers, tramps, and loafers, in meetings he often prized. Most of all, surveying reinforced the deep, concentrated, instinctive nature of his observation. "The man who is bent upon his work is frequently in the best attitude to observe what is irrelevant to his work" (III, 123). After a long day's surveying in Lincoln and a wait of an hour and a half at the depot for the "cars," Thoreau recorded:

> . . . it is when I have been intently, and it may be laboriously at work, and am somewhat listless or abandoned after it, reposing, that the muse visits me. . . . It is from out the shadow of my toil that I look into the light. (VI, 194)

Here, as respects the glance from one space of sense and feeling into another, Thoreau expresses an essential principle of his habits of observing, as he might read a level of his inner life.

In his philosophy of seeing, no law of the excluded middle impedes his intuitionist logic. The observer is required to be wholly respectful of outward fact, while aware that his presence and the state of his belief impart identity to what he sees.

The veracity of the fact to be ascertained is the primary value not only of that fact but of its successors, to which it is the clue. "If you make the least correct observation of nature this year, you will have occasion to repeat it with illustrations the next, and the season and life itself is prolonged." Observation, like nature itself, is generative, and begins with simply seeing.

> The woman who sits in the house and *sees* is a match for a stirring captain. Those still piercing eyes, as faithfully exercised on their talent, will keep her even with Alexander or Shakespeare. . . . We are as much as we see. Faith is sight and knowledge. . . . The farthest blue streak in the horizon I can see, I may reach before many sunsets. What I saw alters not. . . . (I, 247-48)

As this passage reveals, seeing is an inclusive name for what is far more than any purely optical phenomenon. Thoreau could have said to himself, as Virginia Woolf does to herself, "The look of things has a great power over me."[2] Yet the power of seeing has its own conditions:

> Many an object is not seen, though it falls within the range of our visual ray, because it does not come within the range of our intellectual ray, i.e., we are not looking for it. (IX, 466)

Thus, although what exists to be known does not alter, the discovery of it needs some precedent favour.

> The scarlet oak must, in a sense, be in your eye when you go forth. . . . In my botanical rambles I find that first the idea, or image of a plant occupies my thoughts, though it may at first seem very foreign to this locality, and for some weeks or months I go thinking of it and expecting it unconsciously, and at length I surely see it, and it is henceforth an actual neighbor of mine. This is the history of my finding a score . . . of rare plants. . . . (XI, 285-86)

[2]Virginia Woolf, *A Writer's Diary* (New York: Harcourt, Brace & Co., 1954), p. 131.

Thoreau convinces us that it is not by chance, but by an intention of his mind to the object, his bringing it into the "intellectual ray," that he finds his rarities. Nevertheless, good observation must not be governed by an intent that is set or mechanical or self-willed. A respect for the actual is synonymous with acknowledgment of its mystery. For this reason, I think, Thoreau emphasizes to himself, repeatedly, that it is best to saunter to his task. As, from out the shadow of his toil, he looked into the light, he found that a walk of which little was expected, a walk that had some necessary purpose, might turn out best. To be receptive to his truest sense of things, the observer looks from a detached perspective, both of space and of time—waits for himself, as it were. "So in my botanizing or natural history walks, going for one thing, I get another thing." Many of Thoreau's fulminations against organized research or the habits of the laboratory worker sound callow enough. But at the root of all of them, lies his refusal to allow a utilitarian aim, or even such an attitude, to distort his impressions.

The task, then, as incidental to the observation—the discovery to be foreseen, but not commanded, these are the conditions of attention heeded by Thoreau; and when he had in any interval been distracted from them, he recreated them in his earliest moment of freedom. Observation that is too deliberate disappoints him, and he frequently reminds himself of the advantage to the poet or philosopher or naturalist "of pursuing from time to time some other business than his chosen one,— seeing with the side of the eye" (VIII, 314).

For a similar reason, Thoreau loved certain states of weather as witnessing the never-ceasing individuality of the world. Mist, snow, dew, moonlight, he welcomed not only for themselves, but because they summon the senses to new perception, perception from another point of view. Herein he paid respect to the reserve of nature:

Man cannot afford . . . to look at Nature directly, but only with the side of his eye. He must look through her and beyond her. To look at her is fatal as to look at the head of Medusa. It turns the man of science to stone. (V, 45)

All these means of seeing "with the side of the eye" might be termed modes of reflection; and reflection interested Thoreau greatly, so much so that he found in it the principle of composition itself. The difference between a hillside seen looking straight on, and its reflection, exhibits different angles; when one sees the reflection of a tree, different pieces of sky appear between the branches. Thus Nature avoids repetition. For

> the reflection is never a true copy or repetition of its substance, but a new composition, and this may be the source of its novelty and attractiveness . . . I doubt if you can ever get Nature to repeat herself exactly. (X, 97)

Reflection then, (or a modulation of it, the landscape seen in fog or haze) reveals the infinite variability of nature. Looking at the image of button bushes, in the river, Thoreau sees them appearing against the sky, whereas when they are looked at directly only the meadow or hill stands behind them.

> . . . at twilight [we] dream that the light has gone down into the bosom of the waters; for in the reflection the sky comes up to the very shore or edge and appears to extend under it. . . . *In the reflection you have an infinite number of eyes to see for you and report the aspect of things each from its own point of view.* (XI, 213, italics added)

In the observation itself we must find a means to realize the infinitude of relations that constitute actuality. Reflection is such a means to observe the seemingly familiar in "unsuspected lights and relations" (XI, 293). It is like a rhyme, or metaphor, in nature itself. It impresses us "with a sense of harmony and symmetry, as when you fold a blotted paper and produce regular figures—a dualism which nature loves. What you commonly see is but half" (III, 51).

An interval in time may produce a similar effect. By making two distinct reports of the same event at different times, by recurring to an experience after a day or two, he apprehends it more significantly. "I begin to see such an object when I cease to understand it." Writing itself can be improved by distancing oneself from it in time—even by planning revision without the manuscript at hand:

I find that I can criticise my composition best when I stand at a little distance from it,—when I do not see it, for instance. I make a little chapter of contents which enables me to recall it page by page to my mind. . . . The distraction of surveying enables me rapidly to take new points of view. A day or two surveying is equal to a journey. (VI, 190)

A re-flection, then, or second image in time of the life contained in the composition, afforded a chance of novelty, the possibility of sentences "which do not merely report an old, but make a new, impression . . . not mere repetition, but creation." (II, 418-19).

Thoreau instinctively relished small appearances, for example, the study of lichens—so seemingly minimal and marginal in their existence, as to be informative of "Nature in her everyday mood and dress." The lichenist "has the appetite of the worm that never dies"; he is fitted for the "barrenist and rockiest experience." On a wet day—best for this study—the effect of the lichens is a minor phenomenon of reflection; thus "a little moisture, a fog, or rain, or melted snow makes his wilderness to blossom like the rose" (XI, 440). And a day of low mist in the woods may be counted on to be a good lichen day, since the confined view "compels [the] attention to near objects" (III, 166).

Ice or snow wrote new legends. When a fine rain begins to freeze on twig or culm, Thoreau remarks "a white glaze (reflecting the snow or sky), rhyming with the vegetable core" (XI, 372). Ice is "graphic" (XI, 430) in its structuring. It makes the heavens a road for man; we walk upon the sky. In effect, it reminds us of correspondences in time, as in vision:

How few are aware that in winter, when the earth is covered with snow and ice, . . . the sunset sky is double. The winter is coming when I shall walk the sky. . . . There is an annual light in the darkness of the winter night. (XIII, 141-42)

The love of correspondence here, the interest in reflections, haze, fog, ice, as conditions for scanning the variations that "rhyme" with their precursors, or with more frequently seen, sunlit vistas—has nothing in common with the Platonizing theory of correspondences of which Emerson is the exponent. Thoreau did, like Emerson, have an affinity with seventeenth century writers whose intuitions were magnetized by reading in the "Book of Nature" the hieroglyphics of invisible things. This literary and temperamental filiation has been honored by Mr. Matthiessen's unwinding of it in *American Renaissance*. But in observing the ever-new, the "other half" of any substance shown in its rhymed appearances, reflected in water or apparelled in ice, differently related to surrounding objects in moonlight or in haze, Thoreau is not in search of the idea or archetype of these phenomena. Even more than those seventeenth century writers he most resembles—Henry Vaughan and Sir Thomas Browne— his interest not merely begins with but stays with the particular, the minute, the unseen or unnoticed resemblances or differences among concrete objects. He is a veritable seeker of *thisness;* the individual, unduplicatable object can be discerned in its uniqueness when any seeming repetition of it shows it slightly changed.

Herein Thoreau parts company with Emerson in a way that has been little understood. Emerson's mind passes rapidly from perception to abstraction. He thinks philosophically, though not with a philosopher's purpose; he *feels* as a man would who believed throughout his nature what Plato taught. With Emerson the divining of the idea in the concrete fact is not an outcome of the process of dialectic. It is, rather, the *terra firma* of his temperament, the ground he starts from. To Thoreau, as genius of the wood, such assumptions were of course familiar, and it would seem, from some vague ackowledgments of the "ideal," were not uncongenial. But Thoreau's business was with relatedness: of lichen to rock, disintegrated rock to soil, soil to tree, tree to sky, and himself, a man, to each of these in each phase of change. Individuality is significant alone, it needs analogy to identify it, does not itself merely serve to provide an analogy for themes more abstract.

Here is a major difference in emphasis between Emerson and Thoreau. Thoreau had learned so much from Emerson that he

could advance on his own path emancipated from much that
might have impeded him. Both men, sensitive to and respectful
of realities that evade recognition, use some of the same short-
hand terms: especially *Nature*. But in the direction and quality
of his observation, intent on thisness, *haecceitas*, Thoreau is more
akin to Gerard Manley Hopkins. "Let me not be in haste to
detect the *universal law*, let me see more clearly a particular
instance of it!" (III, 157). Nature depends upon and favours
the individual thing, "strews her nuts and flowers broadcast,
and never collects them into heaps." He follows this statement
by a comment that "A man does not tell us all he has thought
upon truth or beauty at a sitting." This might seem like a neo-
Platonist train of thought, but is not: Thoreau is emphasizing
for the thinking man his discovery of truth at individual moments of time. Essentially, then, the second statement reinforces
the first. And in one of a number of passages contrasting Nature
and Man (counterpoint to his other theme, that "Nature must
be viewed humanly to be viewed at all"), he praises Nature

> *because* she is not man. . . . None of his institutions control or
> pervade her. . . . He makes me wish for another world. *She makes
> me content with this.* (IV, 445, last italics added)

In his ardent pursuit of the uniqueness, particularity, to be
observed in every changing phase, Thoreau markedly resembles Hopkins. An inevitable difference lies between them—
temperamental and artistic. The descriptions of clouds, trees,
shadows, river lights, in Hopkins' *Note-Books* have, as compared
with any similar descriptions in Thoreau's *Journal*, an effect
that is at once more static, more specialized. But in allowing for
dissimilarities of conviction, habit, and opportunity between the
two men, we shall find them to be like explorers of the same
terrain, explorers approaching from different directions and on
tangential lines. On November 17, 1869, Hopkins relates that
after a damp fog

> . . . the trees being drenched with wet a sharp frost that followed in
> the night candied them with ice. Before the sun . . . melted the
> ice . . . I looked at the cedar on the left of the portico and found

every needle edged with a blade of ice made of fine horizontal bars of spars all pointing one way, N. and S. . . . There was also an edging of frost in the clematis . . . and . . . the little bars of which the blades or pieces of frost were made up though they lay all along the hairy threads with which the seed vessels of the clematis are set did not turn with their turnings but lay all in parallels N. and S.[3]

Looking at a lunar halo, Hopkins' eye is alert to a composition of light that he records in language strikingly similar to passages in Thoreau's journal:

The halo was not quite round, . . . what is more it fell in on the nether left hand side to rhyme the moon itself, which was not quite at full. I could not but strongly feel in my fancy the odd instress of this, the moon leaning on her side, as if fallen back, in the cheerful light floor within the ring, after with magical rightness and success tracing round her . . . the steady copy of her own out-line.[4]

Hopkins' notion of "instress" or of "inscape" is more strict and more restricted than Thoreau's freer search for form in his study of reflections, of the rhyming of appearances, and of parallel facts or moments. But where in an occasional entry Hopkins treats inscape casually, one is struck by the closeness of intention:

The chestnuts . . . were a beautiful sight: each spike had its own pitch, yet each followed in its place in the sweep with a deeper and deeper stoop. When the wind tossed them they plunged and crossed one another without losing their inscape. (Observe that motion multiplies inscape only when inscape is discovered . . .)[5]

Words come into Hopkins' mind in figures of sound even when he is writing prose: "in the sweep, with a deeper and deeper stoop . . . tossed and crossed." In language as in seeing he has this innate sense for the *sake* of it, "the sake of things, the being a thing has outside itself, . . . a voice by its echo . . . a body by

[3]Humphry House (ed.), *The Note-Books and Papers of Gerard Manley Hopkins* (New York: Oxford University Press, 1937), p. 125.

[4]*Ibid.*, p. 158.

[5]*Ibid.*, p. 133. Cf. also his observations on freezing ice crystals in wind, etc. (p. 136), the "idiom" of snow (p. 128), and the reflection in the sky of planets (p. 125).

its shadow.''[6] In the structure of verse, that which constitutes it, and lacking which poetry is absent, Hopkins found the fundamental principle to be parallelism:

> But what the character of poetry is will best be found by looking at the structure of verse. The artificial part of poetry, perhaps we shall be right to say all artifice, reduces itself to the principle of parallelism. Only the first kind, that of marked parallelism, is concerned with the structure of verse—in rhythm, the recurrence of a certain sequence of syllables, . . . in alliteration, in assonance and in rhyme. Now the force of this recurrence is to beget a . . . parallelism answering to it in the words or thought. . . . To the marked or abrupt kind of parallelism belong metaphor, simile, parable, and so on, where the effect is sought in likeness of things, and antithesis, contrast, . . . where it is sought in unlikeness.[7]

To the astute generalizing of this principle as a foundation for poetics Thoreau could not have attained; he seemingly did not comprehend the possible structures of verse, or the verse he wrote would have been somewhat better. But his choice of a similar principle as providing, in essence, a transition from nature to art—essential both to the veracity of observation and to the veracity of the statement of it, the "report," puts him on a track going in the same direction. Both were observers of things in their "beautiful changes."[8]

The insight into individuality possessed by both Thoreau and Hopkins is the faith that "Nature is never spent." The form of Hopkins' religion would have been antipathetic to Thoreau, for whom religion is "that which is never spoken" (XI, 113). But as students of all that is not man, all that lies before him, that "shines out, like the shining of shook foil," they are prophets of a concept of nature with which man's freedom is linked. For nature, all the more because not man, reflects him. A true knowledge of Nature is not obtained inhumanely—as by killing a snake (VI, 311). Respect for the freedom of other men enters

---

[6]Claude Colleer Abbott (ed.), *Letters of Gerard Manley Hopkins to Robert Bridges* (London: Oxford University Press, 1935), p. 83.

[7]Hopkins, *op. cit.*, pp. 92-93.

[8]*Ibid.*, p. 140.

our awareness of nature too; and if that freedom is injured, we cannot absent ourselves from knowledge of the loss, and desire to repair it. Although Thoreau wrote that he would not so soon despair of the world for the fragrance of the white water-lily, "notwithstanding slavery, and the cowardice and want of principle in the North" (VI, 352), he looked sternly at such evils when they were in the foreground. "There was a remarkable sunset, I think the 25th of October," he wrote in his journal some three weeks later. "But it was hard for me to see its beauty then, when my mind was filled with Capt. Brown" (XII, 443).

Ultimately, the relation betweeen man and nature is reciprocal. An injury done to man impairs his relation to nature; and an injury done to nature lessens the scope of man. Rarely is it granted to the writer to be a prophet in his art; yet on this theme the writing of Thoreau has prophetic meaning for all Americans today, all others. Where we see daily the bulldozers and earthmovers invading the woodlands and meadows, with no thought taken for the best preservation of the natural contours of the land, we must learn again "to love the crust of earth on which [we] dwell" (X, 258). Many fine lines of the incantations necessary for our new learning are in Hopkins: "Long live the weeds and the wilderness yet!" ("Inversnaid"). But Thoreau is the composer of chorales in their honor. Every town should have a park, he directed, or rather a primitive forest, of five hundred or a thousand acres,

> where a stick should never be cut for fuel, a common possession forever, for instruction and recreation. . . . Let us keep the New World *new*, preserve all the advantages of living in the country. (XII, 387)

In the age of the supermarket, superhighway, and the be-stuccoed acres of superbungalows called ranch houses, these are words of revolutionary comfort and counsel. For in the banishing of the wilderness, the destruction of the country, Thoreau saw human destruction, the diminution of consciousness. This realization prompted his careful notes on the oaks and chestnuts, in the last volumes of his journal, notes on the oldest trees, the trees it takes longest to produce, but which often are first to be destroyed or to become extinct. A man who is contemporary with an oak that has been growing a hundred years, shares some of its past, some of its future. Sometimes the cutting of a tree, he said, "lays waste the air for two centuries" (III, 162-64).

Because he would live in antiquity as well as in the present, in order to sound eternity in the present moment, he would preserve for the future some at least of the woods that were here before the country was discovered. And not at a distance, not remote from our daily living. What makes a township handsome? He answers, "A river, with is waterfalls and meadows, a lake, a hill, a cliff or individual rocks, a forest, and ancient trees standing singly. . . . I do not think him fit to be the founder of a state or even a town who does not foresee the use of these things" (XIV, 304). And, in proclaiming that the top of Mt Washington should not be private property, Thoreau explained that parts of the land should be forever unappropriated, for modesty and for reverence's sake, "or if only to suggest that earth has higher uses than we put her to" (XIV, 305).

Children have a right to know the trees and revel in their colour.

> Blaze away! . . . A village is not complete unless it has these trees to mark the season. . . . Such a village will not . . . work well. . . . Let us have willows for spring, elms for summer, maples and walnuts and tupelos for autumn, evergreens for winter, and oaks for all seasons. An avenue of elms as large as our largest . . . would seem to lead to some admirable place, though only Concord were at the end of it. (XI, 220-21)

Only Concord! Although it had taken him forty years and more to know its six square miles and, as he says, thereby to "acquire his language" (XI, 137), Thoreau did not sentimentalize Concord. He invested it with a universal significance, because he had taken its soundings in time, because he knew it better than its selectmen or census takers, understood how to be a stranger there.

One of Thoreau's most mysterious, indispensable themes is the prehension of time. In bringing the works of antiquity to the test of the present, he seeks the living words that abolish distances in time. But the consideration of antiquity as a whole —of what has disappeared from ken as well as what remains to view—strikes him as melancholy, because "we forget that it had any other future than our present. As if it were not as near to the future as ourselves" (I, 294-95). A modern metaphysician pondering time's complexities, and possible infinities of outcome —a Meade, a McTaggart, or an Alexander—would not have to be dissatisfied with this: Thoreau's contemplation of the multiple futures existing for any slice of the past—and finally the glimpse that they have not all been realized.

In hunting for arrowheads ("one of the regular pursuits of the spring"), he imagines this crop as dragon seed that are to create a race—if from the past, no less new to modern man.

> Like the dragon's teeth, which bore a crop of soldiers, these bear crops of philosophers and poets. . . . Each one yields me a thought. . . . It is humanity inscribed on the face of the earth. . . . the Indian arrowhead will balk [Time's] efforts and Eternity will have to come to his aid. . . . I would fain know that I am on the trail of mind. . . . When I see these signs I know that the subtle spirits that made them are not far off. . . . The footprint, the mind-print of the oldest men. (XII, 90-92)

Time, and the past, are balked by eternity, which the Indian arrowhead, found in a present moment, reveals. "The immortals are swift,"—that is to say, each present moment brings to the alert observer an untold immensity of content.

> Nature never lost a day, nor a moment. . . . In the moment, in the aeon, well employed, time ever advances with this rapidity. . . . The plant that waited a whole year, and then blossomed the instant it was ready and the earth was ready for it, . . . was rapid. (IV, 350)

In his frequent, unaffected sorties into a past that unwittingly liberates this instant, as well as in his concentration on the intensity of life within it, Thoreau greatly resembles Virginia Woolf.

The window was all sky without color. The house had lost its shelter. It was night before roads were made, or houses. It was the night that dwellers in caves had watched from some high place among rocks.[9]

And Mrs. Swithin reads, "Once there was a sea . . . between us and the continent. . . . There were rhododendrons in the Strand, and mammoths in Piccadilly.[10]" This is not incidental illustration; it is an extension of feeling essential to the book as a whole. Just as in *Jacob's Room*, the sunrise moving from Greece to London provides in the context a stratification of time as well as spatial omnipresence:

But the wind was rolling the darkness through the streets of Athens. . . . All faces—Greek, Levantine, Turkish, English— would have looked much the same in that darkness. At length the columns and the temples whiten, turn rose; and the Pyramids and St. Peter's arise, and at last sluggish St. Paul's looms up.[11]

This awareness of the past, of antiquity, ancient time, America before it was discovered, prehistory, in Thoreau as in Virginia Woolf backs up an intense love of life. "Life like some gay pavilion"—the phrase is Thoreau's (I, 224)—but it would not be a surprise to find it in *Mrs. Dalloway*. Like Thoreau, Mrs. Woolf noted in her diary the stimulating power of dissatisfaction as of enjoyment: "If I never felt these extraordinary pervasive strains—of unrest or rest or happiness or discomfort— I should sink down into acquiesence."[12] The selection from her journals that has been published provides remarkable evidence of the discipline that she, like Thoreau, evolved for herself, to win or conscript truthful impressions. She notes that she marked "Henry James' sentence: observe perpetually."[13] Yet, as Thoreau discovered, this should not be a method too

[9]Virginia Woolf, *Between the Acts* (New York: Harcourt, Brace & Co., 1941), p. 219.
[10]*Ibid.*, p. 38.
[11]Virginia Woolf, *Jacob's Room* (New York: Harcourt, Brace & Co., 1922), p. 276.
[12]Virginia Woolf, *A Writer's Diary*, pp. 147-48.
[13]*Ibid.*, p. 365.

methodical; the "true paths to perception and enjoyment" lie in the direction of freedom of attention. Hence Thoreau commanded:

> Obey the spur of the moment. These accumulated it is that make the impulse and the impetus of the life of genius. . . . Let the spurs of countless moments goad us incessantly into life. I feel the spur of the moment thrust deep into my side. . . . My life as essentially belongs to the present as that of a willow tree in the spring. (III, 231-32)

"More and more," said Mrs. Woolf to herself, "do I repeat my own version of Montaigne—'It's life that matters.' "[14]

> I don't often trouble now to describe cornfields and groups of harvesting women in loose blues and reds, and little staring yellow-frocked girls. But . . . coming back the other evening from Charleston, again all my nerves stood upright, flushed, electrified (what's the word) with the sheer beauty . . . astounding and super-abounding.
>
> . . . And I don't describe encounters with herds of Alderneys any more—. . . how they barked and belled like stags round Grizzle; and how I waved my stick and stood at bay; and thought of Homer as they came flourishing and trampling towards me; some mimic battle. . . . Ajax? That Greek, for all my ignorance, has worked its way into me.[15]

I know nothing that so much resembles the first part of this passage as Thoreau's description of himself, in a similar moment of entire perception: "At sight of this my spirit is like a lit tree" (X, 205). Or more like the second, than his description of the thrush's singing:

> This thrush's song is a *ranz des vaches* to me . . . where the hours are early morning ones, . . . and the day is forever unproved. . . . I would go after the cows, I would watch the flocks of Admetus there forever, only for my board and clothes. (V, 293)

At another moment of exhilaration in the present, as he watches a pine tree waving like a feather in the gale, the light flashing upward incessantly from its base, he wrote, "I feel somewhat

---

[14]*Ibid.*, p. 72.
[15]*Ibid.*, pp. 65-66.

like the young Astyanax at sight of his father's flashing crest" (XII, 64). The ancient past backs up the present, identifies its immediacy, the mythological figure lively in the new scene.

Emerson rightly advised (in his "Biographical Sketch") that Thoreau did not systematize or define what he represented to himself by the term, Nature. Thoreau confirms this: "I do not know where to find in any literature, whether ancient or modern, any adequate account of that Nature with which I am acquainted. Mythology comes nearest to it of any" (II, 152). For this reason Thoreau as artist (though not always as thinker) is free of any limiting moral perspective. In lamenting the limited existence of so many of his fellow townsmen, the prejudices of the farmers and pretences of the merchants, the tyranny of money-grubbing, money-seeking, and money-prizing that destroyed the finer promise of America, Thoreau's message deserves our hearing. But it reflects a less accurate appreciation of the incli-nations, successes, and defeats of the individual human life than is indispensable to a great imaginative writer. Thoreau himself was not deceived about this: "The best thought is not only without sombreness, but even without morality" (I, 265). "The artist must work with indifference" (I, 349); he must let "Repentance and Co." go (XII, 344). One reason, he decides, that farmers are less interesting than sportsmen and loafers is that "for society a man must not be too *good* or well-disposed, to spoil his natural disposition. The bad are frequently good enough to let you see how bad they are" (VI, 21). Not among the lawyers or learned ones of Concord did Thoreau find the features of nature in men, but in those sportsmen and loafers, the musquash hunters, or in a little Irish boy like Johnny Riordan, who "revives . . . the worthies of antiquity" (III, 149).

If Thoreau had had time to write another book, it would have been very different, I believe, from any he had hitherto composed. The latter volumes of his *Journal* are full of the raw material for his book on Concord—a Concord mythology—it would have become. Everything about the inhabitants—from human beings to frogs, mosquitoes, kinds of fish, mice, birds, trees, weeds, and special grasses—would have had its place in a scheme of relatedness. For whether the man acknowledged it or the frog, Henry Thoreau who had been auditor to both recognized the difference it made to each that the other lived nearby. As to the people, I venture the guess that a directory of Concord in Thoreau's time would list few names about which there is not some note—however seemingly insignificant the fact put down—in the volumes of the journal. Hall, the telegraph operator, or Ferrar, the blacksmith, Lewis, the blind man, Ai Hale and his dog—we do not meet them in the pages of Emerson's journal, but Thoreau wished to record some event of each one's life.

What form this Concord book might have taken we cannot determine. But human scenes with the intensity of life, "like some gay pavilion," could not have failed to include the sportsmen and loafers, woodchoppers and musquash hunters.

> Now that the Indian is gone, [the woodchopper] stands nearest to nature. Who has written the history of his day? . . . Homer refers to the progress of the woodcutter's work, to mark the time of day on the plains of Troy. . . . (III, 245)

Minott, "the most poetical farmer," got out his own wood, and knew the history of every stump on his lot, and the age of every sapling. He was one of the worthies. Another farmer, Cyrus Hubbard, was a potential character in Thoreau's Concord mythology.

> I see the old pale-faced farmer out again on his sled now for the five-thousandth time . . . a man of a certain New England probity . . . immortal and natural. . . . He rides on the sled drawn by oxen, world-wise, yet comparatively so young . . . He does not melt the snow where he treads . . . Moderate, natural, true, as if he were made of earth, stone, wood, snow. I thus meet in this Universe kindred of mine, composed of these elements. I see men like frogs; their peeping I partially understand. (IX, 144-45)

Thus, in the journal at least, Cyrus Hubbard's sketch resolves into a metamorphosis. At another time, Thoreau, sailing on the river towards night, sees the fisherman, John Goodwin, loading driftwood into his cart, and that man's employment, so simple and direct,—though he is regarded by most as a vicious character,—. . . charmed me unspeakably. So much do we love actions that are simple. They are all poetic. (V, 444-46)

Elsewhere, Thoreau christens John Goodwin "the one-eyed Ajax."

Melvin, the hunter, is always accompanied by his dog:

Saw Melvin's lank bluish-white-black-spotted hound, and Melvin with his gun near. . . . He follows hunting . . . as regularly . . . as the farmers follow farming. . . . How I . . . thank him for [it]. . . . Few know how to take the census. I thank my stars for Melvin . . . awkward, gawky, loose-hung, dragging his legs after him. He is my contemporary and neighbor. He is one tribe, I am another, and we are not at war. (IX, 148)

Few know how to take the census! Thoreau had expressed his desire for a book of worthies, a more intelligible directory of men worth seeing, than had been provided. Increasingly his journal contained sections in which the census of the woodcutter, the poetical farmer, the fisherman, and hunter is put together with the census of frogs and mice, buds and sprouts. Not only might Thoreau perceive these worthies in, or perceive in them, a metamorphosis, but sometimes such a man could verily produce one himself, such a man as Minott, who, Thoreau noted,

. . . adorns whatever part of nature he touches. . . . If a common man speaks of Walden pond to me, I see only a shallow, dull-coloured body of water . . . but if Minott speaks of it, I see the green water and reflected hills at once, for he *has been* there. I hear the rustle of the leaves from woods which he goes through. (X, 168)

But above all, the coming of the musquash hunters excites Thoreau's admiration, as if a more primitive race appeared in the spring:

The musquash hunter (last night), with his . . . powder and shot and boat turned up . . . even he, dark, dull, and battered flint that he is, is an inspired man to his extent now . . . and the Musquetaquid meadows cannot spare him. . . . [The hunters] keep up their fires by means unknown to me. . . . I know them wild and ready to risk all when their muse invites. . . . I meet these gods of the river and woods with sparkling faces (like Apollo's) late from the house of correction, it may be carrying whatever mystic and forbidden bottles concealed. . . . What care I to see galleries full of representatives of heathen gods, when I can see natural living ones. . . . These aboriginal men cannot be repressed, but under some guise or other they survive and reappear continually. (XI, 423-25)

Such passages suggest a work in prose, somewhat like the *Georgics*—for if Thoreau's notes in the journal are any guide, the human figures when they appear serve not merely their own purposes but to set the leaves rustling, alert the muskrat who is as immortal as the hunters. They provide incidents he finds allegorical, "like myths or passages in a myth" (V, 203). The relation of one such happening, the hunter Melvin's reluctantly leading Thoreau to the site of the rare azalea which he has kept secret for many years, is one of the most high-spirited and amusing passages in the *Journal*.

Thoreau, it is clear, used the journal for books he was writing or about to write (as Leonard Woolf says of Mrs. Woolf's use of her diary), although he never talks as directly about the planning of a book, or his way of working on it as distinct from keeping his journal. Like Mrs. Woolf, he found that "writing for my own eye only is good practice."[16] Necessarily much in it would be unfinished. But the context, thought allied to thought as in life, less arbitrarily connected than in the framework of an essay, gave it to him a unique character.

Perhaps this is the main value of . . . keeping a journal. . . . Having by chance recorded a few disconnected thoughts and then brought them into juxtaposition, they suggest a whole new field in which . . . to labor and to think. Thought begat thought. (III, 217)

A Herculean task he found it: no exercise could be more vigorous than "joining thought to thought," than to "think a thought about this life and then get it expressed" (X, 405).

While it is hardly possible to exaggerate the value of Thoreau's journal, he did himself tend to overestimate the general value

[16] *Ibid.*, p. 13.

of this form of writing—thinking for example that had Shakespeare kept a journal it would excel his plays and poetry. Here Thoreau the warrior vaunting his own prowess interferes with Thoreau the writer—as, for the same reason, when he claims that "one man shall derive from the fisherman's story more than the fisherman has got who tells it" (X, 404). Only a writer of Shakespeare's potential power of sympathy with so many kinds of men, could see that the fisherman who tells the story has precisely as much—no more and no less—of life than the best recreator of his story. Unless he knows this, the writer must be allegorist, essayist, pastoral poet. The other kind of writer, the true novelist or dramatist, must disappear into his work; and the more perfectly that transformation occurs, the more completely does he fulfill Thoreau's highest counsel, "Say the thing with which you labor" (III, 144).

But as Thoreau, if we taxed him, would, I think, admit, each kind of writing has its own necessities. His is the very best of its kind we have; his limitations were necessary to it. They are transcended on those remarkable pages when he realizes that not awe, but the intensity of life gives true relatedness (IX, 377). Not "natural history," but the history of true relatedness is the motif of all his Concord explorations, the minute appearances of buds and sprouts as well as the larger scenes of the musquash hunters gathering in the dark. At last to find one hitherto unknown species of pickerel in Walden Pond: of what moment? Because it had been there all the while, without anyone's awareness: "And all these years I have known Walden, these striped breams have skulked in it without my knowledge!" (XI, 351). His becoming conscious of a relation with this aboriginal, first-found creature altered, if ever so slightly, the nexus of relationship with all other Concord beings. In the new relatedness, the intensity; in the intensity, the true relatedness: thus to report life "tried out of the fat of my experience and joy" (IX, 195). And these unique moments, facts, occasions, that he conferred with and confederated, he rescued from the lapse of time because he made his first report to himself. Unmistakably, his is a writer's journal.

SELECTED BIBLIOGRAPHY

WRITINGS

Bode, Carl (ed.). *Collected Poems of Henry Thoreau.* New York: Hendricks House, Inc., 1943.

Harding, Walter and Bode, Carl (ed.). *The Correspondence of Henry David Thoreau.* New York: New York University Press, 1958.

Miller, Perry (ed.). *Consciousness in Concord.* The Text of Thoreau's Hitherto " Lost " Journal (1840-41). Together with Notes and a Commentary. Boston : Houghton Mifflin Company, 1958.

Thoreau, Henry D. *The Writings of Henry David Thoreau.* 20 vols. Boston: Houghton Mifflin and Company, 1906. Vols. VII-XX contain the *Journal of Henry D. Thoreau*, ed. Bradford Torrey and Francis H. Allen.

BIOGRAPHY

Canby, Henry S. *Thoreau.* Boston: Houghton Mifflin Company, 1939.

Channing, William E. *Thoreau, the Poet-Naturalist.* Boston: Roberts Brothers, 1873. Revised edition, ed. F. B. Sanborn. Boston: Charles E. Goodspeed, 1902.

Emerson, Ralph Waldo. "Thoreau," in *Works.* 12 vols. Boston and New York: Houghton Mifflin and Company, 1883-87. (Vol. X).

Krutch, Joseph W. *Henry David Thoreau.* New York: William Sloane Associates, 1948.

Salt, Henry. *The Life of Henry David Thoreau.* London: Richard Bentley & Son, 1890. Revised edition, London: Walter Scott, Ltd., 1896. (Great Writers Series).

CRITICAL STUDIES
(especially those relating to the *Journal*)

Cook, Reginald. *Passage to Walden.* Boston: Houghton Mifflin Company, 1949.

Harding, Walter (ed.). *Thoreau: A Century of Criticism.* Dallas: Southern Methodist University Press, 1954.

Leary, Lewis. "Thoreau," in *Eight American Authors*, ed. Floyd Stovall. New York: Modern Language Association of America, 1956.

Matthiessen, F. O. *American Renaissance: Art and Expression in the Age of Emerson and Whitman*. New York: Oxford University Press, 1941.

Paul, Sherman. *The Shores of America: Thoreau's Inward Exploration*. Urbana: University of Illinois Press, 1958.

Seybold, Ethel. *Thoreau: The Quest and the Classics*. New Haven: Yale University Press, 1951.

Shanley, J. Lyndon. *The Making of Walden*. Chicago: University of Chicago Press, 1957.

Shepard, Odell. *The Heart of Thoreau's Journals*. New York: Dover Publications, Inc, 1961.

H. D. THOREAU:
A WRITER'S JOURNAL

I

SIMPLY SEEING

March 7, 1838. We should not endeavor coolly to analyze our thoughts, but, keeping the pen even and parallel with the current, make an accurate transcript of them. Impulse is, after all, the best linguist, and for his logic, if not conformable to Aristotle, it cannot fail to be most convincing. The nearer we approach to a complete but simple transcript of our thought the more tolerable will be the piece, for we can endure to consider ourselves in a state of passivity or in involuntary action, but rarely our efforts, and least of all our rare efforts.

December. A good book is the plectrum with which our silent lyres are struck. In all epics, when, after breathless attention, we come to the significant words "He said," then especially our inmost man is addressed. We not unfrequently refer the interest which belongs to our own unwritten sequel to the written and comparatively lifeless page. Of all valuable books this same sequel makes an indispensable part. It is the author's aim to say once and emphatically, "He said." This is the most the book-maker can attain to. If he make his volume a foil whereon the waves of silence may break, it is well. It is not so much the sighing of the blast as that pause, as Gray expresses it, "when the gust is recollecting itself," that thrills us, and is infinitely grander than the importunate howlings of the storm.

Feb. 13, 1840. An act of integrity is to an act of duty what the French verb *être* is to *devoir*. Duty is *ce que devrait être.*

Duty belongs to the understanding, but genius is not dutiful, the highest talent is dutiful. Goodness results from the wisest use of talent.

The perfect man has both genius and talent. The one is his head, the other his foot; by one he is, by the other he lives.

1

The unconsciousness of man is the consciousness of God, the end of the world.

The very thrills of genius are disorganizing. The body is never quite acclimated to *its* atmosphere, but how often succumbs and goes into a decline!

Feb. 14. Beauty lives by rhymes. Double a deformity is a beauty. Draw this blunt quill over the paper, and fold it once transversely to the line, pressing it suddenly before the ink dries, and a delicately shaded and regular figure is the result which art cannot surpass.

June 23. I cannot see the bottom of the sky, because I cannot see to the bottom of myself. It is the symbol of my own infinity. My eye penetrates as far into the ether as that depth is inward from which my contemporary thought springs.

Not by constraint or severity shall you have access to true wisdom, but by abandonment, and childlike mirthfulness. If you would know aught, be gay before it.

Feb. 8, 1841. My Journal is that of me which would else spill over and run to waste, gleanings from the field which in action I reap. I must not live for it, but in it for the gods.

They are my correspondent, to whom daily I send off this sheet postpaid. I am clerk in their counting-room, and at evening transfer the account from day-book to ledger. It is as a leaf which hangs over my head in the path. I bend the twig and write my prayers on it; then letting it go, the bough springs up and shows the scrawl to heaven. As if it were not kept shut in my desk, but were as public a leaf as any in nature. It is papyrus by the riverside; it is vellum in the pastures; it is parchment on the hills. I find it everywhere as free as the leaves which troop along the lanes in autumn. The crow, the goose, the eagle carry my quill, and the wind blows the leaves as far as I go. Or, if my imagination does not soar, but gropes in slime and mud, then I write with a reed.

Feb. 20. Saturday. I suspect the moral discrimination of the oldest and best authors. I doubt if Milton distinguished greatly between his Satan and his Raphael. In Homer and Aeschylus and Dante I miss a nice discrimination of the *important* shades of character.

When I am going out for an evening, I arrange the fire in my stove so that I do not fail to find a good one when I return, though it would have engaged my frequent attention present. So that, when I know I am to be at home, I sometimes make believe that I may go out, to save trouble. And this is the art of living, too,—to leave our life in a condition to go alone, and not to require a constant supervision. We will then sit down serenely to live, as by the side of a stove.

Feb. 27. Saturday. Life looks as fair at this moment as a summer's sea, or a blond dress in a saffron light, with its sun and grass and walled towns so bright and chaste, as fair as my own virtue which would adventure therein. Like a Persian city or hanging gardens in the distance, so washed in light, so untried, only to be thridded by clean thoughts. All its flags are flowing, and tassels streaming, and drapery flapping, like some gay pavilion. The heavens hang over it like some low screen, and seem to undulate in the breeze.

Through this pure, unwiped hour, as through a crystal glass, I look out upon the future, as a smooth lawn for my virtue to disport in. It shows from afar as unrepulsive as the sunshine upon walls and cities, over which the passing life moves as gently as a shadow. I see the course of my life, like some retired road, wind on without obstruction into a country maze.

I am attired for the future so, as the sun setting presumes all men at leisure and in contemplative mood,—and am thankful that it is thus presented blank and indistinct. It still o'ertops my hope. My future deeds bestir themselves within me and move grandly towards a consummation, as ships go down the Thames. A steady onward motion I feel in me, as still as that, or like some vast, snowy cloud, whose shadow first is seen across the fields. It is the material of all things loose and set afloat that makes my sea.

Feb. 28. Nothing goes by luck in composition. It allows of no tricks. The best you can write will be the best you are. Every sentence is the result of a long probation. The author's character is read from title-page to end. Of this he never corrects the proofs. We read it as the essential character of a handwriting without regard to the flourishes. And so of the rest of our actions; it runs as straight as a ruled line through them all, no matter how many curvets about it. Our whole life is taxed for the least thing well done; it is its net result. How we eat, drink, sleep, and use our desultory hours, now in these indifferent days, with no eye to observe and no occasion [to] excite us, determines our authority and capacity for the time to come.

March 3. I hear a man blowing a horn this still evening, and it sounds like the plaint of nature in these times. In this, which I refer to some man, there is something greater than any man. It is as if the earth spoke. It adds a great remoteness to the horizon, and its very distance is grand, as when one draws back the head to speak. That which I now hear in the west seems like an invitation to the east. It runs round the earth as a whisper gallery. It is the spirit of the West calling to the spirit of the East, or else it is the rattling of some team lagging Day's train. Coming to me through the darkness and silence, all things great seem transpiring there. It is friendly as a distant hermit's taper. When it is trilled, or undulates, the heavens are crumpled into time, and successive waves flow across them.

It is a strangely healthy sound for these disjointed times. It is a rare soundness when cow-bells and horns are heard from over the fields.

March 13. Saturday. There is a sort of homely truth and naturalness in some books, which is very rare to find, and yet looks quite cheap. There may be nothing lofty in the sentiment, or polished in the expression, but it is careless, countrified talk. The scholar rarely writes as well as the farmer talks. Homeliness is a great merit in a book; it is next to beauty and a high art. Some have this merit only. A few homely expressions redeem them. Rusticity is pastoral, but affection merely civil. The scholar does not make his most familiar experience come gracefully to the aid of his expression, and hence, though he live in it, his books contain no tolerable pictures of the country and simple life. Very few men can speak of Nature with any truth. They confer no favor; they do not speak a good word for her. Most cry better than they speak. You can get more nature out of them by pinching than by addressing them. It is naturalness, and not simply good nature, that interests. I like better the surliness with which the woodchopper speaks of his woods, handling them as indifferently as his axe, than the mealy-mouthed enthusiasm of the lover of nature.

March 15. A great cheerfulness have all great wits possessed, almost a prophane levity to such as understood them not, but their religion had the broader basis in proportion as it was less prominent. The religion I love is very laic. The clergy are as diseased, and as much possessed with a devil, as the reformers. They make their topic as offensive as the politician, for our religion is as unpublic and incommunicable as our poetical vein, and to be approached with as much love and tenderness.

April 9. Friday. How much virtue there is in simply seeing! We may almost say that the hero has striven in vain for his pre-eminency, if the student oversees him. The woman who sits in the house and *sees* is a match for a stirring captain. Those still, piercing eyes, as faithfully exercised on their talent, will keep her even with Alexander or Shakespeare. They may go to Asia with parade, or to fairyland, but not beyond her ray. We are as much as we see. Faith is sight and knowledge. The hands only serve the eyes. The farthest blue streak in the horizon I can see, I may reach before many sunsets. What I saw alters not; in my night, when I wander, it is still steadfast as the star which the sailor steers by.

April 25. We return from the lyceum and caucus with such stir and excitement, as if a crisis were at hand; but no natural scene or sound sympathizes with us, for Nature is always silent and unpretending as at the break of day. She but rubs her eyelids.

April 26. Monday. At R. W. E.'s.

The charm of the Indian to me is that he stands free and unconstrained in Nature, is her inhabitant and not her guest, and wears her easily and gracefully. But the civilized man has the habits of the house. His house is a prison, in which he finds himself oppressed and confined, not sheltered and protected. He walks as if he sustained the roof; he carries his arms as if the walls would fall in and crush him, and his feet remember the cellar beneath. His muscles are never relaxed. It is rare that he overcomes the house, and learns to sit at home in it, and roof and floor and walls support themselves, as the sky and trees and earth.

It is a great art to saunter.

April 27. It is only by a sort of voluntary blindness, and omitting to see, that we know ourselves, as when we see stars with the side of the eye. The nearest approach to discovering what we are is in dreams. It is as hard to see one's self as to look backwards without turning round. And foolish are they that look in glasses with that intent.

April 29. Better a monosyllabic life than a ragged and muttered one; let its report be short and round like a rifle, so that it may hear its own echo in the surrounding silence.

April 30. Where shall we look for standard English but to the words of any man who has a depth of feeling in him? Not in any smooth and leisurely essay. From the gentlemanly windows of the country-seat no sincere eyes are directed upon nature, but from the peasant's horn windows a true glance and greeting occasionally. "For summer being ended, all things," said the Pilgrim, "stood in appearance with a weather-beaten face, and the whole country full of woods and thickets represented a wild and savage hue." Compare this with the agricultural report.

July 10 to 12. A slight sound at evening lifts me up by the ears, and makes life seem inexpressibly serene and grand. It may be in Uranus, or it may be in the shutter. It is the original sound of which all literature is but the echo. It makes all fear superfluous. Bravery comes from further than the sources of fear.

Aug. 1. Sunday. I never met a man who cast a free and healthy glance over life, but the best live in a sort of Sabbath light, a Jewish gloom. The best thought is not only without sombreness, but even without morality. The universe lies outspread in floods of white light to it. The moral aspect of nature is a jaundice reflected from man. To the innocent there are no cherubim nor angels. Occasionally we rise above the necessity of virtue into an unchangeable morning light, in which we have not to choose in a dilemma between right and wrong, but simply to live right on and breathe the circumambient air. There is no name for this life unless it be the very vitality of *vita*. Silent is the preacher about this, and silent must ever be, for he who knows it will not preach.

Aug. 6. Of what moment are facts that can be lost,—which need to be commemorated? The monument of death will outlast the memory of the dead. The Pyramids do not tell the tale confided to them. The living fact commemorates itself. Why look in the dark for light? Look in the light rather. Strictly speaking, the Societies have not recovered one fact from oblivion, but they themselves are instead of the fact that is lost. The researcher is more memorable than the researched. The crowd stood admiring the mist and the dim outline of the trees seen through it, and when one of their number advanced to explore the phenomenon, with fresh admiration all eyes were turned on his dimly retreating figure. Critical acumen is exerted in vain to uncover the past; the *past* cannot be *presented*; we cannot know what we are not. But one veil hangs over past, present, and future, and it is the province of the historian to find out, not what was, but what is. Where a battle has been fought, you will find nothing but the bones of men and beasts; where a battle is being fought, there are hearts beating. We will sit on a mound and muse, and not try to make these skeletons stand on their legs again.

[Dec.] 13. Monday. We constantly anticipate repose. Yet it surely can only be the repose that is in entire and healthy activity. It must be a repose without rust. What is leisure but

opportunity for more complete and entire action? Our energies pine for exercise. That time we spend in our duties is so much leisure, so that there is no man but has sufficient of it.

I make my own time, I make my own terms. I cannot see how God or Nature can ever get the start of me.

[*Dec.*] *14. Tuesday.* To hear the sunset described by the old Scotch poet Douglas as I have seen it repays me for many weary pages of antiquated Scotch. Nothing so restores and humanizes antiquity and makes it blithe as the discovery of some natural sympathy between it and the present. Why is it that there is something melancholy in antiquity? We forget that it had any other future than our present. As if it were not as near to *the* future as ourselves! No, thank heavens, these ranks of men to right and left, posterity and ancestry, are not to be thridded by any earnest mortal. The heavens stood over the heads of our ancestors as near as to us. Any living word in their books abolishes the difference of time.

[*Dec.*] *15. Wednesday.* A mild summer sun shines over forest and lake. The earth looks as fair this morning as the Valhalla of the gods. Indeed our spirits never go beyond nature. In the woods there is an inexpressible happiness. Their mirth is but just repressed. In winter, when there is but one green leaf for many rods, what warm content is in them! They are not rude, but tender, even in the severest cold. Their nakedness is their defense. All their sounds and sights are elixir to my spirit. They possess a divine health. God is not more well. Every sound is inspiriting and fraught with the same mysterious assurance, from the creaking of the boughs in January to the soft sough of the wind in July.

How much of my well-being, think you, depends on the condition of my lungs and stomach,—such cheap pieces of Nature as they, which, indeed, she is every day reproducing with prodigality. Is the arrow indeed fatal which rankles in the breast of the bird on the bough, in whose eye all this fair landscape is reflected, and whose voice still echoes through the wood?

The trees have come down to the bank to see the river go by. This old, familiar river is renewed each instant; only the channel is the same. The water which so calmly reflects the fleeting clouds and the primeval trees I have never seen before....

I seem to see somewhat more of my own kith and kin in the lichens on the rocks than in any books. It does seem as if mine were a peculiarly wild nature, which so yearns toward all wildness. I know of no redeeming qualities in me but a sincere love for some things, and when I am reproved I have to fall back on to this ground. This is my argument in reserve for all cases. My love is invulnerable. Meet me on that ground, and you will find me strong. When I am condemned, and condemn myself utterly, I think straightway, "But I rely on my love for some things." Therein I am whole and entire. Therein I am God-propped.

When I see the smoke curling up through the woods from some farmhouse invisible, it is more suggestive of the poetry of rural and domestic life than a nearer inspection can be. Up goes the smoke as quietly as the dew exhales in vapor from these pine leaves and oaks; as busy, disposing itself in circles and in wreaths, as the housewife on the hearth below. It is cotemporary with a piece of human biography, and waves as a feather in some *man's* cap....

I can at length stretch me when I come to Chaucer's breadth; and I think, "Well, I could be *that* man's acquaintance," for he walked in that low and retired way that I do, and was not too good to live. I am grieved when they hint of any unmanly submissions he may have made, for that subtracts from his breadth and humanity.

Dec. 30. Thursday. I admire Chaucer for a sturdy English wit. The easy height he speaks from in his Prologue to the Canterbury Tales is as good as anything in it,—as if he were indeed better than any of the company there assembled.

The poet does not have to go out of himself and cease to tattle of his domestic affairs, to win our confidence, but is so broad that we see no limits to his sympathy.

Great delicacy and gentleness of character is constantly displayed in Chaucer's verse. The simplest and humblest words come readily to his lips. The natural innocence of the man appears in the simple and pure spirit in which "The Prioresses Tale" is conceived, in which the child sings *O alma redemtoris mater*, and in the account of the departure of Custance with her child upon the sea, in "The Man of Lawes Tale." The whole story of Chanticleer and Dame Partlet in "The Nonnes Preestes Tale" is genuine humanity. I know nothing better in its kind. The poets seem to be only more frank and plain-spoken than other men. Their verse is but confessions. They always confide in the reader, and speak privily with him, keeping nothing back.

Jan. 5, 1842. Wednesday. I find that whatever hindrances may occur I write just about the same amount of truth in my Journal; for the record is more concentrated, and usually it is some very real and earnest life, after all, that interrupts. All flourishes are omitted. If I saw wood from morning to night, though I grieve that I could not observe the train of my thoughts during that time, yet, in the evening, the few scrannel lines which describe my day's occupations will make the creaking of the saw more musical than my freest fancies could have been. I find incessant labor with the hands, which engrosses the attention also, the best method to remove palaver out of one's style. One will not dance at his work who has wood to cut and cord before the night falls in the short days of winter; but every stroke will be husbanded, and ring soberly through the wood; and so will his lines ring and tell on the ear, when at evening he settles the accounts of the day. I have often been astonished at the force and precision of style to which busy laboring men, unpracticed in writing, easily attain when they are required to make the effort. It seems as if their sincerity and plainness were the main thing to be taught in schools,—and yet not in the schools, but in the fields, in actual service, I should say. The scholar not unfrequently envies the propriety and emphasis with which the farmer calls to his team, and confesses that if that lingo were written it would surpass his labored sentences.

Who is not tired of the weak and flowing periods of the politician and scholar, and resorts not even to the Farmer's Almanac, to read the simple account of the month's labor, to restore his tone again? I want to see a sentence run clear through to the end, as deep and fertile as a well-drawn furrow which shows that the plow was pressed down to the beam. If our scholars would lead more earnest lives, we should not witness those lame conclusions to their ill-sown discourses, but their sentences would pass over the ground like loaded rollers, and not mere hollow and wooden ones, to press in the seed and make it germinate.

A well-built sentence, in the rapidity and force with which it works, may be compared to a modern corn-planter, which furrows out, drops the seed, and covers it up at one movement.

March 23. After all, I believe it is the style of thought entirely, and not the style of expression, which makes the difference in books. For if I find any thought worth extracting, I do not wish to alter the language. Then the author seems to have had all the graces of eloquence and poetry given him. . . .

I occasionally find myself to be nothing at all, because the gods give me nothing to do. I cannot brag; I can only congratulate my masters.

In idleness I am of no thickness, I am thinnest wafer. I never compass my own ends. God schemes for me.

March 24. Thursday. Those authors are successful who do not *write down* to others, but make their own taste and judgment their audience. By some strange infatuation we forget that we do not approve what yet we recommend to others. It is enough if I please myself with writing; I am then sure of an audience. . . .

The artist must work with indifferency. Too great interest vitiates his work.

March 26. Saturday. The wise will not be imposed on by wisdom. You can tell, but what do you know?

I thank God that the cheapness which appears in time and

the world, the trivialness of the whole scheme of things, is in my own cheap and trivial moment. I am time and the world. I assert no independence. In me are summer and winter, village life and commercial routine, pestilence, and famine and refreshing breezes, joy and sadness, life and death. How near is yesterday! How far tomorrow! I have seen nails which were driven before I was born. Why do they look old and rusty? Why does not God make some mistake to show to us that time is a delusion? Why did I invent time but to destroy it?

March 27. Sunday. See what a life the gods have given us, set round with pain and pleasure. It is too strange for sorrow; it is too strange for joy. One while it looks as shallow, though as intricate, as a Cretan labyrinth, and again it is a pathless depth. I ask for bread incessantly,—that my life sustain me, as much as meat my body.

March 28. Monday. How often must one feel, as he looks back on his past life, that he has gained a talent but lost a character! My life has got down into my fingers. My inspiration at length is only so much breath as I can breathe. . . .

One may well feel chagrined when he finds he can do nearly all he can conceive.

Some books ripple on like a stream, and we feel that the author is in the full tide of discourse. Plato and Jamblichus and Pythagoras and Bacon halt beside them. Long, stringy, slimy thoughts which flow or run together. They read as if written for military men or men of business, there is such a dispatch in them, and a double-quick time, a Saratoga march with beat of drum. But the grave thinkers and philosophers seem not to have got their swaddling-clothes off; they are slower than a Roman army on its march, the rear encampment tonight where the van camped last night. The wise Jamblichus eddies and gleams like a watery slough.

But the reviewer seizes the pen and shouts, "Forward! Alamo and Fanning!" and after rolls the tide of war. Immediately the author discovers himself launched, and if the slope was easy and the grease good, does not go to the bottom. . . .

If I cannot chop wood in the yard, can I not chop wood in my journal? Can I not give vent to that appetite so? I wish to relieve myself of superfluous energy.

March 31. Thursday. The really efficient laborer will be found not to crowd his day with work, but will saunter to his task surrounded by a wide halo of ease and leisure. There will be a wide margin for relaxation to his day. He is only earnest to secure the kernels of time, and does not exaggerate the value of the husk. Why should the hen set all day? She can lay but one egg, and besides she will not have picked up materials for a new one. Those who work much do not work hard.

Nothing is so rare as sense. Very uncommon sense is poetry, and has a heroic or sweet music. But in verse, for the most part, the music now runs before and then behind the sense, but is never coincident with it. Given the metre, and one will make music while another makes sense. But good verse, like a good soldier, will make its own music, and it will march to the same with one consent. In most verse there is no inherent music. The man should not march, but walk like a citizen. It is not time of war but peace. Boys study the metres to write Latin verses, but it does not help them to write English.

Lydgate's "Story of Thebes," intended for a Canterbury Tale, is a specimen of most unprogressive, unmusical verse. Each line rings the knell of its brother, as if it were introduced but to dispose of him. No mortal man could have breathed to that cadence without long intervals of relaxation; the repetition would have been fatal to the lungs. No doubt there was much healthy exercise taken in the meanwhile. He should forget his rhyme and tell his story, or forget his story and breathe himself.

In Shakespeare and elsewhere the climax may be somewhere along the line, which runs as varied and meandering as a country road, but in Lydgate it is nowhere but in the rhyme. The couplets slope headlong to their confluence.

August 6, 1845. How can he remember well his ignorance who has so often to use his knowledge.

1845–47. The way to compare men is to compare their respective ideals. The actual man is too complex to deal with. . . .

Carlyle is an earnest, honest, heroic worker as literary man and sympathizing brother of his race. . . .

Emerson again is a critic, poet, philosopher, with talent not so conspicuous, not so adequate to his task; but his field is still higher, his task more arduous. Lives a far more intense life; seeks to realize a divine life; his affections and intellect equally developed. Has advanced farther, and a new heaven opens to him. Love and Friendship, Religion, Poetry, the Holy are familiar to him. The life of an Artist; more variegated, more observing, finer perception; not so robust, elastic; practical enough in his own field; faithful, a judge of men. There is no such general critic of men and things, no such trustworthy and faithful man. More of the divine realized in him than in any. A poetic critic, reserving the unqualified nouns for the gods.

Alcott is a geometer, a visionary, the Laplace of ethics, more intellect, less of the affections, sight beyond talents, a substratum of practical skill and knowledge unquestionable, but overlaid and concealed by a faith in the unseen and impracticable. Seeks to realize an entire life; a catholic observer; habitually takes in the farthest star and nebula into his scheme. Will be the last man to be disappointed as the ages revolve. His attitude is one of greater faith and expectation than that of any man I know; with little to show; with undue share, for a philosopher, of the weaknesses of humanity. The most hospitable intellect, embracing high and low. For children how much that means, for the insane and vagabond, for the poet and scholar!

Emerson has special talents unequalled. The divine in man has had no more easy, methodically distinct expression. His personal influence upon young persons greater than any man's. In his world every man would be a poet, Love would reign, Beauty would take place, Man and Nature would harmonize.

When Alcott's day comes, laws unsuspected by most will take effect, the system will crystalize according to them, all seals and falsehood will slough off, everything will be in its place.

Feb. 22 [*No year*]. Emerson does not consider things in respect to their essential utility, but an important partial and relative one, as works of art perhaps. His probes pass one side of their centre of gravity. His exaggeration is of a part, not of the whole.

How many an afternoon has been stolen from more profitable, if not more attractive, industry,—afternoons when a good run of custom might have been expected on the main street, such as tempt the ladies out a-shopping,—spent, I say, by me away in the meadows, in the well-nigh hopeless attempt to set the river on fire or be set on fire by it, with such tinder as I had, with such flint as I was. Trying at least to make it flow with milk and honey, as I had heard of, or liquid gold, and drown myself without getting wet,—a laudable enterprise, though I have not much to show for it.

So many autumn days spent outside the town, trying to hear what was in the wind, to hear it and carry it express. I well-nigh sunk all my capital in it, and lost my own breath into the bargain, by running in the face of it. Depend upon it, if it concerned either of the parties, it would have appeared in the yeoman's gazette, the *Freeman*, with other earliest intelligence.

For many years I was self-appointed inspector of snow-storms and rain-storms, and did my duty faithfully, though I never received one cent for it.

Surveyor, if not of higher ways, then of forest paths and all across-lot routes, keeping many open ravines bridged and passable at all seasons, where the public heel had testified to the importance of the same, all not only without charge, but even at considerable risk and inconvenience. Many a mower would have forborne to complain had he been aware of the invisible public good that was in jeopardy.

So I went on, I may say without boasting, I trust, faithfully minding my business without a partner, till it became more and more evident that my townsmen would not, after all, admit me into the list of town officers, nor make the place a sinecure with moderate allowance.

I have looked after the wild stock of the town, which pastures in common, and every one knows that these cattle give you a good deal of trouble in the way of leaping fences. I have counted and registered all the eggs I could find at least, and have had an eye to all nooks and corners of the farm, though I didn't always know whether Jonas or Solomon worked in a particular field today; that was none of my business. I only knew him for one of the men, and trusted that he was as well employed as I was. I had to make my daily entries in the general farm book, and my duties may sometimes have made me a little stubborn and unyielding.

Many a day spent on the hilltops waiting for the sky to fall, that I might catch something, though I never caught much, only a little, manna-wise, that would dissolve again in the sun.

My accounts, indeed, which I can swear to have been faithfully kept, I have never got audited, still less accepted, still less paid and settled. However, I haven't set my heart upon *that*.

I have watered the red huckleberry and the sand cherry and the hoopwood [?] tree, and the cornel and spoonhunt and yellow violet, which might have withered else in dry seasons. The white grape.

To find the bottom of Walden Pond, and what inlet and outlet it might have.

I found at length that, as they were not likely to offer me any office in the court-house, any curacy or living anywhere else, I must shift for myself, I must furnish myself with the necessaries of life.

Now watching from the observatory of the Cliffs or Annursnack to telegraph any new arrival, to see if Wachusett, Watatic, or Monadnock had got any nearer. Climbing trees for the same purpose. I have been reporter for many years to one of the journals of no very wide circulation, and, as is too common, got only my pains for my labor. Literary contracts are little binding.

[*1837–47*].[1] I hold in my hands a recent volume of essays and poems, in its outward aspect like the thousands which the press

[1]The passages that follow are from a commonplace book containing copies of entries made in earlier notebooks kept over a period of years, all apparently before 1847.

sends forth, and, if the gods permitted their own inspiration to be breathed in vain, this might be forgotten in the mass, but the accents of truth are as sure to be heard on earth as in heaven. The more I read it the more I am impressed by its sincerity, its depth and grandeur. It already seems ancient and has lost the traces of its modern birth. It is an evidence of many virtues in the writer. More serenely and humbly confident, this man has listened to the inspiration which all may hear, and with greater fidelity reported it. It is therefore a true prophecy, and shall at length come to pass. It has the grandeur of the Greek tragedy, or rather its Hebrew original, yet it is not necessarily referred to any form of faith. The slumbering, heavy depth of its sentences is perhaps without recent parallel. It lies like the sward in its native pasture, where its roots are never disturbed, and not spread over a sandy embankment. . . .

It is one great and rare merit in the old English tragedy that it says something. The words slide away very fast, but toward some conclusion. It has to do with things, and the reader feels as if he were advancing. It does not make much odds what message the author has to deliver at this distance of time, since no message can startle us, but how he delivers it,—that it be done in a downright and manly way. They come to the point and do not waste the time.

They say that Carew was a laborious writer, but his poems do not show it. They are finished, but do not show the marks of the chisel. Drummond was indeed a quiddler, with little fire or fibre, and rather a taste *for* poetry than a taste *of* it.

After all, we draw on very gradually in English literature to Shakespeare, through Peele and Marlowe, to say nothing of Raleigh and Spenser and Sidney. We hear the same great tone already sounding to which Shakespeare added a serener wisdom and clearer expression. Its chief characteristics of reality and unaffected manliness are there. The more we read of the literature of these times, the more does acquaintance divest the genius of Shakespeare of the in some measure false mystery which has thickened around it, and leave it shrouded in the grander mystery of daylight. His critics have for the most part made their [*sic*] comtemporaries less that they might make Shakespeare more.

The distinguished men of those times had a great flow of spirits, a cheerful and elastic wit far removed from the solemn wisdom of later days. What another thing was fame and a name then than now! This is seen in the familiar manner in which they were spoken of by each other and the nation at large,— *Kit* Marlowe, and *George* (Peele), and *Will* Shakespeare, and *Ben* Jonson,—great *fellows*,—*chaps*. . . .

Daniel deserves praise for his moderation, and sometimes has risen into poetry before you know it. Strong sense appears in his epistles, but you have to remember too often in what age he wrote, and yet that Shakespeare was his contemporary. His style is without the tricks of the trade and really in advance of his age. We can well believe that he was a retired scholar, who would keep himself shut up in his house two whole months together.

Donne was not a poet, but a man of strong sense, a sturdy English thinker, full of conceits and whimsicalities, hammering away at his subject, be it eulogy or epitaph, sonnet or satire, with the patience of a day laborer, without taste but with an occasional fine distinction or poetic phrase. He was rather *Doctor* Donne, than the *poet* Donne. His letters are perhaps best. . . .

We read Marlowe as so much poetical pabulum. It is food for poets, water from the Castalian Spring, some of the atmosphere of Parnassus, raw and crude indeed, and at times breezy, but pure and bracing. Few have so rich a phrase! He had drunk deep enough, and had that fine madness, as Drayton says,

"Which justly should possess a poet's brain."

We read his "Dr. Faustus," "Dido, Queen of Carthage," and "Hero and Leander," especially the last, without being wearied. He had many of the qualities of a great poet, and was in some degree worthy to precede Shakespeare. But he seems to have run to waste for want of seclusion and solitude, as if mere pause and deliberation would have added a new element of greatness to his poetry. . . .

All matter, indeed, is capable of entertaining thought.

March 13, 1846. The song sparrow and blackbird heard today. The snow going off. The ice in the pond one foot thick.

1850. The Hindoos are more serenely and thoughtfully religious than the Hebrews. They have perhaps a purer, more independent and impersonal knowledge of God. Their religious books describe the first inquisitive and contemplative access to God; the Hebrew bible a conscientious return, a grosser and more personal repentance. Repentance is not a free and fair highway to God. A wise man will dispense with repentance. It is shocking and passionate. God prefers that you approach him thoughtful, not penitent, though you are the chief of sinners. It is only by forgetting yourself that you draw near to him. . . .

I do not prefer one religion or philosophy to another. I have no sympathy with the bigotry and ignorance which make transient and partial and puerile distinctions between one man's faith or form of faith and another's,—as Christian and heathen. I pray to be delivered from narrowness, partiality, exaggeration, bigotry. To the philosopher all sects, all nations, are alike. I like Brahma, Hari, Buddha, the Great Spirit, as well as God.

The names of those who bought these fields of the red men, the wild men of the woods, are Buttrick, Davis, Barrett, Bulkley, etc., etc. (*Vide* History.) Here and there still you will find a man with Indian blood in his veins, an eccentric farmer descended from an Indian chief; or you will see a solitary pure-blooded Indian, looking as wild as ever among the pines, one of the last of the Massachusetts tribes, stepping into a railroad car with his gun.

Still here and there an Indian squaw with her dog, her only companion, lives in some lone house, insulted by school-children, making baskets and picking berries her employment. You will meet her on the highway, with few children or none, with melancholy face, history, destiny; stepping after her race; who had stayed to tuck them up in their long sleep. For whom berries condescend to grow. I have not seen one on the Musketaquid for many a year, and some who came up in their canoes and camped on its banks a dozen years ago had to ask me where it came from. A lone Indian woman without children, accompanied by her dog, wearing the shroud of her race, performing the last offices for her departed race. Not yet absorbed into the elements again; a daughter of the soil; one of the nobility of the land. The white man an imported weed,— burdock and mullein, which displace the ground-nut. . . .

I find the actual to be far less real to me than the imagined. Why this singular prominence and importance is given to the former, I do not know. In proportion as that which possesses my thoughts is removed from the actual, it impresses me. I have never met with anything so truly visionary and accidental as some actual events. They have affected me less than my dreams. Whatever actually happens to a man is wonderfully trivial and insignificant,—even to death itself, I imagine. He complains of the fates who drown him, that they do not touch *him*. They do not deal directly with him. I have in my pocket a button which I ripped off the coat of the Marquis of Ossoli on the seashore the other day. Held up, it intercepts the light and casts a shadow,—an *actual* button so called,—and yet all the life it is connected with is less substantial to me than my faintest dreams. This stream of events which we consent to call actual, and that other mightier stream which alone carries us with it,—what makes the difference? On the one our bodies float, and we have sympathy with it through them; on the other, our spirits. We are ever dying to one world and being born into another, and possibly no man knows whether he is at any time dead in the sense in which he affirms that phenomenon of another, or not. Our thoughts are the epochs of our life; all else is but as a journal of the winds that blew while we were here. . . .

Do a little more of that work which you have sometimes confessed to be good, which you feel that society and your justest judge rightly demands of you. Do what you reprove yourself for not doing. Know that you are neither satisfied nor dissatisfied with yourself without reason. Let me say to you and to myself in one breath, Cultivate the tree which you have found to bear fruit in your soil. Regard not your past failures nor successes. All the past is equally a failure and a success; it is a success in as much as it offers you the present opportunity. . . .

Do not read the newspapers. Improve every opportunity to be melancholy. Be as melancholy as you can be, and note the result. Rejoice with fate. As for health, consider yourself well, and mind your business. Who knows but you are dead already? Do not stop to be scared yet; there are more terrible things to come, and ever to come. Men die of fright and live of confidence. Be not simply obedient like the vegetables; set up your own Ebenezer. Of man's "*dis*obedience and the fruit," etc. Do not engage to find things as you think they are. Do what nobody can do for you. Omit to do everything else. . . .

From time to time I overlook the promised land, but I do not feel that I am travelling toward it. The moment I begin to look there, men and institutions get out of the way that I may see. I see nothing permanent in the society around me, and am not quite committed to any of its ways. . . .

I walk over the hills, to compare *great* things with *small*, as through a gallery of pictures, ever and anon looking through a gap in the wood, as through the frame of a picture, to a more distant wood or hillside, painted with several more coats of air. . . .

A field of water betrays the spirit that is in the air. It has new life and motion. It is intermediate between land and sky. On land, only the grass and trees wave, but the water itself is *rippled* by the wind. I see the breeze dash across it in streaks and flakes of light. It is somewhat singular that we should *look down* on the surface of water. We shall look down on the surface of air next, and mark where a still subtler spirit sweeps over *it*. . . .

Roman wormwood, pigweed, amaranth, polygonum, and one or two coarse kinds of grass reign now in the cultivated fields.

Though the potatoes have man with all his implements on their side, these rowdy and rampant weeds completely bury them, between the last hoeing and the digging. The potatoes hardly succeed with the utmost care: these weeds only ask to be *let alone* a little while. I judge that they have not got the rot. I sympathize with all this luxuriant growth of weeds. Such is the year. The weeds grow as if in sport and frolic.

Sept. 19. It is pleasant to have been to a place by the way a river went.

The forms of trees and groves change with every stroke of the oar. . . .

What does education often do? It makes a straight-cut ditch of a free, meandering brook.

You must walk like a camel, which is said to be the only beast which ruminates when it walks.

The actual life of men is not without a dramatic interest to the thinker. It is not in all its respects prosaic. Seventy thousand pilgrims proceed annually to Mecca from the various nations of Islam.

I was one evening passing a retired farmhouse which had a smooth green plat before it, just after sundown, when I saw a hen turkey which had gone to roost on the front fence with her wings outspread over her young now pretty well advanced, who were roosting on the next rail a foot or two below her. It completed a picture of rural repose and happiness such as I had not seen for a long time. A particularly neat and quiet place, where the very ground was swept around the woodpile. The neighboring fence of roots, agreeable forms for the traveller to study, like the bones of marine monsters and the horns of mastodons or megatheriums.

You might say of a philosopher that he was in this world as a spectator.

A squaw came to our door today with two pappooses, and said, "Me want a pie." Theirs is not common begging. You are merely the rich Indian who shares his goods with the poor. They merely offer you an opportunity to be generous and hospitable.

Nov. 16. In literature it is only the wild that attracts us. Dullness is only another name for tameness. It is the untamed, uncivilized, free, and wild thinking in Hamlet, in the Iliad, and in all the scriptures and mythologies that delights us,—not learned in the schools, not refined and polished by art. A truly good book is something as wildly natural and primitive, mysterious and marvellous, ambrosial and fertile, as a fungus or a lichen. Suppose the muskrat or beaver were to turn his views [*sic*] to literature, what fresh views of nature would be present! The fault of our books and other deeds is that they are too humane, I want something speaking in some measure to the condition of muskrats and skunk-cabbage as well as of men, —not merely to a pining and complaining coterie of philanthropists. . . .

My Journal should be the record of my love. I would write in it only of the things I love, my affection for any aspect of the world, what I love to think of. I have no more distinctness or pointedness in my yearnings than an expanding bud, which does indeed point to flower and fruit, to summer and autumn, but is aware of the warm sun and spring influence only. I feel ripe for something, yet do nothing, can't discover what that thing is. I feel fertile merely. It is seedtime with me. I have lain fallow long enough.

Notwithstanding a sense of unworthiness which possesses me, not without reason, notwithstanding that I regard myself as a good deal of a scamp, yet for the most part the spirit of the universe is unaccountably kind to me, and I enjoy perhaps an unusual share of happiness. Yet I question sometimes if there is not some settlement to come.

Nov. 21. I saw Fair Haven Pond with its island, and meadow between the island and the shore, and a strip of perfectly still and smooth water in the lee of the island, and two hawks, fish hawks perhaps, sailing over it. I did not see how it could be improved. Yet I do not see what these things can be. I begin to see such an object when I cease to *understand* it and see that I did not realize or appreciate it before, but I get no further than this. How adapted these forms and colors to my eye! A meadow and an island! What are these things? Yet the hawks and the ducks keep so aloof! and Nature is so reserved! I am made to love the pond and the meadow, as the wind is made to ripple the water.

Nov. 23. I find it to be the height of wisdom not to endeavor to oversee myself and live a life of prudence and common sense, but to see over and above myself, entertain sublime conjectures, to make myself the thoroughfare of thrilling thoughts, live all that can be lived. The man who is dissatisfied with himself, what can he not do?

Nov. 25. I feel a little alarmed when it happens that I have walked a mile into the woods bodily, without getting there in spirit. I would fain forget all my morning's occupation, my obligations to society. But sometimes it happens that I cannot easily shake off the village; the thought of some work, some surveying, will run in my head, and I am not where my body is. I am out of my senses. In my walks I would return to my senses like a bird or a beast. What business have I in the woods, if I am thinking of something out of the woods? . . .

I saw a muskrat come out of a hole in the ice. He is a man wilder than Ray or Melvin. While I am looking at him, I am thinking what he is thinking of me. He is a different sort of a man, that is all. He would dive when I went nearer, then reappear again, and had kept open a place five or six feet square so that it had not frozen, by swimming about in it. Then he would sit on the edge of the ice and busy himself about something. I could not see whether it was a clam or not. What a cold-blooded fellow! thoughts at a low temperature, sitting perfectly still so long on ice covered with water, mumbling a cold, wet clam in its shell. What safe, low, moderate thoughts it must have! It does not get on to stilts. The generations of muskrats do not fail. They are not preserved by the legislature of Massachusetts.

Jan. 7, 1851. I felt my spirits rise when I had got off the road into the open fields, and the sky had a new appearance. I stepped along more buoyantly. There was a warm sunset over the wooded valleys, a yellowish tinge on the pines. Reddish dun-colored clouds like dusky flames stood over it. And then streaks of blue sky were seen here and there. The life, the joy, that is in blue sky after a storm! There is no account of the blue sky in history. Before I walked in the ruts of travel; now I adventured.

Jan. 10. [Perhaps I am more] than usually jealous of my freedom. I feel that my connections with and obligations to society are at present very slight and transient. Those slight labors which afford me a livelihood, and by which I am serviceable to my contemporaries, are as yet a pleasure to me, and I am not often reminded that they are a necessity. So far I am successful, and only he is successful in his business who makes that pursuit which affords him the highest pleasure sustain him. But I foresee that if my wants should be much increased the labor required to supply them would become a drudgery. If I should sell both my forenoons and afternoons to society, neglecting my peculiar calling, there would be nothing left worth living for. I trust that I shall never thus sell my birthright for a mess of pottage. . . .

The arts teach us a thousand lessons. Not a yard of cloth can be woven without the most thorough fidelity in the weaver. The ship must be made *absolutely* tight before it is launched.

It is an important difference between two characters that the one is satisfied with a happy but level success but the other as constantly elevates his aims. Though my life is low, if my spirit looks upward habitually at an elevated angle, it is as it were redeemed. When the desire to be better than we are is really sincere we are instantly elevated, and so far better already. . . .

I would fain keep a journal which should contain those thoughts and impressions which I am most liable to forget that I have had; which would have in one sense the greatest remoteness, in another, the greatest nearness to me.

'Tis healthy to be sick sometimes.

I do not know but the reason why I love some Latin verses more than whole English poems is simply in the elegant terseness and conciseness of the language, an advantage which the individual appears to have shared with his nation. . . .

English literature from the days of the minstrels to the Lake Poets, Chaucer and Spenser and Shakespeare and Milton included, breathes no quite fresh and, in this sense, wild strain. It is an essentially tame and civilized literature, reflecting Greece and Rome. Her wilderness is a greenwood, her wild man a Robin Hood. There is plenty of genial love of nature in her poets, but [not so much of nature herself]. Her chronicles inform us when her wild animals, but not when the wild man in her, became extinct. There was need of America.

Feb. 9. I have heard that there is a Society for the Diffusion of Useful Knowledge. It is said that knowledge is power and the like. Methinks there is equal need of a Society for the Diffusion of Useful Ignorance, for what is most of our boasted so-called knowledge but a conceit that we know something, which robs us of the advantages of our actual ignorance.

For a man's ignorance sometimes is not only useful but beautiful, while his knowledge is oftentimes worse than useless, besides being ugly. In reference to important things, whose knowledge amounts to more than a consciousness of his ignorance? Yet what more refreshing and inspiring knowledge than this?

How often are we wise as serpents without being harmless as doves!

Donne says, "Who are a little wise the best fools be." Cudworth says, "We have all of us by nature μάντευμά τε (as both Plato and Aristotle call it), a certain divination, presage and parturient vaticination in our minds, of some higher good and perfection than either power or knowledge." Aristotle himself declares, that there is λόγου τι κρεῖττον, which is λόγου ἀρχή,—(something better than reason and knowledge, which is the principle and original of all). Lavater says, "Who finds the clearest not clear, thinks the darkest not obscure."

My desire for knowledge is intermittent; but my desire to commune with the spirit of the universe, to be intoxicated even with the fumes, call it, of that divine nectar, to bear my head through atmospheres and over heights unknown to my feet, is perennial and constant.

It is remarkable how few events or crises there are in our minds' histories, how little *exercised* we have been in our minds, how few experiences we have had.

A thousand assemble about the fountain in the public square, —the town pump,—be it full or dry, clear or turbid, every morning, but not one in a thousand is in the meanwhile drinking at that fountain's head. It is hard for the young, aye, and the old, man in the outskirts to keep away from the mill-dam a whole day; but he will find some excuse, as an ounce of cloves that might be wanted, or a *New England Farmer* still in the office, to tackle up the horse, or even go afoot, but he will go at some rate. This is not bad comparatively; this is because he cannot do better. In spite of his hoeing and chopping, he is unexpressed and undeveloped.

I do not know where to find in any literature, whether ancient or modern, any adequate account of that Nature with which I am acquainted. Mythology comes nearest to it of any.

Feb. 12. Wednesday. A beautiful day, with but little snow or ice on the ground. Though the air is sharp, as the earth is half bare the hens have strayed to some distance from the barns. The hens, standing around their lord and pluming themselves and still fretting a little, strive to fetch the year about.

A thaw has nearly washed away the snow and raised the river and the brooks and flooded the meadows, covering the old ice, which is still fast to the bottom.

I find that it is an excellent walk for variety and novelty and wildness, to keep round the edge of the meadow,—the ice not being strong enough to bear and transparent as water,—on the bare ground or snow, just between the highest water mark and the present water line,—a narrow, meandering walk, rich in unexpected views and objects. The line of rubbish which marks the higher tides—withered flags and reeds and twigs and cranberries—is to my eyes a very agreeable and significant line, which Nature traces along the edge of the meadows. It is a strongly marked, enduring natural line, which in summer reminds me that the water has once stood over where I walk.

Sometimes the grooved trees tell the same tale. The wrecks of the meadow, which fill a thousand coves, and tell a thousand tales to those who can read them. Our prairial, mediterranean shore. The gentle rise of water around the trees in the meadow, where oaks and maples stand far out in the sea, and young elms sometimes are seen standing close around some rock which lifts its head above the water, as if protecting it, preventing it from being washed away, though in truth they owe their origin and preservation to it. It first invited and detained their seed, and now preserves the soil in which they grow. A pleasant reminiscence of the rise of waters, to go up one side of the river and down the other, following this way, which meanders so much more than the river itself. If you cannot go on the ice, you are then gently compelled to take this course, which is on the whole more beautiful,—to follow the sinuosities of the meadow. Between the highest water mark and the present water line is a space generally from a few feet to a few rods in width. When the water comes over the road, then my spirits rise,—when the fences are carried away. A prairial walk. Saw a caterpillar crawling about on the snow.

The earth is so bare that it makes an impression on me as if it were catching cold.

Feb. 14. Consider the farmer, who is commonly regarded as the healthiest man. He may be the toughest, but he is not the healthiest. He has lost his elasticity; he can neither run nor jump. Health is the free use and command of all our faculties, and equal development. His is the health of the ox, an overworked buffalo. His joints are stiff. The resemblance is true even in particulars. He is cast away in a pair of cowhide boots, and travels at an ox's pace. Indeed, in some places he puts his foot into the skin of an ox's shin. It would do him good to be thoroughly shampooed to make him supple. His health is an insensibility to all influence. But only the healthiest man in the world is sensible to the finest influence; he who is affected by more or less of electricity in the air.

We shall see but little way if we require to understand what we see. How few things can a man measure with the tape of his understanding! How many greater things might he be seeing in the meanwhile!

One afternoon in the fall, November 21st, I saw Fair Haven Pond with its island and meadow; between the island and the shore, a strip of perfectly smooth water in the lee of the island; and two hawks sailing over it; and something more I saw which cannot easily be described, which made me say to myself that the landscape could not be improved. I did not see how it could be improved. Yet I do not know what these things can be; I begin to see such objects only when I leave off understanding them, and afterwards remember that I did not appreciate them before.

Feb. 18. There is little or nothing to be remembered written on the subject of getting an honest living. Neither the New Testament nor Poor Richard speaks to our condition. I cannot think of a single page which entertains, much less answers, the questions which I put to myself on this subject. How to make the getting our living poetic! for if it is not poetic, it is not life but death that we get. Is it that men are too disgusted with their experience to speak of it? or that commonly they do not question the common modes? The most practically important of all questions, it seems to me, is how shall I get my living, and yet I find little or nothing said to the purpose in any book. Those who are living on the interest of money inherited, or dishonestly, i.e. by false methods, acquired, are of course incompetent to answer it. I consider that society with all its arts, has done nothing for us in this respect. One would think, from looking at literature, that this question had never disturbed a solitary individual's musings. Cold and hunger seem more friendly to my nature than those methods which men have adopted and advise to ward them off. If it were not that I desire to do something here,—accomplish some work,—I should certainly prefer to suffer and die rather than be at the pains to get a living by the modes men propose.

Feb. 27. Of two men, one of whom knows nothing about a subject, and, what is extremely rare, knows that he knows nothing, and the other really knows something about it, but thinks that he knows all,—what great advantage has the latter over the former? which is the best to deal with? I do not know that knowledge amounts to anything more definite than a novel and grand surprise, or a sudden revelation of the insufficiency of all that we had called knowledge before; an indefinite sense of the grandeur and glory of the universe. . . .

A culture which imports much muck from the meadows and deepens the soil, not that which trusts to heating manures and improved agricultural implements only.

How, when a man purchases a thing, he is determined to get and get hold of it, using how many expletives and how long a string of synonymous or similar terms signifying possession, in the legal process! What's mine's my own. An old deed of a small piece of swamp land, which I have lately surveyed at the risk of being mired past recovery, says that "The said Spaulding his Heirs and Assigns, shall and may from this [?] time, and at all times forever hereafter, by force and virtue of these presents, lawfullly, peaceably and quietly have, hold, use, occupy, possess and enjoy the said swamp," etc. . . .

Walking in the woods, it may be, some afternoon, the shadow of the wings of a thought flits across the landscape of my mind, and I am reminded how little eventful are our lives. What have been all these wars and rumors of wars, and modern discoveries and improvements so-called? A mere irritation in the skin. But this shadow which is so soon past, and whose substance is not detected, suggests that there are events of importance whose interval is to us a true historic period. . . .

Obey the law which reveals, and not the law revealed.

Carrying Off Sims [A Slave]

A recent English writer (De Quincey), endeavoring to account for the atrocities of Caligula and Nero, their monstrous and anomalous cruelties, and the general servility and corruption which they imply, observes that it is difficult to believe that "the descendants of a people so severe in their habits" as the Romans had been "could thus rapidly" have degenerated and that, "in reality, the citizens of Rome were at this time a new race, brought together from every quarter of the world, but especially from Asia." A vast "proportion of the ancient citizens had been cut off by the sword," and such multitudes of emancipated slaves from Asia had been invested with the rights of citizens "that, in a single generation, Rome became almost transmuted into a baser metal." As Juvenal complained, "the Orontes . . . had mingled its impure waters with those of the Tiber." And "probably, in the time of Nero, not one man in six was of pure Roman descent." Instead of such, says another, "came Syrians, Cappadocians, Phrygians, and other enfranchised slaves." "These in half a century had sunk so low, that Tiberius pronounced her [Rome's] very senators to be *homines ad servitutem natos*, men born to be slaves."

So one would say, in the absence of particular genealogical evidence, that the vast majority of the inhabitants of the city of Boston, even those of senatorial dignity,—the Curtises, Lunts, Woodburys, and others,—were not descendants of the men of the Revolution,—the Hancocks, Adamses, Otises,—but some "Syrians, Cappadocians, and Phrygians," merely, *homines ad servitutem natos*, men born to be slaves. But I would have done with comparing ourselves with our ancestors, for on the whole I believe that even they, if somewhat braver and less corrupt than we, were not men of so much principle and generosity as to go to war in behalf of another race in their midst. I do not believe that the North will soon come to blows with the South on this question. It would be too bright a page to be written in the history of the race at present. . . .

In '75 two or three hundred of the inhabitants of Concord assembled at one of the bridges with arms in their hands to assert the right of three millions to tax themselves, to have a voice in governing themselves. About a week ago the authorities of Boston, having the sympathy of many of the inhabitants of Concord, assembled in the gray of the dawn, assisted by a still larger armed force, to send back a perfectly innocent man, and one whom they knew to be innocent, into a slavery as complete as the world ever knew. Of course it makes not the least difference—I wish you to consider this—who the man was,—whether he was Jesus Christ or another,—for inasmuch as ye did it unto the least of these his brethren ye did it unto him. Do you think *he* would have stayed here in liberty and let the black man go into slavery in his stead? They sent him back, I say, to live in slavery with other three millions—mark that—whom the same slave power, or slavish power, North and South, holds in that condition,—three millions who do not, like the first mentioned, assert the right to govern themselves but simply to run away and stay away from their prison.

Just a week afterward, those inhabitants of this town who especially sympathize with the authorities of Boston in this their deed caused the bells to be rung and the cannon to be fired to celebrate the courage and the love of liberty of those men who assembled at the bridge. As if *those* three millions had fought for the right to be free themselves, but to hold in slavery three million others. Why, gentlemen, even consistency, though it is much abused, is sometimes a virtue. Every humane and intelligent inhabitant of Concord, when he or she heard those bells and those cannon, thought not so much of the events of the 19th of April, 1775, as of the event of the 12th of April, 1851.

I wish my townsmen to consider that, whatever the human law may be, neither an individual nor a nation can ever deliberately commit the least act of injustice without having to pay the penalty for it. A government which deliberately enacts injustice, and persists in it!—it will become the laughing-stock of the world. . . .

When I read the account of the carrying back of the fugitive into slavery, which was read last Sunday evening, and read also what was not read here, that the man who made the prayer on the wharf was Daniel Foster of *Concord*, I could not help feeling a slight degree of pride because, of all the towns in the Commonwealth, Concord was the only one distinctly named as being represented in that new tea-party, and, as she had a place in the first, so would have a place in this, the last and perhaps next most important chapter of the History of Massachusetts. But my second feeling, when I reflected how short a time that gentleman has resided in this town, was one of doubt and shame, because the *men* of Concord in recent times have done nothing to entitle them to the honor of having their town named in such a connection. . . .

I think that we are not commonly aware that man is our contemporary,—that in this strange, outlandish world, so barren, so prosaic, fit not to live in but merely to pass through, that even here so divine a creature as man does actually live. Man, the crowning fact, the god we know. While the earth supports so rare an inhabitant, there is somewhat to cheer us. Who shall say that there is no God, if there is a *just* man. It is only within a year that it has occurred to me that there is such a being actually existing on the globe. Now that I perceive that it is so, many questions assume a new aspect.

May 27. I saw an organ-grinder this morning before a rich man's house, thrilling the street with harmony, loosening the very paving-stones and tearing the routine of life to rags and tatters, when the lady of the house shoved up a window and in a semiphilanthropic tone inquired if he wanted anything to eat. But he, very properly it seemed to me, kept on grinding and paid no attention to her question, feeding her ears with melody unasked for.

June 11. Wednesday. Last night a beautiful summer night, not too warm, moon not quite full, after two or three rainy days. Walked to Fair Haven by railroad, returning by Potter's pasture and Sudbury road. I feared at first that there would be too much white light, like the pale remains of daylight, and not a yellow, gloomy, dreamier light; that it would be like a candlelight by day; but when I got away from the town and deeper into the night, it was better. I hear whip-poor-wills, and see a few fireflies in the meadow.

I saw by the shadows cast by the inequalities of the clayey sand-bank in the Deep Cut that it was necessary to see objects by moonlight as well as sunlight, to get a complete notion of them. This bank had looked much more flat by day, when the light was stronger, but now the heavy shadows revealed its prominences. The prominences are light, made more remarkable by the dark shadows which they cast.

When I rose out of the Deep Cut into the old pigeon-place field, I rose into a warmer stratum of air, it being lighter. It told of the day, of sunny noontide hours,—an air in which work had been done, which men had breathed. It still remembered the sunny banks,—of the laborer wiping his brow, of the bee humming amid flowers, the hum of insects. Here is a puff of warmer air which has taken its station on the hills; which has come up from the sultry plains of noon.

I hear the nighthawks uttering their squeaking notes high in the air now at nine o'clock P.M., and occasionally—what I do not remember to have heard so late—their booming note. It sounds more as if under a cope than by day. The sound is not so fugacious, going off to be lost amid the spheres, but is echoed hollowly to earth, making the low roof of heaven vibrate. Such a sound is more confused and dissipated by day.

The whip-poor-will suggests how wide asunder [are] the woods and the town. Its note is very rarely heard by those who live on the street, and then it is thought to be of ill omen. Only the dwellers on the outskirts of the village hear it occasionally. It sometimes comes into their yards. But go into the woods in a warm night at this season, and it is the prevailing sound. I hear now five or six at once. It is no more of ill omen therefore here than the night and the moonlight are. It is a bird not only of the woods, but of the night side of the woods.

New beings have usurped the air we breathe, rounding Nature, filling her crevices with sound. To sleep where you may hear the whip-poor-will in your dreams!

I hear from this upland, from which I see Wachusett by day, a wagon crossing one of the bridges. I have no doubt that in some places tonight I should be sure to hear every carriage which crossed a bridge over the river within the limits of Concord, for in such an hour and atmosphere the sense of hearing is wonderfully assisted and asserts a new dignity, and

[we] become the Hearalls of the story. The late traveller cannot drive his horse across the distant bridge, but this still and resonant atmosphere tells the tale to my ear. Circumstances are very favorable to the transmission of such a sound. In the first place, planks so placed and struck like a bell swung near the earth emit a very resonant and penetrating sound; add that the bell is, in this instance, hung over water, and that the night air, not only on account of its stillness, but perhaps on account of its density, is more favorable to the transmission of sound. If the whole town were a raised planked floor, what a din there would be!

I hear some whip-poor-wills on hills, others in thick wooded vales, which ring hollow and cavernous, like an apartment or cellar, with their note. As when I hear the working of some artisan from within an apartment.

I now descend round the corner of the grain-field, through the pitch pine wood into a lower field, more inclosed by woods, and find myself in a colder, damp and misty atmosphere, with much dew on the grass. I seem to be nearer to the origin of things. There is something creative and primal in the cool mist. This dewy mist does not fail to suggest music to me, unaccountably; fertility, the origin of things. An atmosphere which has forgotten the sun, where the ancient principle of moisture prevails. It is laden with the condensed fragrance of plants and, as it were, distilled in dews.

The woodland paths are never seen to such advantage as in a moonlight night, so embowered, still opening before you almost against expectation as you walk; you are so completely in the woods, and yet your feet meet no obstacles. It is as if it were not a path, but an open, winding passage through the bushes, which your feet find.

Now I go by the spring, and when I have risen to the same level as before, find myself in the warm stratum again.

The woods are about as destitute of inhabitants at night as the streets. In both there will be some nightwalkers. There are but few wild creatures to seek their prey. The greater part of its inhabitants have retired to rest.

Ah, that life that I have known! How hard it is to remember what is most memorable! We remember how we itched, not how our hearts beat. I can sometimes recall to mind the quality, the immortality, of my youthful life, but in memory is the only relation to it.

The very cows have now left their pastures and are driven home to their yards. I meet no creature in the fields.

I hear the night-warbler breaking out as in his dreams, made so from the first for some mysterious reason.

Our spiritual side takes a more distinct form, like our shadow which we see accompanying us.

I do not know but I feel less vigor at night; my legs will not carry me so far; as if the night were less favorable to muscular exertion,—weakened us, somewhat as darkness turns plants pale. But perhaps my experience is to be referred to being already exhausted by the day, and I have never tried the experiment fairly. Yet sometimes after a hard day's work I have found myself unexpectedly vigorous. It was so hot summer before last that the Irish laborers on the railroad worked by night instead of day for a while, several of them having been killed by the heat and cold water. I do not know but they did as much work as ever by day. Yet methinks Nature would not smile on such labors.

Only the Hunter's and Harvest moons are famous, but I think that each full moon deserves to be and has its own character well marked. One might be called the Midsummer-Night Moon.

The wind and water are still awake. At night you are sure to hear what wind there is stirring. The wind blows, the river flows, without resting. There lies Fair Haven Lake, undistinguishable from fallen sky. The pines seem forever foreign, at least to the civilized man,—not only their aspect but their scent, and their turpentine.

So still and moderate is the night! No scream is heard, whether of fear or joy. No great comedy nor tragedy is being enacted. The chirping of crickets is the most universal, if not the loudest, sound. There is no French Revolution in Nature, no excess. She is warmer or colder by a degree or two.

By night no flowers, at least no variety of colors. The pinks are no longer pink; they only shine faintly, reflecting more light. Instead of flowers underfoot, stars overhead.

My shadow has the distinctness of a second person a certain black companion bordering on the imp, and I ask, "Who is this?" which I see dodging behind me as I am about to sit down on a rock.

No one, to my knowledge, has observed the minute differences in the seasons. Hardly two nights are alike. The rocks do not feel warm tonight, for the air is warmest; nor does the sand particularly. A book of the seasons, each page of which should be written in its own season and out-of-doors, or in its own locality wherever it may be.

When you get into the road, though far from the town, and feel the sand under your feet, it is as if you had reached your own gravel walk. You no longer hear the whip-poor-will, nor regard your shadow, for here you expect a fellow-traveller. You catch yourself walking merely. The road leads your steps and thoughts alike to the town. You see only the path, and your thoughts wander from the objects which are presented to your senses. You are no longer in place. It is like conformity,— walking in the ways of men. . . .

June 22. The birch is the surveyor's tree. It makes the best stakes to look at through the sights of a compass, except when there is snow on the ground. Their white bark was not made in vain. In surveying wood-lots I have frequent occasion to say this is what they were made for.

I see that Dugan has trimmed off and peeled the limbs of the willows on the Turnpike as well as the Acton powder-mill. I believe they get eight dollars a cord for this wood.

I. Hapgood of Acton got me last Friday to compare the level of his cellar-bottom with his garden, for, as he says, when Robbins & Wetherbee keep the water of Nashoba Brook back so as to flood his garden, it comes into his cellar. I found that part of the garden five inches lower than the cellar-bottom. Men are affected in various ways by the actions of others. If a man far away builds a dam, I have water in my cellar. . . .

We are enabled to criticise others only when we are different from, and in a given particular superior to, them ourselves. By our aloofness from men and their affairs we are enabled to overlook and criticise them. There are but few men who stand on the hills by the roadside. I am sane only when I have risen above my common sense, when I do not take the foolish view of things which is commonly taken, when I do not live for the low ends for which men commonly live. Wisdom is not common. To what purpose have I senses, if I am thus absorbed in affairs? My pulse must beat with Nature. After a hard day's work without a thought, turning my very brain into a mere tool, only in the quiet of evening do I so far recover my senses as to hear the cricket, which in fact has been chirping all day. In my better hours I am conscious of the influx of a serene and unquestionable wisdom which partly unfits, and if I yielded to it more rememberingly would wholly unfit me, for what is called the active business of life, for that furnishes nothing on which the eye of reason can rest. What is that other kind of life to which I am thus continually allured? which alone I love? Is it a life for this world? Can a man feed and clothe himself gloriously who keeps only the truth steadily before him? who calls in no evil to his aid? Are there duties which necessarily interfere with the serene perception of truth? Are our serene moments mere foretastes of heaven,—joys gratuitously vouchsafed to us as a consolation,—or simply a transient realization of what might be the whole tenor of our lives?

To be calm, to be serene! There is the calmness of the lake when there is not a breath of wind; there is the calmness of a stagnant ditch. So it is with us. Sometimes we are clarified and calmed healthily, as we never were before in our lives, not by an opiate, but by some unconscious obedience to the all-just laws, so that we become like a still lake of purest crystal and without an effort out depths are revealed to ourselves. All the world goes by us and is reflected in our deeps. Such clarity! obtained by such pure means! by simple living, by honesty of purpose. We live and rejoice. I awoke into a music which no one about me heard. Whom shall I thank for it? The luxury of wisdom! the luxury of virtue! Are there any intemperate in these things? I feel my Maker blessing me.

June 23. There is some advantage in being the humblest, cheapest, least dignified man in the village, so that the very stable boys shall damn you. Methinks I enjoy that advantage to an unusual extent. There is many a coarsely well-meaning fellow, who knows only the skin of me, who addresses me familiarly by my Christian name. I get the whole good of him and lose nothing myself. There is "Sam" the jailer,—whom I never call Sam, however,—who exclaimed last evening: "Thoreau, are you going up the street pretty soon? Well, just take a couple of these handbills along and drop one in at Hoar's piazza and one at Holbrook's and I'll do as much for you another time." I am not above being used, aye abused, sometimes.

July 7. I have been tonight with Anthony Wright to look through Perez Blood's telescope a second time. A dozen of Blood's neighbors were swept along in the stream of our curiosity. One who lived half a mile this side said that Blood had been down that way within a day or two with his terrestrial, or day, glass, looking into the eastern horizon [at] the hills of Billerica, Burlington, and Woburn. I was amused to see what sort of respect this man with a telescope had obtained from his neighbors, something akin to that which savages award to civilized men, though in this case the interval between the parties was very slight. Mr. Blood, with his skull-cap on, his short figure, his north European figure, made me think of Tycho Brahe. He did not invite us into his house this cool evening,— men nor women,—nor did he ever before to my knowledge. I am still contented to see the stars with my naked eye. Mr. Wright asked him what his instrument cost. He answered, "Well, that is something I don't like to tell." (Stuttering or hesitating in his speech a little as usual.) "It is a very proper question, however." "Yes," said I, "and you think that you have given a very proper answer. . . ."

With a certain wariness, but not without a slight shudder at the danger oftentimes, I perceive how near I had come to admitting into my mind the details of some trivial affair, as a case at court; and I am astonished to observe how willing men are to lumber their minds with such rubbish,—to permit idle rumors, tales, incidents, even of an insignificant kind, to intrude upon what should be the sacred ground of the thoughts. Shall the temple of our thought be a public arena where the most trivial affairs of the market and the gossip of the tea-table is discussed,—a dusty, noisy trivial place? Or shall it be a quarter of heaven itself, a place consecrated to the service of the gods, a hypaethral temple? I find it so difficult to dispose of the few facts which to me are significant that I hesitate to burden my mind with the most insignificant which only a divine mind could illustrate. . . .

I think that we should treat our minds as innocent and ingenuous children whose guardians we are,—be careful what objects and what subjects we thrust on their attention. Even the facts of science may dust the mind by their dryness, unless they are in a sense effaced each morning, or rather rendered fertile by the dews of fresh and living truth. Every thought that passes through the mind helps to wear and tear it, and to deepen the ruts, which, as in the streets of Pompeii, evince how much it has been used. How many things there are concerning which we might well deliberate whether we had better know them! Routine, conventionality, manners, etc., etc.,—how insensibly an undue attention to these dissipates and impoverishes the mind, robs it of its simplicity and strength, emasculates it!

Knowledge does not come to us by details but by *lieferungs* from the gods. . . .

I can express adequately only the thought which I *love* to express. All the faculties in repose but the one you are using, the whole energy concentrated in that. Be ever so little distracted, your thoughts so little confused, your engagements so few, your attention so free, your existence so mundane, that in all places and in all hours you can hear the sound of crickets in those seasons when they are to be heard.

II

WALKING BY NIGHT

July 11, 1851. Friday. At 7.15 P.M. with W. E. C. go forth to see
the moon, the glimpses of the moon. We think she is not quite
full; we can detect a little flatness on the eastern side. Shall we
wear thick coats? The day has been warm enough, but how
cool will the night be? It is not sultry, as the last night. As a
general rule, it is best to wear your thickest coat even in a July
night. Which way shall we walk? Northwest, that we may see
the moon returning? But on that side the river prevents our
walking in the fields, and on other accounts that direction is not
so attractive. We go toward Bear Garden Hill. The sun is
setting. The meadow-sweet has bloomed. These dry hills and
pastures are the places to walk by moonlight. The moon is
silvery still, not yet inaugurated. The tree-tops are seen against
the amber west. I seem to see the outlines of one spruce among
them distinguishable afar. My thoughts expand and flourish
most on this barren hill, where in the twilight I see the moss
spreading in rings and prevailing over the short, thin grass,
carpeting the earth, adding a few inches of green to its circle
annually while it dies within.

As we round the sandy promontory, we try the sand and rocks
with our hands. The sand is cool on the surface but warmer a
few inches beneath, though the contrast is not so great as it was
in May. The larger rocks are perceptibly warm. I pluck the
blossom of the milkweed in the twilight and find how sweet it
smells. The white blossoms of the Jersey tea dot the hillside,
with the yarrow everywhere. Some woods are black as clouds;
if we knew not they were green by day, they would appear
blacker still. When we sit, we hear the mosquitoes hum. The
woodland paths are not the same by night as by day, if they are
a little grown up, the eye cannot find them, but must give the

reins to the feet, as the traveller to his horse. So we went through the aspens at the base of the Cliffs, their round leaves reflecting the lingering twilight on the one side, the waxing moonlight on the other. Always the path was unexpectedly open.

Now we are getting into moonlight. We see it reflected from particular stumps in the depths of the darkest woods, and from the stems of trees, as if it selected what to shine on,—a silvery light. It is a light, of course, which we have had all day, but which we have not appreciated, and proves how remarkable a lesser light can be when a greater has departed. How simply and naturally the moon presides! 'Tis true she was eclipsed by the sun, but now she acquires an almost equal respect and worship by reflecting and representing him, with some new quality, perchance, added to his light, showing how original the disciple may be who still in midday is seen, though pale and cloud-like, beside his master. Such is a worthy disciple. In his master's presence he still is seen and preserves a distinct existence; and in his absence he reflects and represents him, not without adding some new quality to his light, not servile and never rival. As the master withdraws himself, the disciple, who was a pale cloud before, begins to emit a silvery light, acquiring at last a tinge of golden as the darkness deepens, but not enough to scorch the seeds which have been planted or to dry up the fertilizing dews which are falling.

Passing now near Well Meadow Head toward Baker's orchard. The sweet-fern and indigo-weed fill the path up to one's middle, wetting us with dews so high. The leaves are shining and flowing. We wade through the luxuriant vegetation, seeing no bottom. Looking back toward the Cliffs, some dead trees in the horizon, high on the rocks, make a wild New Hampshire prospect. There is the faintest possible mist over the pond-holes, where the frogs are eructating, like the falling of huge drops, the bursting of mephitic air-bubbles rising from the bottom, a sort of blubbering,—such conversation as I *have* heard between men, a belching conversation, expressing a sympathy of stomachs and abdomens. The peculiar appearance of the indigo-weed, its misty massiveness, is striking. In Baker's orchard the thick grass looks like a sea of mowing in this weird moonlight, a bottomless sea of grass. Our feet must be imaginative, must know the earth in imagination only, as well as our heads. We sit on the fence, and, where it is broken and interrupted, the fallen and slanting rails are lost in the grass (really thin and wiry) as in water. We even see our tracks a long way behind, where we have brushed off the dew. The clouds are peculiarly wispy tonight, somewhat like fine flames, not massed and dark nor downy, not thick, but slight, thin wisps of mist.

I hear the sound of Heywood's Brook falling into Fair Haven Pond, inexpressibly refreshing to my senses. It seems to flow through my very bones. I hear it with insatiable thirst. It allays some sandy heat in me. It affects my circulations; methinks my arteries have sympathy with it. What is it I hear but the pure waterfalls within me, in the circulation of my blood, the streams that fall into my heart? What mists do I ever see but such as hang over and rise from my blood? The sound of this gurgling water, running thus by night as by day, falls on all my dashes, fills all my buckets, overflows my float-boards, turns all the machinery of my nature, makes me a flume, a sluice-way, to the springs of nature. Thus I am washed; thus I drink and quench my thirst. Where the streams fall into the lake, if they are only a few inches more elevated, all walkers may hear.

On the high path through Baker's wood I see, or rather feel, the tephrosia. Now we come out into the open pasture. And under those woods of elm and buttonwood, where still no light is seen, repose a family of human beings. By night there is less to distinguish this locality from the woods and meadows we have threaded. We might go very near to farmhouses covered with ornamental trees and standing on a highroad, thinking that [we] were in the most retired woods and fields still. Having yielded to sleep, man is a less obtrusive inhabitant of nature. Now, having reached the dry pastures again, we are surrounded by a flood of moonlight. The dim cart-path over the sward curves gracefully through the pitch pines, ever to some more fairy-like spot. The rails in the fences shine like silver. We know not whether we are sitting on the ruins of a wall, or the materials which are to compose a new one. I see, half a mile off, a phosphorescent arc on the hillside, where Bartlett's Cliff reflects the moonlight. Going by the shanty, I smell the excrements of its inhabitants, which I had never smelt before.

And now, at half-past 10 o'clock, I hear the cockerels crow in Hubbard's barns, and morning is already anticipated. It is the feathered, wakeful thought in us that anticipates the following day. This sound is wonderfully exhilarating at all times. These birds are worth far more to me for their crowing and cackling than for their drumsticks and eggs. How singular the connection of the hen with man,—that she leaves her eggs in his barns always! She is a domestic fowl, though still a little shyish of him. I cannot [help] looking at the whole as an experiment still and wondering that in each case it succeeds. There is no doubt at last but hens may be kept. They will put their eggs in your barn by a tacit agreement. They will not wander far from your yard.

July 12. 8 P.M. Now at least the moon is full, and I walk alone, which is best by night, if not by day always. Your companion must sympathize with the present mood. The conversation must be located where the walkers are, and vary exactly with the scene and events and the contour of the ground. Farewell to those who will talk of nature unnaturally, whose presence is an interruption. I know but one with whom I can walk. I might as well be sitting in a bar-room with them as walk and talk with most. We are never side by side in our thoughts, and we cannot hear each other's silence. Indeed, we cannot be silent. We are forever breaking silence, that is all, and mending nothing. How can they keep together who are going different ways!

I start a sparrow from her three eggs in the grass, where she had settled for the night. The earliest corn is beginning to show its tassels now, and I scent it as I walk,—its peculiar dry scent. (This afternoon I gathered ripe blackberries, and felt as if the autumn had commenced.) Now perchance many sounds and sights only remind me that they once said something to me, and are so by association interesting. I go forth to be reminded of a previous state of existence, if perchance any memento of it is to be met with hereabouts. I have no doubt that Nature preserves her integrity. Nature is in as rude health as when Homer sang. We may at last by our sympathies be well. I see a skunk on Bear Garden Hill stealing noiselessly away from me, while the moon shines over the pitch pines, which send long shadows down the hill. Now, looking back, I see it shining on the south side of farmhouses and barns with a weird light, for I pass here half an hour later than last night. I smell the huckleberry bushes. I hear a human voice, some laborer singing after his day's toil, —which I do not often hear. Loud it must be, for it is far away. Methinks I should know it for a white man's voice. Some strains have the melody of an instrument. Now I hear the sound of a bugle in the "Corner," reminding me of poetic wars; a few flourishes and the bugler has gone to rest. At the foot of the Cliff hill I hear the sound of the clock striking nine, as distinctly as within a quarter of a mile usually, though there is no wind. The moonlight is more perfect than last night; hardly a cloud in the sky, only a few fleecy ones. There is more serenity and more light. I hear that sort of throttled or chuckling note as of a bird flying high, now from this side, then from that. Methinks when I turn my head I see Wachusett from the side of the hill, I smell butter-and-eggs as I walk. I am startled by the rapid transit of some wild animal across my path, a rabbit or a fox,—or you hardly know if it be not a bird. Looking down from the cliffs, the leaves of the tree-tops shine more than ever by day. Here and there a lightning-bug shows his greenish light over the tops of the trees.

As I return through the orchard, a foolish robin bursts away from his perch unnaturally, with the habits of man. The air is remarkably still and unobjectionable on the hilltop, and the whole world below is covered as with a gossamer blanket of moonlight. It is just about as yellow as a blanket. It is a great dimly burnished shield with darker blotches on its surface. You have lost some light, it is true, but you have got this simple and magnificent stillness, brooding like genius.

July 16. Wednesday. Methinks my present experience is nothing; my past experience is all in all. I think that no experience which I have today comes up to, or is comparable with, the experiences of my boyhood. And not only this is true, but as far back as I can remember I have unconsciously referred to the experiences of a previous state of existence. "For life is a forgetting," etc. Formerly, methought, nature developed as I developed, and grew up with me. My life was ecstasy. In youth, before I lost any of my senses, I can remember that I was all alive, and inhabited my body with inexpressible satisfaction; both its weariness and its refreshment were sweet to me. This earth was the most glorious musical instrument, and I was audience to its strains. To have such sweet impressions made on us, such ecstasies begotten of the breezes! I can remember how I was astonished. I said to myself,—I said to others,—"There comes into my mind such an indescribable, infinite, all-absorbing, divine, heavenly pleasure, a sense of elevation and expansion, and [I] have had nought to do with it. I perceive that I am dealt with by superior powers. This is a pleasure, a joy, an existence which I have not procured myself. I speak as a witness on the stand, and tell what I have perceived." The morning and the evening were sweet to me, and I led a life aloof from society of men. I wondered if a mortal had ever known what I knew. I looked in books for some recognition of a kindred experience, but, strange to say, I found none. Indeed, I was slow to discover that other men had had this experience, for it had been possible to read books and to associate with men on other grounds. The maker of me was improving me. When I detected this interference I was profoundly moved. For years I marched as to a music in comparison with which the military music of the streets is noise and discord. I was daily intoxicated, and yet no man could call me intemperate. With all your science can you tell how it is, and whence it is, that light comes into the soul? . . .

When formerly I was looking about to see what I could do for a living, some sad experience in conforming to the wishes of friends being fresh in my mind to tax my ingenuity, I thought often and seriously of picking huckleberries; that surely I could do, and its small profits might suffice, so little capital it required, so little distraction from my wonted thoughts, I foolishly thought. While my acquaintances went unhesitatingly into trade or the professions, I thought of this occupation as most like theirs; ranging the hills all summer to pick the berries which came in my way, which I might carelessly dispose of; so to keep the flocks of King Admetus. My greatest skill has been to want but little. I also dreamed that I might gather the wild herbs, or carry evergreens to such villagers as loved to be reminded of the woods, and so find my living got. But I have since learned that trade curses everything it handles; and though you *trade* in messages from heaven, the whole curse of trade attaches to the business.

July 21. 8 A.M. The forenoon is fuller of light. The butterflies on the flowers look like other and frequently larger flowers themselves. Now I yearn for one of those old, meandering, dry, uninhabited roads, which lead away from towns, which lead us away from temptation, which conduct to the outside of earth, over its uppermost crust; where you may forget in what country you are travelling; where no farmer can complain that you are treading down his grass, no gentleman who has recently constructed a seat in the country that you are trespassing; on which you can go off at half-cock and wave adieu to the village; along which you may travel like a pilgrim, going nowhither; where travellers are not too often to be met; where my spirit is free; where the walls and fences are not cared for, where your head is more in heaven than your feet are on earth; which have long reaches where you can see the approaching traveller half a mile off and be prepared for him; not so luxuriant a soil as to attract men; some root and stump fences which do not need attention; where travellers have no occasion to stop, but pass along and leave you to your thoughts; where it makes no odds which way you face, whether you are going or coming, whether it is morning or evening, mid-noon or midnight; where earth is cheap enough by being public; where you can walk and think with least obstruction, there being nothing to measure progress by; where you can pace when your breast is full, and cherish your moodiness; where you are not in false relations with men, are not dining nor conversing with them; by which you may go to the uttermost parts of the earth. It is wide enough, wide as the thoughts it allows to visit you. Sometimes it is some particular half-dozen rods which I wish to find myself pacing over, as where certain airs blow; then my life will come to me, methinks; like a hunter I walk in wait for it. When I am against this bare promontory of a huckleberry hill, then forsooth my thoughts will expand. Is it some influence, as a vapor which exhales from the ground, or something in the gales which blow there, or in all things there brought together agreeably to my spirit? The walls must not be too high, imprisoning me, but low, with numerous gaps. The trees must not be too numerous, nor the hills too near, bounding the view, nor the soil too rich, attracting the attention to the earth. It must simply be the way and the life,—a way that was never known to be repaired, nor to need repair, within the memory of the oldest inhabitant. I cannot walk habitually in those ways that are liable to be mended; for sure it was the devil only that wore them. Never by the heel of thinkers (of thought) were they worn; the zephyrs could repair that damage. The saunterer wears out no road, even though he travel on it, and therefore should pay no highway, or rather *low* way tax. He may be taxed to construct a higher way than men travel. A way which no geese defile, nor hiss along it, but only sometimes their wild brethren fly far overhead; which the kingbird and the swallow twitter over, and the song sparrow sings on its rails; where the small red butterfly is at home on the yarrow, and no boys threaten it with imprisoning hat. There I can walk and stalk and pace and plod. Which nobody but Jonas Potter travels beside me; where no cow but his is tempted to linger for the herbage by its side; where the guide-board is fallen, and now the hand points to heaven significantly,—to a Sudbury and Marlborough in the skies. That's a road I can travel, that the particular Sudbury I am bound for, six miles an hour, or two, as you please; and few

there be that enter thereon. There I can walk, and recover the
lost child that I am without any ringing of a bell; where there
was nothing ever discovered to detain a traveller, but all went
through about their business; where I never passed the time
of day with any,—indifferent to me were the arbitrary divisions
of time; where Tullus Hostilius might have disappeared,—at
any rate has never been seen. The road to the Corner! the
ninety and nine acres that you go through to get there! I would
rather see it again, though I saw it this morning, than Gray's
churchyard. The road whence you may hear a stake-driver, a
whip-poor-will, a quail in a midsummer day, a—yes, a quail
comes nearest to the *gum-c* bird heard there; where it would not
be sport for a sportsman to go. And the mayweed looks up in
my face,—not there; the pale lobelia, the Canada snapdragon,
rather. A little hardhack and meadowsweet peep over the
fence,—nothing more serious to obstruct the views,—and
thimble-berries are the food of thought, before the drought,
along by the walls.

It is they who go to Brighton and to market that wear out the
roads, and they should pay all the tax. The deliberate pace of a
thinker never made a road the worse for travelling on.

There I have freedom in my thought, and in my soul am
free. Excepting the omnipresent butcher with his calf-cart,
followed by a distracted and anxious cow.

Be it known that in Concord, where the first forcible resistance to British agression was made in the year 1775, they chop
up the young calves and give them to the hens to make them
lay, it being considered the cheapest and most profitable food
for them, and they sell the milk to Boston.

On the promenade deck of the world, an outside passenger.
The inattentive, ever strange baker, whom no weather detains,
that does not bake his bread in this hemisphere,—and therefore
it is dry before it gets here. Ah! there is a road where you might
advertise to fly, and make no preparations till the time comes;
where your wings will sprout if anywhere, where your feet are
not confined to earth. An airy head makes light walking.

Where I am not confined and balked by the sight of distant

farmhouses which I have not gone past. In roads the obstructions are not under my feet,—I care not for rough ground or
wet even,—but they are in my vision and in the thoughts or
associations which I am compelled to entertain. I must be
fancy-free; I must feel that, wet or dry, high or low, it is the
genuine surface of the planet, and not a little chip-dirt or a
compost-heap, or made land or redeemed. Where I can sit by
the wall-side and not be peered at by any old ladies going a-
shopping, not have to bow to one whom I may have seen in my
youth,—at least, not more than once. I am engaged and cannot
be polite. Did you ever hear of such a thing as a man sitting in the
road and then have four eyes levelled at you? Have we any more
right sometimes to look at one than to point a revolver at him;
it might go off; and so perchance we might see him—though
there is not so much danger of *that*,—which would be equally
fatal, if it *should* ever happen, though perhaps it never has.

A thinker's weight is in his thought, not in his tread: when
he thinks freely, his body weighs nothing. He cannot tread
down your grass, farmers.

I thought to walk this forenoon instead of this afternoon, for
I have not been in the fields and woods much of late except
when surveying, but the least affair of that kind is as if you had
[a] black veil drawn over your face which shut out nature, as
that eccentric and melancholy minister whom I have heard of.
It may be the fairest day in all the year and you shall not know
it. One little chore to do, one little commission to fulfill, one
message to carry, would spoil heaven itself. Talk about a lover
being engaged! He is the only man in all the world who is free.
And all you get is your dollars. To go forth before the heat is
intolerable, and see what is the difference between forenoon and
afternoon. It seems there is a little more coolness in the air;
there is still some dew, even on this short grass in the shade of
the walls and woods; and a feeling of vigor the walker has.
There are few sounds but the slight twittering of swallows, and
the *springy* note of the sparrow in the grass or trees, and a lark in
the meadow (now at 8 A.M.), and the cricket under all to ally
the hour to night. Day is, in fact, about as still as night. Draw

the veil of night over this landscape, and these sounds would not disturb nor be inconsistent for their loudness with the night. It is a difference of white and black. Nature is in a white sleep. It threatens to be a hot day, and the haymakers are whetting their scythes in the fields, where they have been out since 4 o'clock. When I have seen them in the twilight commencing their labors, I have been impressed as if it were last night. There is something ghastly about such very early labor. I cannot detect the whole and characteristic difference between this and afternoon, though it is positive and decided enough, as my instincts know. By 2 o'clock it will be warmer and hazier, obscuring the mountains, and the leaves will curl, and the dust will rise more readily. Every herb is fresher now, has recovered from yesterday's drought. The cooler air of night still lingers in the fields, as by night the warm air of day. The noon is perchance the time to stay in the house.

There is no glory so bright but the veil of business can hide it effectually. With most men life is postponed to some trivial business, and so therefore is heaven. Men think foolishly they may abuse and misspend life as they please and when they get to heaven turn over a new leaf.

I see the track of a bare human foot in the dusty road, the toes and muscles all faithfully imprinted. Such a sight is so rare that it affects me with surprise, as the footprint on the shore of Juan Fernandez did Crusoe. It is equally rare here. I am affected as if some Indian or South-Sea-Islander had been along, some man who had a foot. I am slow to be convinced that any of my neighbors—the judge on the bench, the parson in the pulpit—might have made that or something like it, however irregular. It is pleasant as it is to see the tracks of cows and deer and birds. I am brought so much nearer to the tracker —when again I think of the sole of my own foot—than when I behold that of his shoe merely, or am introduced to him and converse with him in the usual way. I am disposed to say to the judge whom I meet, "Make tracks."

Men are very generally spoiled by being so civil and well-disposed. You can have no profitable conversation with them, they are so conciliatory, determined to agree with you. They exhibit such long-suffering and kindness in a short interview. I would meet with some provoking strangeness, so that we may be guest and host and refresh one another. It is possible for a man wholly to disappear and be merged in his manners. The thousand and one gentlemen whom I meet, I meet despairingly and but to part from them, for I am not cheered by the hope of any rudeness from them. A cross man, a coarse man, an eccentric man, a silent, a man who does not drill well,—of him there is some hope. Your gentlemen, they are all alike. They utter their opinions as if it was not a man that uttered them. It is "just as you please;" they are indifferent to everything. They will talk with you for nothing. The interesting man will rather avoid [you], and it is a rare chance if you get so far as talk with him. The laborers whom I know, the loafers, fishers, and hunters, I can spin yarns with profitably, for it is hands off; they are they and I am I still; they do not come to me and quarter themselves on me for a day or an hour to be treated politely, they do not approach me with a flag of truce. They do not go out of themselves to meet me. I am never electrified by my gentleman; he is not an electric eel, but one of the common kind that slip through your hands, however hard you clutch them, and leave them covered with slime. He is a man, every inch of him; is worth a groom.

To eat berries on the dry pastures of Conantum, as if they were the food of thought, dry as itself! Berries are now thick enough to pick.

July 23. 8 A.M. A comfortable breeze blowing. Methinks I can write better in the afternoon, for the novelty of it, if I should go abroad this morning. My genius makes distinctions which my understanding cannot, and which my senses do not report. If I should reverse the usual—go forth and saunter in the fields all the forenoon, then sit down in my chamber in the afternoon, which it is so unusual for me to do,—it would be like a new season to me, and the novelty of it [would] inspire me. The wind has fairly blown me outdoors; the elements were so lively and active, and I so sympathized with them, that I could not sit while the wind went by. . . .

You must walk so gently as to hear the finest sounds, the faculites being in repose. Your mind must not perspire. True, out of doors my thought is commonly drowned, as it were, and shrunken, pressed down by stupendous piles of light ethereal influences, for the pressure of the atmosphere is still fifteen pounds to a square inch. I can do little more than preserve the equilibrium and resist the pressure of the atmosphere. I can only nod like the ryeheads in the breeze. I expand more surely in my chamber, as far as expression goes, as if that pressure were taken off, but here outdoors is the place to store up influences. . . .

The influences which make for one walk more than another, are much more ethereal than terrestrial. It is the quality of the air much more than the quality of the ground that concerns the walker,—cheers or depresses him. What he may find in the air, not what he may find on the ground.

On such a road (the Corner) I walk securely, seeing far and wide on both sides, as if I were flanked by light infantry on the hills, to rout the provincials, as the British marched into Concord, while my grenadier thoughts keep the main road. That is, my light-armed and wandering thoughts scour the neighboring fields, and so I know if the coast is clear. With what a breadth of van I advance! I am not bounded by the walls, I think more than the road full. (Going southwesterly.)

While I am abroad, the ovipositors plant their seeds in me; I am fly-blown with thought, and go home to hatch and brood over them.

I was too discursive and rambling in my thoughts for the chamber, and must go where the wind blows on me walking. . . .

The mind is subject to moods, as the shadows of clouds pass over the earth. Pay not too much heed to them. Let not the traveller stop for them. They consist with the fairest weather. By the mood of my mind, I suddenly felt dissuaded from continuing my walk, but I observed at the same instant that the shadow of a cloud was passing over [the] spot on which I stood, though it was of small extent, which, if it had no connection with my mood, at any rate suggested how transient and little to be regarded that mood was. I kept on, and in a moment the sun shone on my walk within and without.

The button-bush in blossom. The tobacco-pipe in damp woods. Certain localities only a few rods square in the fields and on the hills, sometimes the other side of a wall, attract me as if they had been the scene of pleasure in another state of existence.

But this habit of close observation,—in Humboldt, Darwin, and others. Is it to be kept up long, this science? Do not tread on the heels of your experience. Be impressed without making a minute of it. Poetry puts an interval between the impression and the expression,—waits till the seed germinates naturally.

Aug. 5. 7.30 P.M. Moon half full. I sit beside Hubbard's Grove...

As the twilight deepens and the moonlight is more and more bright, I begin to distinguish myself, who I am and where; as my walls contract, I become more collected and composed, and sensible of my own existence, as when a lamp is brought into a dark apartment and I see who the company are. With the coolness and the mild silvery light, I recover some sanity, my thoughts are more distinct, moderated, and tempered. Reflection is more possible while the day goes by. The intense light of the sun unfits me for meditation, makes me wander in my thoughts; my life is too diffuse and dissipated; routine succeeds and prevails over us; the trivial has greater power then, and most at noon-day, the most trivial hour of the twenty-four. I am sobered by the moonlight. I bethink myself. It is like a cup of cold water to a thirsty man. The moonlight is more favorable to meditation than sunlight.

The sun lights this world from without, shines in at a window, but the moon is like a lamp within an apartment. It shines for us. The stars themselves make a more visible, and hence a nearer and more domestic, roof at night. Nature broods us, and has not left our germs of thought to be hatched by the sun. We feel her heat and see her body darkening over us. Our thoughts are not dissipated, but come back to us like an echo.

The different kinds of moonlight are infinite. This is not a night for contrasts of light and shade, but a faint diffused light in which there is light enough to travel, and that is all. . . .

Ah, what a poor, dry compilation is the "Annual of Scientific Discovery!" I trust that observations are made during the year which are not chronicled there,—that some mortal may have caught a glimpse of Nature in some corner of the earth during the year 1851. . . . The question is not what to look at, but what you see.

I hear now from Bear Garden Hill—I rarely walk by moonlight without hearing—the sound of a flute, or a horn, or a human voice. It is a performer I never see by day; should not recognize him if pointed out; but you may hear his performance in every horizon. He plays but one strain and goes to bed early, but I know by the character of that single strain that he is deeply dissatisfied with the manner in which he spends his day. He is a slave who is purchasing his freedom. He is Apollo watching the flocks of Admetus on every hill, and this strain he plays every evening to remind him of his heavenly descent. . . .

What an entertainment for the traveller, this incessant motion apparently of the moon traversing the clouds! Whether you sit or stand, it is always preparing new developments for you. It is event enough for simple minds. You all alone, the moon all alone, overcoming with incessant victory whole squadrons of clouds above the forests and the lakes and rivers and the mountains. You cannot always calculate which one the moon will undertake next.

I see a solitary firefly over the woods.

The moon wading through clouds; though she is eclipsed by this one, I see her shining on a more distant but lower one. The entrance into Hubbard's Wood above the spring, coming from the hill, is like the entrance to a cave; but when you are within, there are some streaks of light on the edge of the path.

All these leaves so still, none whispering, no birds in motion, —how can I be else than still and thoughtful?

Aug. 6. The motions of circus horses are not so expressive of music, do not harmonize so well with a strain of music, as those of animals of the cat kind. An Italian has just carried a hand-organ through the village. I hear it even at Walden Wood. It is as if a cheeta had skulked, howling, through the streets of the village, with knotted tail, and left its perfume there.

Neglected gardens are full of fleabane (?) now, not yet in blossom. Thoroughwort has opened, and golden-rod is gradually opening. The smooth sumach shows its red fruit. The berries of the bristly aralia are turning dark. The wild holly's scarlet fruit is seen and the red cherry (*Cerasus*). After how few steps, how little exertion, the student stands in pine woods above the Solomon's-seal and the cow-wheat, in a place still unaccountably strange and wild to him, and to all civilization! This so easy and so common, though our literature implies that this is rare! . . .

Why does not man sleep all day as well as all night, it seems so very natural and easy? For what is he awake? . . .

I am, perchance, most and most profitably interested in the things which I already know a little about; a mere and utter novelty is a mere monstrosity to me. I am interested to see the yellow pine, which we have not in Concord, though Michaux says it grows in Massachusetts; or the Oriental plane, having often heard of it and being well acquainted with its sister, the Occidental plane; or the English oak, having heard of the royal oak and having oaks ourselves; but the new Chinese flower, whose cousin I do not happen to know, I pass by with indifference. I do not know that I am very fond of novelty. I wish to get a clearer notion of what I have already some inkling.

These Italian boys with their hand-organs remind me of the keepers of wild beasts in menageries, whose whole art consists in stirring up their beasts from time to time with a pole. I am reminded of bright flowers and glancing birds and striped pards of the jungle; these delicious harmonies tear me to pieces while they charm me. The tiger's musical smile.

How some inventions have spread! Some, brought to perfection by the most enlightened nations, have been surely and rapidly communicated to the most savage. The gun, for instance. How soon after the settlement of America were comparatively remote Indian tribes, most of whose members had never seen a white man, supplied with guns! The gun is invented by the civilized man, and the savage in remote wildernesses on the other side of the globe throws away his bow and arrows and takes up this arm. Bartram, travelling in the Southern States between 1770 and 1780, describes the warriors as so many gun-men.

Ah, yes, even here in Concord horizon Apollo is at work for King Admetus! Who is King Admetus? It is Business, with his four prime ministers Trade and Commerce and Manufacturers and Agriculture. And this is what makes mythology true and interesting to us.

Aug. 12. Tuesday. 1.30 A.M.—Full moon. Arose and went to the river and bathed, stepping very carefully not to disturb the household, and still carefully in the street not to disturb the neighbors. I did not walk naturally and freely till I had got over the wall. Then to Hubbard's Bridge at 2 A.M. There was a whip-poor-will in the road just beyond Goodwin's, which flew up and lighted on the fence and kept alighting on the fence within a rod of me and circling round me with a slight squeak as if inquisitive about me. I do not remember what I observed or thought in coming hither.

The traveller's whole employment is to calculate what cloud will obscure the moon and what she will triumph over. In the after-midnight hours the traveller's sole companion is the moon. All his thoughts are centred in her. She is waging continual war with the clouds on his behalf. What cloud will enter the lists with her next, this employs his thoughts; and when she enters on a clear field of great extent in the heavens, and shines unobstructedly, he is glad. And when she has fought her way through all the squadrons of her foes, and rides majestic in a clear sky, he cheerfully and confidently pursues his way, and rejoices in his heart. But if he sees that she has many new clouds to contend with, he pursues his way moodily, as one disappointed and aggrieved; he resents it as an injury to himself. It is his employment to watch the moon, the companion and guide of his journey, wading through clouds, and calculate what one is destined to shut out her cheering light. He traces her course, now almost completely obscured, through the ranks of her foes, and calculates where she will issue from them. He is disappointed and saddened when he sees that she has many clouds to contend with.

Sitting on the sleepers of Hubbard's Bridge, which is being repaired, now, 3 o'clock A.M., I hear a cock crow. How admirably adapted to the dawn is that sound! as if made by the first rays of light rending the darkness, the creaking of the sun's axle heard already over the eastern hills.

Though màn's life is trivial and handselled, Nature is holy and heroic. With what infinite faith and promise and moderation begins each new day! It is only a little after 3 o'clock, and already there is evidence of morning in the sky.

He rejoices when the moon comes forth from the squadrons of the clouds unscathed and there are no more any obstructions in her path, and the cricket also seems to express joy in his song. It does not concern men who are asleep in their beds, but it is very important to the traveller, whether the moon shines bright and unobstructed or is obscured by clouds. It is not easy to realize the serene joy of all the earth when the moon commences to shine unobstructedly, unless you have often been a traveller by night.

The traveller also resents it if the wind rises and rustles the leaves or ripples the water and increases the coolness at such an hour.

A solitary horse in his pasture was scared by the sudden sight of me, an apparition to him, standing still in the moonlight, and moved about, inspecting with alarm, but I spoke and he heard the sound of my voice; he was at once reassured and expressed his pleasure by wagging his stump of a tail, though still half a dozen rods off. How wholesome the taste of huckleberries, when now by moonlight I feel for them amid the bushes!

And now the first signs of morning attract the traveller's

attention, and he cannot help rejoicing, and the moon begins gradually to fade from his recollection. The wind rises and rustles the copses. The sand is cool on the surface but warm two or three inches beneath, and the rocks are quite warm to the hand, so that he sits on them or leans against them for warmth, though indeed it is not cold elsewhere. As I walk along the side of Fair Haven Hill, I see a ripple on the river, and now the moon has gone behind a large and black mass of clouds, and I realize that I may not see her again in her glory this night, that perchance ere she rises from this obscurity, the sun will have risen, and she will appear but as a cloud herself, and sink unnoticed into the west (being a little after full (a day?)). As yet no sounds of awakening men; only the more frequent crowing of cocks, still standing on their perches in the barns. The milkmen are the earliest risers,—though I see no lanthorns carried to their barns in the distance,—preparing to carry the milk of cows in their tin cans for men's breakfasts, even for those who dwell in distant cities. In the twilight now, by the light of the stars alone, the moon being concealed, they are pressing the bounteous streams from full udders into their milk-pails, and the sound of the streaming milk is all that breaks the sacred stillness of the dawn; distributing their milk to such as have no cows. I perceive no mosquitoes now. Are they vespertinal, like the singing of the whip-poor-will? I see the light of the obscured moon reflected from the river brightly. With what mild emphasis Nature marks the spot!—so bright and serene a sheen that does not more contrast with the night.

4 A.M.—It adds a charm, a dignity, a glory, to the earth to see the light of the moon reflected from her streams. There are but us three, the moon, the earth which wears this jewel (the moon's reflection) in her crown, and myself. Now there has come round the Cliff (on which I sit), which faces the west, all unobserved and mingled with the dusky sky of night, a lighter and more ethereal living blue, whispering of the sun still far, far away, behind the horizon. From the summit of our atmosphere, perchance, he may already be seen by soaring spirits that inhabit those thin upper regions, and they communicate the glorious intelligence to us lower ones. The real *divine*, the heavenly, blue, the Jove-containing air, it is, I see through this dusky lower stratum. The sun gilding the summits of the air. The broad artery of light flows over all the sky. Yet not without sadness and compassion I reflect that I shall not see the moon again in her glory. (Not far from four, still in the night, I heard a nighthawk squeak and *boom*, high in the air, as I sat on the Cliff. What is said about this being less of a night bird than the whip-poor-will is perhaps to be questioned. For neither do I remember to have heard the whip-poor-will *sing* at 12 o'clock, though I met one sitting and flying between two and three this morning. I believe that both may be heard at midnight, though very rarely.) Now at *very earliest* dawn the nighthawk booms and the whip-poor-will sings. Returning down the hill by the path to where the woods [are] cut off, I see the signs of the day, the morning red. There is the lurid morning star, soon to be blotted out by a cloud.

There is an early redness in the east which I was not prepared for, changing to amber or saffron, with clouds beneath in the horizon and also above this clear streak.

The birds utter a few languid and yawning notes, as if they had not left their perches, so sensible to light to wake so soon,—a faint peeping sound from I know not what kind, a slight, innocent, half-awake sound, like the sounds which a quiet housewife makes in the earliest dawn. Nature preserves her innocence like a beautiful child. I hear a wood thrush even now, long before sunrise, as in the heat of the day. And the pewee and the catbird and the vireo, red-eyed? I do not hear—or do not mind, perchance—the crickets now. Now whip-poor-wills commence to sing in earnest, considerably *after* the wood thrush. The wood thrush, that beautiful singer, inviting the day once more to enter his pine woods. (So you may hear the wood thrush and whip-poor-will at the same time.) Now go by two whip-poor-wills, in haste seeking some coverts from the eye of day. And the bats are flying about on the edge of the wood, improving the last moments of their day in catching insects. The moon appears at length, not yet as a cloud, but with a frozen light, ominous of her fate. The early cars sound like a wind in the woods. The chewinks make a business now of waking each other up with their low *yorrick* in the neighboring low copse. The sun would have shown before but for the cloud. Now, on his rising, not the clear sky, but the cheeks of the clouds high and wide, are tinged with red, which, like the sky before, turns gradually to saffron and then to the white light of day.

Aug. 17. For a day or two it has been quite cool, a coolness that was felt even when sitting by an open window in a thin coat on the west side of the house in the morning, and you naturally sought the sun at that hour. The coolness concentrated your thought, however. As I could not command a sunny window, I went abroad on the morning of the 15th and lay in the sun in the fields in my thin coat, though it was rather cool even there. I feel as if this coolness would do me good. If it only makes my life more pensive! Why should pensiveness be akin to sadness? There is a certain fertile sadness which I would not avoid, but rather earnestly seek. It is positively joyful to me. It saves my life from being trivial. My life flows with a deeper current, no longer as a shallow and brawling stream. . . . Ah! if I could so live that there should be no desultory moment in all my life! that in the trivial season, when small fruits are ripe, my fruits might be ripe also! that I could match nature always with my moods! that in each season when some part of nature especially flourishes, then a corresponding part of me may not fail to flourish! Ah! I would walk, I would sit and sleep, with natural piety! What if I could pray aloud or to myself as I went along by the brooksides a cheerful prayer like the birds! For joy I could embrace the earth; I shall delight to be buried in it. And then to think of those I love among men, who will know that I love them though I tell them not! I sometimes feel as if I were rewarded merely for expecting better hours. I did not despair of worthier moods, and now I have occasion to be grateful for the flood of life that is flowing over me. I am not so poor: I can smell the ripening apples; the very rills are deep; the autumnal flowers, the *Trichostema dichotomum,*—not only its bright blue flower above the sand, but its strong wormwood scent which belongs to the season,—feed my spirit, endear the earth to me, make me value myself and rejoice; the quivering of pigeons' wings reminds me of the tough fibre of the air which they rend. I thank you, God. I do not deserve anything, I am unworthy of the least regard; and yet I am made to rejoice.

Aug. 19. P.M.—To Marlborough Road *via* Clamshell Hill, Jenny Dugan's, Round Pond, Canoe Birch Road, (Deacon Dakin's), and White Pond.

How many things concur to keep a man at home, to prevent his yielding to his inclination to wander! If I would extend my walk a hundred miles, I must carry a tent on my back for shelter at night or in the rain, or at least I must carry a thick coat to be prepared for a change in the weather. So that it requires some resolution, as well as energy and foresight, to undertake the simplest journey. Man does not travel as easily as the birds migrate. He is not everywhere at home, like flies. When I think how many things I can conveniently carry, I am wont to think it most convenient to stay at home. My home, then, to a certain extent is the place where I keep my thick coat and my tent and some books which I cannot carry; where, next, I can depend upon meeting some friends; and where, finally, I, even I, have established myself in business. But this last in my case is the least important qualification of a home.

The poet must be continually watching the moods of his mind, as the astronomer watches the aspects of the heavens. What might we not expect from a long life faithfully spent in this wise? The humblest observer would see some stars shoot. A faithful description as by a disinterested person of the thoughts which visited a certain mind in threescore years and ten, as when one reports the number and character of the vehicles which pass a particular point. As travellers go round the world and report natural objects and phenomena, so faithfully let another stay at home and report the phenomena of his own life,—catalogue stars, those thoughts whose orbits are as rarely calculated as comets. It matters not whether they visit my mind or yours,—

whether the meteor falls in my field or in yours,—only that it come from heaven. (I am not concerned to express that kind of truth which Nature has expressed. Who knows but I may suggest some things to her? Time was when she was indebted to such suggestions from another quarter, as her present advancement shows. I deal with the truths that recommend themselves to me, —please me,—not those merely which any system has voted to accept.) A meteorological journal of the mind. You shall observe what occurs in your latitude, I in mine.

Some institutions—most institutions, indeed—have had a divine origin. But of most that we see prevailing in society nothing but the form, the shell, is left; the life is extinct, and there is nothing divine in them. Then the reformer arises inspired to reinstitute life, and whatever he does or causes to be done is a reestablishment of that same or a similar divineness. But some, who never knew the significance of these instincts, are, by a sort of false instinct, found clinging to the shells. Those who have no knowledge of the divine appoint themselves defenders of the divine, as champions of the church, etc. I have been astonished to observe how long some audiences can endure to hear a man speak on a subject which he knows nothing about, as religion for instance, when one who has no ear for music might with the same propriety take up the time of a musical assembly with putting through his opinions on music. This young man who is the main pillar of some divine institution,— does he know what he has undertaken? If the saints were to come again on earth, would they be likely to stay at his house? would they meet with his approbation even? *Ne sutor ultra crepidam.* They who merely have a talent for affairs are forward to express their opinions. A Roman soldier sits there to decide upon the righteousness of Christ. The world does not long endure such blunders, though they are made every day. The weak-brained and pusillanimous farmers would fain abide by the institutions of their fathers. Their argument is they have not long to live, and for that little space let them not be disturbed in their slumbers; blessed are the peacemakers; let this cup pass from me, etc.

How vain it is to sit down to write when you have not stood up to live! Methinks that the moment my legs begin to move, my thoughts begin to flow, as if I had given vent to the stream at the lower end and consequently new fountains flowed into it at the upper. A thousand rills which have their rise in the sources of thought burst forth and fertilize my brain. You need to increase the draught below, as the owners of meadows on Concord River say of the Billerica Dam. Only while we are in action is the circulation perfect. The writing which consists with habitual sitting is mechanical, wooden, dull to read. . . .

What if a man were earnestly and wisely to set about recollecting and preserving the thoughts which he has had! How many perchance are now irrecoverable! Calling in his neighbors to aid him.

Aug. 22. It is the fault of some excellent writers—De Quincey's first impressions on seeing London suggest it to me—that they express themselves with too great fullness and detail. They give the most faithful, natural, and lifelike account of their sensations, mental and physical, but they lack moderation and sententiousness. They do not affect us by an ineffectual earnestness and a reserve of meaning, like a stutterer; they say all they mean. Their sentences are not concentrated and nutty. Sentences which suggest far more than they say, which have an atmosphere about them, which do not merely report an old, but make a new, impression; sentences which suggest as many things and are as durable as a Roman aqueduct; to frame these, that is the *art* of writing. Sentences which are expensive, towards which so many volumes, so much life, went; which lie like boulders on the page, up and down or across; which contain the seed of other sentences, not mere repetition, but creation; which a man might sell his grounds and castles to build. If De Quincey had suggested each of his pages in a sentence and passed on, it would have been far more excellent writing. His style is nowhere kinked and knotted up into something hard and significant, which you could swallow like a diamond, without digesting.

Aug. 23. P.M.—Walk to Annursnack and back over stone bridge.

I sometimes reproach myself because I do not find anything attractive in certain mere trivial employments of men,—that I skip men so commonly, and their affairs,—the professions and the trades,—do not elevate them at least in my thought and get some material for poetry out of them directly. I will not avoid, then, to go by where these men are repairing the stone bridge,—see if I cannot see poetry in that, if that will not yield me a reflection. It is narrow to be confined to woods and fields and grand aspects of nature only. The greatest and wisest will still be related to men. Why not see men standing in the sun and casting a shadow, even as trees? May not some light be reflected from them as from the stems of trees? I will try to enjoy them as animals, at least. They are perhaps better animals than men. Do not neglect to speak of men's low life and affairs with sympathy, though you ever so speak as to suggest a contract between them and the ideal and divine. You may be excused if you are always pathetic, but do not refuse to recognize.

Resolve to read no book, to take no walk, to undertake no enterprise, but such as you can endure to give an account of to yourself. Live thus deliberately for the most part.

Aug. 31. Half an hour before sunset I was at Tupelo Cliff, when, looking up from my botanizing (I had been examining the *Ranunculus filiformis*, the *Sium latifolium* (? ?), and the obtuse galium on the muddy shore), I saw the seal of evening on the river. There was a quiet beauty in the landscape at that hour which my senses were prepared to appreciate. The sun going down on the west side, that hand being already in shadow for the most part, but his rays lighting up the water and the willows and pads even more than before. His rays then fell at right angles on their stems. I sitting on the old brown geologic rocks, their feet submerged and covered with weedy moss (utricularia roots?) . . . . The cardinal-flowers standing by me. The trivialness of the day is past. The greater stillness, the *serenity* of the

air, its coolness and transparency, the mistiness being condensed,
are favorable to thought. . . . When I have walked all day in
vain under the torrid sun, and the world has been all trivial,—
as well field and wood as highway,—then at eve the sun goes
down westward, and the wind goes down with it, and the dews
begin to purify the air and make it transparent, and the lakes
and rivers acquire a glassy stillness, reflecting the skies, the
reflex of the day. . . . The attractive point is that line where
the water meets the land, not distinct, but known to exist. The
willows are not the less interesting because of their nakedness
below. How rich, like what we love to read of South American
primitive forests, is the scenery of this river! What luxuriance of
weeds, what depth of mud along its sides! These old antehis-
toric, geologic, antediluvian rocks, which only primitive wading
birds, still lingering among us, are worthy to tread.

Sept. 2. We cannot write well or truly but what we write with
gusto. The body, the senses, must conspire with the mind.
Expression is the act of the whole man, that our speech may be
vascular. The intellect is powerless to express thought without
the aid of the heart and liver and of every member. Often I feel
that my head stands out too dry, when it should be immersed.
A writer, a man writing, is the scribe of all nature; he is the corn
and the grass and the atmosphere writing. It is always essential
that we love to do what we are doing, do it with a heart. The
maturity of the mind, however, may perchance consist with a
certain dryness.

Sept. 4. It is wise to write on many subjects, to try many themes,
that so you may find the right and inspiring one. Be greedy of
occasions to express your thought. Improve the opportunity to
draw analogies. There are innumerable avenues to a perception
of the truth. Improve the suggestion of each object however
humble, however slight and transient the provocation. What
else is there to be improved? Who knows what opportunities he
may neglect? It is not in vain that the mind turns aside this way
or that; follow its leading; apply it whither it inclines to go.
Probe the universe in a myriad points. Be avaricious of these

impulses. You must try a thousand themes before you find the right one, as nature makes a thousand acorns to get one oak. He is a wise man and experienced who has taken many views; to whom stones and plants and animals and a myriad objects have each suggested something, contributed something.

Sept. 7. We are receiving our portion of the infinite. The art of life! Was there ever anything memorable written upon it? By what disciplines to secure the most life, with what care to watch our thoughts. To observe what transpires, not in the street, but in the mind and heart of me! I do not remember any page which will tell me how to spend this afternoon. I do not so much wish to know how to economize time as how to spend it, by what means to grow rich, that the day may not have been in vain. . . .

The scenery, when it is truly seen, reacts on the life of the seer. How to live. How to get the most life. As if you were to teach the young hunter how to entrap his game. How to extract its honey from the flower of the world. That is my every-day business. I am as busy as a bee about it. I ramble over all fields on that errand, and am never so happy as when I feel myself heavy with honey and wax. I am like a bee searching the live-long day for the sweets of nature. Do I not impregnate and intermix the flowers, produce rare and finer varieties by trans-ferring my eyes from one to another? I do as naturally and as joyfully, with my own humming music, seek honey all the day. With what honeyed thought any experience yields me I take a bee line to my cell. It is with flowers I would deal. . . . Did not the young Achilles (?) spend his youth learning how to hunt? The art of spending a day. If it is possible that we may be addressed, it behooves us to be attentive. If by watching all day and all night I may detect some trace of the Ineffable, then will it not be worth the while to watch? Watch and pray without ceasing, but not necessarily in sadness. Be of good cheer. Those Jews were too sad; to another people a still deeper revelation may suggest only joy. Don't I know what gladness is? Is it but the reflex of sadness, its back side?

Sept. 8. No fog this morning. Shall I not have words as fresh as my thoughts? Shall I use any other man's word? A genuine thought or feeling can find expression for itself, if it have to invent hieroglyphics. It has the universe for type-metal. It is for want of original thought that one man's style is like another's.

Sept. 9. 2 A.M.—The moon not quite full. To Conantum *via* road.

There is a low vapor in the meadows beyond the depot, dense and white, though scarcely higher than a man's head, concealing the stems of the trees. I see that the oaks, which are so dark and distinctly outlined, are illumined by the moon on the opposite side. This as I go up the back road. A few thin, ineffectual clouds in the sky. I come out thus into the moonlit night, where men are not, as if into a scenery anciently deserted by men. The life of men is like a dream. It is three thousand years since night has had possession. Go forth and hear the crickets chirp at midnight. Hear if their dynasty is not an ancient one and well founded. I feel the antiquity of the night. She surely repossesses herself of her realms, as if her dynasty were uninterrupted, or she had underlain the day. No sounds but the steady creaking of crickets and the occasional crowing of cocks.

I go by the farmer's houses and barns, standing there in the dim light under the trees, as if they lay at an immense distance or under a veil. The farmer and his oxen now all asleep. Not even a watch-dog awake. The human slumbers. There is less of man in the world.

The fog in the lowlands on the Corner road is never still. It now advances and envelops me as I stand to write these words, then clears away, with ever noiseless step. It covers the meadows like a web. I hear the clock strike three.

Now at the clayey bank. The light of Orion's belt seems to show traces of the blue day through which it came to us. The sky at least is lighter on that side than in the west, even about the moon. Even by night the sky is blue and not black, for we see through the veil of night into the distant atmosphere of day.

Sept. 11. Every artisan learns positively something by his trade. Each craft is familiar with a few simple, well-known, well-established facts, not requiring any genius to discover, but mere use and familiarity. You may go by the man at his work in the street every day of your life, and though he is there before you, carrying into practice certain essential information, you shall never be the wiser. Each trade is in fact a craft, a cunning, a covering an ability; and its methods are the result of a long experience. There sits a stone-mason, splitting Westford granite for fence-posts. Egypt has perchance taught New England something in this matter. His hammer, his chisels, his wedges, his shims or half-rounds, his iron spoon,—I suspect that these tools are hoary with age as with granite dust. He learns as easily where the best granite comes from as he learns how to erect that screen to keep off the sun. He knows that he can drill faster into a large stone than a small one, because there is less jar and yielding. He deals in stone as the carpenter in lumber. In many of his operations only the materials are different. His work is slow and expensive. Nature is here hard to be overcome. He wears up one or two drills in splitting a single stone. He must sharpen his tools oftener than the carpenter. He fights with granite. He knows the temper of the rocks. He grows stony himself. His tread is ponderous and steady like the fall of a rock.

Sept. 12. After I have spent the greater part of a night abroad in the moonlight, I am obliged to sleep enough more the next night to make up for it,—*Endymionis somnum dormire* (to sleep an Endymion sleep), as the ancients expressed it. And there is something gained still by thus turning the day into night. Endymion is said to have obtained of Jupiter the privilege of sleeping as much as he would. Let no man be afraid of sleep, if his weariness comes of obeying his Genius. He who has spent the night with the gods sleeps more innocently by day than the sluggard who has spent the day with the satyrs sleeps by night. He who has travelled to fairyland in the night sleeps by day more innocently than he who is fatigued by the merely trivial labors of the day sleeps by night. That kind of life which, sleeping, we dream that we live awake, in our walks by night, we, waking, live, while our daily life appears as a dream.

2 P.M.—To the Three Friends' Hill beyond Flint's Pond, *via* railroad, R. W. E.'s wood-path south side Walden, George Heywood's cleared lot, and Smith's orchard; return *via* east of Flint's Pond, *via* Goose Pond and my old home to railroad.

I go to Flint's Pond for the sake of the mountain view from the hill beyond, looking over Concord. I have thought it the best, especially in the winter, which I can get in this neighborhood. It is worth the while to see the mountains in the horizon once a day. I have thus seen some earth which corresponds to my least earthly and trivial, to my most heavenward-looking, thoughts. . . . I wish to see the earth through the medium of much air or heaven, for there is no paint like the air.

Oct. 1. 5 P.M.—Just put a fugitive slave, who has taken the name of Henry Williams, into the cars for Canada. He escaped from Stafford County, Virginia, to Boston last October; has been in Shadrach's place at the Cornhill Coffee-House; had been corresponding through an agent with his master, who is his father, about buying himself, his master asking $600, but he having been able to raise only $500. Heard that there were writs out for two Williamses, fugitives, and was informed by his fellow-servants and employer that Augerhole Burns and others of the police had called for him when he was out. Accordingly fled to Concord last night on foot, bringing a letter to our family from Mr. Lovejoy of Cambridge and another which Garrison had formerly given him on another occasion. He lodged with us, and waited in the house till funds were collected with which to forward him. Intended to dispatch him at noon through to Burlington, but when I went to buy his ticket, saw one at the depot who looked and behaved so much like a Boston policeman that I did not venture that time. An intelligent and very well-behaved man, a mulatto.

There is art to be used, not only in selecting wood for a withe, but in using it. Birch withes are twisted, I suppose in order that the fibres may be less abruptly bent; or is it only by accident that they are twisted?

The slave said he could guide himself by many other stars than the north star, whose rising and setting he knew. They steered for the north star even when it had got round and appeared to them to be in the south. They frequently followed the telegraph when there was no railroad. The slaves bring many superstitions from Africa. The fugitives sometimes superstitiously carry a turf in their hats, thinking that their success depends on it.

Oct. 4. Minott was telling me to-day that he used to know a man in Lincoln who had no floor to his barn, but waited till the ground froze, then swept it clean in his barn and threshed his grain on it. He also used to see men threshing their buckwheat in the field where it grew, having just taken off the surface down to a hard-pan.

Minott used the word "gavel" to describe a parcel of stalks cast on the ground to dry. His are good old English words, and I am always sure to find them in the dictionary, though I never heard them before in my life.

I was admiring his corn-stalks disposed about the barn to dry, over or astride the braces and the timbers, of such a fresh, clean, and handsome green, retaining their strength and nutritive properties so, unlike the gross and careless husbandry of speculating, money-making farmers, who suffer their stalks to remain out till they are dry and dingy and black as chips.

Minott is, perhaps, the most poetical farmer—who most realizes to me the poetry of the farmer's life—that I know. He does nothing with haste and drudgery, but as if he loved it. He makes the most of his labor, and takes infinite satisfaction in every part of it. He is not looking forward to the sale of his crops or any pecuniary profit, but he is paid by the constant satisfaction which his labor yields him. He has not too much land to trouble him,—too much work to do,— no hired man nor boy,— but simply to amuse himself and live. He cares not so much to raise a large crop as to do his work well. He knows every pin and nail in his barn. If another linter is to be floored, he lets no hired man rob him of that amusement, but he goes slowly to the woods and, at his leisure, selects a pitch pine tree, cuts it, and hauls it or gets it hauled to the mill; and so he knows the history of his barn floor.

Farming is an amusement which has lasted him longer than gunning or fishing. He is never in a hurry to get his garden planted and yet [it] is always planted soon enough, and none in the town is kept so beautifully clean.

He always prophesies a failure of the crops, and yet is satisfied with what he gets. His barn floor is fastened down with oak pins, and he prefers them to iron spikes, which he says will rust and give way. He handles and amuses himself with every ear of his corn crop as much as a child with its playthings, and so his small crop goes a great way. He might well cry if it were carried to market. The seed of weeds is no longer in his soil.

He loves to walk in a swamp in windy weather and hear the wind groan through the pines. He keeps a cat in his barn to catch the mice. He indulges in no luxury of food or dress or furniture, yet he is not penurious but merely simple. If his sister dies before him, he may have to go to the almshouse in his old age; yet he is not poor, for he does not want riches. He gets out of each manipulation in the farmers' operations a fund of entertainment which the speculating drudge hardly knows. With never-failing rheumatism and trembling hands, he seems yet to enjoy perennial health. Though he never reads a book,—since he has finished the "Naval Monument,"—he speaks the best of English.

Oct. 12. Minott shells all his corn by hand. He has got a boxful ready for the mill. He will not winnow it, for he says the chaff (?) makes it lie loose and dry faster. He tells me that Jacob Baker, who raises as fair corn as anybody, gives all the corn of his own raising to his stock, and buys the flat yellow corn of the South for bread; and yet the Northern corn is worth the most per bushel. Minott did not like this kind of farming any better than I. Baker also buys a great quantity of "shorts" below for his cows, to make more milk. He remembers when a Prescott, who lived where E. Hosmer does, used to let his hogs run in the woods in the fall, and they grew quite fat on the acorns, etc., they found, but now there are few nuts, and it is against the law. He tells me of places in the woods which to his eyes are unchanged since he was a boy, as natural as life. He tells me, then, that in some respects he is still a boy. And yet the gray squirrels were ten then to one now. But for the most part, he says, the world is turned upside down.

Nov. 9. I, too, would fain set down something beside facts. Facts should only be as the frame to my pictures; they should be material to the mythology which I am writing; not facts to assist men to make money, farmers to farm profitably, in any common sense; facts to tell who I am, and where I have been or what I have thought: as now the bell rings for evening meeting, and its volumes of sound, like smoke which rises from where a cannon is fired, make the tent in which I dwell. My facts shall be falsehoods to the common sense. I would so state facts that they shall be significant, shall be myths or mythologic. Facts which the mind perceived, thoughts which the body thought,—with these I deal. I, too, cherish vague and misty forms, vaguest when the cloud at which I gaze is dissipated quite and naught but the skyey depths are seen.

Nov. 11. "Says I to myself" should be the motto of my journal. It is fatal to the writer to be too much possessed by his thought. Things must lie a little remote to be described.

Nov. 12. Write often, write upon a thousand themes, rather than long at a time, not trying to turn too many feeble somersets in the air,—and so come down upon your head at last. Antaeus-like, be not long absent from the ground. Those sentences are good and well discharged which are like so many little resiliencies from the spring floor of our life,—a distinct fruit and kernel itself, springing from terra firma. Let there be as many distinct plants as the soil and the light can sustain. Take as many bounds in a day as possible. Sentences uttered

with your back to the wall. Those are the admirable bounds
when the performer has lately touched the springboard. A good
bound into the air from the air [*sic*] is a good and wholesome
experience, but what shall we say to a man's leaping off
precipices in the attempt to fly? He comes down like lead. In
the meanwhile, you have got your feet planted upon the rock,
with the rock also at your back, and, as in the case of King
James and Roderick Dhu, can say,—

> "Come one, come all! this rock shall fly
> From its firm base as soon as I."

Such, uttered or not, is the strength of your sentence. Sentences
in which there is no strain. A fluttering and inconstant and
quasi inspiration, and ever memorable Icarian fall, in which
your helpless wings are expanded merely by your swift descent
into the *pelagos* beneath.

C. is one who will not stoop to rise (to change the subject).
He wants something for which he will not pay the going price.
He will only learn slowly by failure,—not a noble, but dis-
graceful, failure. This is not a noble method of learning, to be
educated by inevitable suffering, like De Quincey, for instance.
Better dive like a muskrat into the mud, and pile up a few
weeds to sit on during the floods, a foundation of your own
laying, a house of your own building, however cold and
cheerless.

Methinks the hawk that soars so loftily and circles so steadily
and apparently without effort has earned this power by faithfully creeping on the ground as a reptile in a former state of
existence. You must creep before you can run; you must run
before you can fly. Better one effective bound upward with
elastic limbs from the valley than a jumping from the mountain-
tops in the attempt to fly. The observatories are not built high
but deep; the foundation is equal to the superstructure. It is
more important to a distinct vision that it be steady than that
it be from an elevated point of view.

Walking through Ebby Hubbard's wood this afternoon, with
Minott, who was actually taking a walk for amusement and

exercise, he said, on seeing some white pines blown down, that you might know that ground had been cultivated, by the trees being torn up so, for otherwise they would have rooted themselves more strongly. Minott has a story for every woodland path. He has hunted in them all. Where we walked last, he had once caught a partridge by the *wing*!

Nov. 13. To Fair Haven Hill.

A cold and dark afternoon, the sun being behind clouds in the west. The landscape is barren of objects, the trees being leafless, and so little light in the sky for variety. Such a day as will almost oblige a man to eat his own heart. A day in which you must hold on to life by your teeth. You can hardly ruck up any skin on Nature's bones. The sap is down; she won't peel. Now is the time to cut timber for yokes and ox-bows, leaving the tough bark on,—yokes for your own neck. Finding yourself yoked to Matter and to Time. Truly a hard day, hard times these! Not a mosquito left. Not an insect to hum. Crickets gone into winter quarters. Friends long since gone there, and you left to walk on frozen ground, with your hands in your pockets. . . . What do the thoughts find to live on? What avails you now the fire you stole from heaven? Does not each thought become a vulture to gnaw your vitals? No Indian summer have we had this November. I see but few traces of the perennial spring. Now is there nothing, not even the cold beauty of ice crystals and snowy architecture, nothing but the echo of your steps over the frozen ground, no voice of birds nor frogs. You are dry as a farrow cow. The earth will not admit a spade. All fields lie fallow. Shall not your mind? . . .

The walker now fares like cows in the pastures, where is no grass but hay; he gets nothing but an appetite. If we must return to hay, pray let us have that which has been stored in barns, which has not lost its sweetness. The poet needs to have more stomachs than the cow, for for him no fodder is stored in barns. He relies upon his instinct, which teaches him to paw away the snow to come at the withered grass.

Methinks man came very near being made a dormant

creature, just as some of these animals. The ground squirrel, for instance, which lays up vast stores, is yet found to be half dormant, if you dig him out. Now for the oily nuts of thought which you have stored up.

Dec. 12. I have been surveying for twenty or thirty days, living coarsely, even as respects my diet,—for I find that that will always alter to suit my employment,—indeed, leading a quite trivial life; and tonight, for the first time, had made a fire in my chamber and endeavored to return to myself. I wished to ally myself to the powers that rule the universe. I wished to dive into some deep stream of thoughtful and devoted life, which meandered through retired and fertile meadows far from towns. I wished to do again, or for once, things quite congenial to my highest inmost and most sacred nature, to lurk in crystalline thought like the trout under verdurous banks, where stray mankind should only see my bubble come to the surface. I wished to live, ah! as far away as a man can think. I wished for leisure and quiet to let my life flow in its proper channels, with its proper currents; when I might not waste the days, might establish daily prayer and thanksgiving in my family; might do my own work and not the work of Concord and Carlisle, which would yield me better than money. (How much forbearance, aye, sacrifice and loss, goes to every accomplishment! I am thinking by what long discipline and at what cost a man learns to speak simply at last.) I bethought myself, while my fire was kindling, to open one of Emerson's books, which it happens that I rarely look at, to try what a chance sentence out of that could do for me; thinking, at the same time, of a conversation I had with him the other night, I finding fault with him for the stress he had laid on some of Margaret Fuller's whims and superstitions, but he declaring gravely that she was one of those persons whose experiences warranted her attaching importance to such things,—as the *Sortes Virgilianae*, for instance, of which her numerous friends could tell remarkable instances. At any rate, I saw that he was disposed [to] regard such things more seriously than I. The first sentence which I opened upon in his book was this: "If, with a high trust, he can thus submit himself, he will find that ample returns are poured into his bosom out of what seemed hours of obstruction and loss. Let him not grieve too much on account of unfit associates. . . . In a society of perfect sympathy, no word, no act, no record, would be. He will learn that it is not much matter what he reads, what he does. Be a scholar, and he shall have the scholar's part of everything." etc., etc.

Most of this responded well enough to my mood, and this would be as good an instance of the *Sortes Virgilianae* as most to quote. But what makes this coincidence very little if at all remarkable to me is the fact of the obviousness of the moral, so that I had, perhaps, *thought* the same thing myself twenty times during the day, and yet had not been *contented* with that account of it, leaving me thus to be amused by the coincidence, rather than impressed as by an intimation out of the deeps.

Dec. 13. Saturday. This varied employment, to which my necessities compel me, serves instead of foreign travel and the lapse of time. If it makes me forget some things which I ought to remember, it no doubt enables me to forget many things which it is well to forget. By stepping aside from my chosen path so often, I see myself better and am enabled to criticise myself. Of this nature is the only true lapse of time. It seems an age since I took walks and wrote in my journal, and when shall I revisit the glimpses of the moon? To be able to see ourselves, not merely as others see us, but as we are, that service a *variety* of absorbing employments does us.

I would not be rude to the fine intimations of the gods for fear of incurring the reproach of superstition. . . .

Saw Perez Blood in his frock,—a stuttering, sure, unpretending man, who does not speak without thinking, does not guess. When I reflected how different he was from his neighbors, Conant, Mason, Hodgman, I saw that it was not so much outwardly, but that I saw an inner form. We do, indeed, see through and through each other, through the veil of the body, and see the real form and character in spite of the garment.

Any coarseness or tenderness is seen and felt under whatever garb. How nakedly men appear to us! for the spiritual assists the natural eye.

Dec. 21. I have seen, in the form, in the expression of face, of a child three years old, the tried magnanimity and grave nobility of ancient and departed worthies. Just saw a little Irish boy, come from the distant shanty in the woods over the bleak railroad to school this morning, take his last step from his last snow-drift on to the schoolhouse door-step, floundering still; saw not his face or his profile, only his mien, and imagined, saw clearly in imagination, his old-worthy face behind the sober visor of his cap. Ah! this little Irish boy, I know not why, revives to my mind the worthies of antiquity. He is not drawn, he never was drawn, in a willow wagon; he progresses by his own brave steps. Has not the world waited for such a generation? Here he condescends to his a-b-c without one smile, who has the lore of worlds uncounted in his brain. He speaks not of the adventures of the causeway. What was the bravery of Leonidas and his three hundred boys at the pass of Thermopylae to this infant's? They but dared to die; he dares to live,—and take his "reward of merit," perchance without relaxing his face into a smile, that overlooks his unseen and unrewardable merits. Little Johnny Riordan, who faces cold and routs it like a Persian army, who, yet innocent, carries in his knees the strength of a thousand Indras. That does not reward the thousandth part of his merit. While the charitable waddle about cased in furs, he, lively as a cricket, passes them on his way to school. I forget for the time Kossuth and his Hungarians. Here's a Kossuth for you!

Dec. 25. It would be a truer discipline for the writer to take the least film of thought that floats in the twilight sky of his mind for his theme, about which he has scarcely one idea (that would be teaching his ideas how to shoot), faintest intimations, shadowiest subjects, make a lecture on this, by assiduity and attention get perchance two views of the same, increase a little the stock of knowledge, clear a new field instead of manuring the old; instead of making a lecture out of such obvious truths, hackneyed to the minds of all thinkers. We seek too soon to ally the perceptions of the mind to the experience of the hand, to prove our gossamer truths practical, to show their connection with our every-day life (better show their distance from our every-day life), to relate them to the cider-mill and the banking institution. Ah, give me pure mind, pure thought! Let me not be in haste to detect the *universal law;* let me see more clearly a particular instance of it! Much finer themes I aspire to, which will yield no satisfaction to the vulgar mind, not one sentence for them. Perchance it may convince such that there are more things in heaven and earth than are dreamed of in their philosophy. Dissolve one nebula, and so destroy the nebular system and hypothesis. Do not seek expressions, seek thoughts to be expressed. By perseverance you get two views of the same rare truth.

That way of viewing things you know of, least insisted on by you, however, least remembered,—take that view, adhere to that, insist on that, see all things from that point of view. Will you let these intimations go unattended to and watch the door-bell or knocker? That is your text. Do not speak for other men; speak for yourself. They show you as in a vision the kingdoms of the world, and of all the worlds, but you prefer to look in upon a puppet-show. Though you should only speak to one kindred mind in all time, though you should not speak to one, but only utter aloud, that you may the more completely realize and live in the idea which contains the reason of your life, that you may build yourself up to the height of your conceptions, that you may remember your Creator in the days of your youth and justify His ways to man, that the end of life may not be its amusement, speak—though your thought presupposes the non-existence of your hearers—thoughts that transcend life and death. What though mortal ears are not fitted to hear absolute truth! Thoughts that blot out the earth are best conceived in the night, when darkness has already blotted it out from sight.

We look upward for inspiration.

Dec. 26. I observed this afternoon that when Edmund Hosmer came home from sledding wood and unyoked his oxen, they made a business of stretching and scratching themselves with their horns and rubbing against the posts, and licking themselves in those parts which the yoke had prevented their reaching all day. The human way in which they behaved affected me even pathetically. They were too serious to be glad that their day's work was done; they had not spirits enough left for that. They behaved as a tired woodchopper might. This was to me a new phase in the life of the laboring ox. It is painful to think how they may sometimes be overworked. I saw that even the ox could be weary with toil.

III

STANDING AT A DISTANCE

Jan. 1, 1852. I have observed that one mood is the natural critic of another. When possessed with a strong feeling on any subject foreign to the one I may be writing on, I know very well what of good and what of bad I have written on the latter. It looks to me now as it will ten years hence. My life is then earnest and will tolerate no makeshifts nor nonsense. What is tinsel or euphuism or irrelevant is revealed to such a touchstone. In the light of a strong feeling, all things take their places, and truth of every kind is seen for such. Now let me read my verses, and I will tell you if the god has had a hand in them. I wish to survey my composition for a moment from the least favorable point of view. I wish to be translated to the future, and look at my work as it were at a structure on the plain, to observe what portions have crumbled under the influence of the elements.

Jan. 20. The farmers nowadays can cart out peat and muck over the frozen meadows. Somewhat analogous, methinks, the scholar does; drives in with tight-braced energy and winter cheer on to his now firm meadowy grounds, and carts, hauls off, the virgin loads of fertilizing soil which he threw up in the warm, soft summer. We now bring our muck out of the meadows, but it was thrown up first in summer. The scholar's and the farmer's work are strictly analogous. Easily he now conveys, sliding over the snow-clad ground, great loads of fuel and of lumber which have grown in many summers, from the forest to the town. *He* deals with the dry hay and cows, the spoils of summer meads and fields, stored in his barns, doling it out from day to day, and manufactures milk for men. When I see the farmer driving into his barn-yard with a load of muck, whose blackness contrasts strangely with the white snow, I have the thoughts which I have described. He is doing like myself. My barn-yard is my journal.

Jan. 22. To set down such choice experiences that my own writings may inspire me and at last I may make wholes of parts. Certainly it is a distinct profession to rescue from oblivion and to fix the sentiments and thoughts which visit all men more or less generally, that the contemplation of the unfinished picture may suggest its harmonious completion. Associate reverently and as much as you can with your loftiest thoughts. Each thought that is welcomed and recorded is a nest egg, by the side of which more will be laid. Thoughts accidentally thrown together become a frame in which more may be developed and exhibited. Perhaps this is the main value of a habit of writing, of keeping a journal,—that so we remember our best hours and stimulate ourselves. My thoughts are my company. They have a certain individuality and separate existence, aye, personality. Having by chance recorded a few disconnected thoughts and then brought them into juxtaposition, they suggest a whole new field in which it was possible to labor and to think. Thought begat thought.

Jan. 26. Whatever wit has been produced on the spur of the moment will bear to be reconsidered and reformed with phlegm. The arrow had best not be loosely shot. The most transient and passing remark must be reconsidered by the writer, made sure and warranted, as if the earth had rested on its axle to back it, and all the natural forces lay behind it. The writer must direct his sentences as carefully and leisurely as the marksman his rifle, who shoots sitting and with a rest, with patent sights and conical balls beside. He must not merely seem to speak the truth. He must really speak it. If you foresee that a part of your essay will topple down after the lapse of time, throw it down now yourself. . . .

Obey the spur of the moment. These accumulated it is that make the impulse and the impetus of the life of genius. These are the spongioles or rootlets by which its trunk is fed. If you neglect the moments, if you cut off your fibrous roots, what but a languishing life is to be expected? Let the spurs of countless moments goad us incessantly into life. I feel the spur of the moment thrust deep into my side. . . .

Jan. 27. I do not know but thoughts written down thus in a journal might be printed in the same form with greater advantage than if the related ones were brought together into separate essays. They are now allied to life, and are seen by the reader not to be far-fetched. It is more simple, less artful. I feel that in the other case I should have no proper frame for my sketches.

Jan. 28. Homer refers to the progress of the woodcutter's work, to mark the time of day on the plains of Troy, and the inference from such passages commonly is that he lived in a more primitive state of society than the present. But I think that this is a mistake. Like proves like in all ages, and the fact that I myself should take pleasure in referring to just such simple and peaceful labors which are always proceeding, that the contrast itself always attracts the civilized poet to what is rudest and most primitive in his contemporaries, all this rather proves a certain interval between the poet and the chopper whose labor he refers to, than an unusual nearness to him, on the principle that familiarity breeds contempt. Homer is to be subjected to a very different kind of criticism from any he has received.

That reader who most fully appreciates the poet, and derives the greatest pleasure from his works, himself lives in circumstances most like those of the poet himself.

Jan. 29. The forcible writer does not go far for his themes. His ideas are not far-fetched. He derives inspiration from his chagrins and his satisfactions. His theme being ever an instant one, his own gravity assists him, gives impetus to what he says. He minds his business. He does not speculate while others drudge for him.

Jan. 30. Do nothing merely out of good resolutions. Discipline yourself only to yield to love; suffer yourself to be attracted. It is in vain to write on chosen themes. We must wait till they

have kindled a flame in our minds. There must be the copula-
ting and generating force of love behind every effort destined
to be successful. The cold resolve gives birth to, begets, nothing.
The theme that seeks me, not I it. The poet's relation to his
theme is the relation of lovers. It is no more to be courted. Obey,
report.

Feb. 18. I have a commonplace-book for facts and another for
poetry, but I find it difficult always to preserve the vague
distinction which I had in my mind, for the most interesting
and beautiful facts are so much the more poetry and that is
their success. They are *translated* from earth to heaven. I see
that if my facts were sufficiently vital and significant,—perhaps
transmuted more into the substance of the human mind,—I
should need but one book of poetry to contain them all.

March 16. Spent the day in Cambridge Library. Walden is not
yet melted round the edge. It is, perhaps, more suddenly warm
this spring than usual. Mr. Bull thinks that the pine grosbeaks,
which have been unusually numerous the past winter, have
killed many branches of his elms by budding them, and that
they will die and the wind bring them down, as heretofore.
Saw a large flock of geese go over Cambridge and heard the
robins in the College Yard.

The Library a wilderness of books. Looking over books on
Canada written within the last three hundred years, could
see how one had been built upon another, each author consul-
ting and referring to his predecessors. You could read most of
them without changing your leg on the steps. It is necessary to
find out exactly what books to read on a given subject. Though
there may be a thousand books written upon it, it is only important to read three or four; they will contain all that is
essential, and a few pages will show which they are. Books
which are books are all that you want, and there are but half
a dozen in any thousand. I saw that while we are clearing the
forest in our westward progress, we are accumulating a forest of
books in our rear, as wild and unexplored as any of nature's
primitive wildernesses. The volumes of the Fifteenth, Sixteenth,

and Seventeenth Centuries, which lie so near on the shelf, are rarely opened, are effectually forgotten and not implied by our literature and newspapers. When I looked into Purchas's Pilgrims, it affected me like looking into an impassable swamp, ten feet deep with sphagnum, where the monarchs of the forest, covered with mosses and stretched along the ground, were making haste to become peat. Those old books suggested a certain fertility, an Ohio soil, as if they were making a humus for new literatures to spring in. I heard the bellowing of bullfrogs and the hum of the mosquitoes reverberating through the thick embossed covers when I had closed the book. Decayed literature makes the richest of all soils.

March 17. I catch myself philosophizing most abstractly when first returning to consciousness in the night or morning. I make the truest observations and distinctions then, when the will is yet wholly asleep and the mind works like a machine without friction. I am conscious of having, in my sleep, transcended the limits of the individual, and made observations and carried on conversations which in my waking hours I can neither recall nor appreciate. As if in sleep our individual fell into the infinite mind, and at the moment of awakening we found ourselves on the confines of the latter.

Apr. 11. I see now the mosses in pastures, bearing their light-colored capsules on the top of red filaments. When I reach the bridge, it is become a serene evening; the broad waters are more and more smooth, and everything is more beautiful in the still light. The view toward Fair Haven, whose woods are now cut off, is beautiful. No obvious sign of spring. The hill now dimly reflected; the air not yet quite still. The wood on Conantum abuts handsomely on the water and can ill be spared. . . . The catkins of the willow are silvery. The shadow of the wood named above at the river end is indispensable in this scene; and, what is remarkable, I see where it has reached across the river and is creeping up the hill with dark pointed spears, though the intermediate river is all sunny, the reflection of the sunny hill covered with withered grass being seen through the invisible shadow. A river is best seen breaking through highlands, issuing from some narrow pass. It imparts a sense of power. The shadow at the end of the wood makes it appear grander in this case. The serenity and warmth are the main thing after the windy and cool days we have had. You may even hear a fish leap in the water now. The lowing of a cow advances me many weeks towards summer. The reflections grow more distinct every moment. At last the outline of the hill is as distinct below as above. And every object appears rhymed by reflection. . . . Now the shadow, reaching across the river, has crept so far up the hill that I see its reflection on the hillside in the water, and in this way it may at length connect itself with its source. Clouds are now distinctly seen in the water. The bridge is a station for walkers. I parted with my companion here; told him not to wait for me. Maple in the swamp answers to maple, birch to birch. There is one clump of three birches particularly picturesque. In a few minutes the wind has thus gone down. At this season the reflections of deciduous trees are more picturesque and remarkable than when they are in leaf, because, the branches being seen, they make with their reflections a more wonderful rhyme. It is not mere mass or outline corresponding to outline, but a kind of geometrical figure.

Apr. 21. On the east side of Ponkawtasset I hear a robin singing cheerily from some perch in the wood, in the midst of the rain, where the scenery is now wild and dreary. His song a singular antagonism and offset to the storm. As if Nature said, "Have faith, these *two* things I can do." . . .

Was that a large shad-bush where Father's mill used to be? There is quite a waterfall beyond where the old dam was. Where the rapids commence, at the outlet of the pond, the water is singularly creased as it rushes to the fall, like braided hair, as the poet has it. I did not see any inequalities in the rock it rushed over which could make it so plaited.

Apr. 25. It is related that Giorgio Barbarelli, Titian's friend, defending painting against the charge of being an incomplete art because it could exhibit but one side of a picture, laid a wager with some sculptor that he could represent the back, face, and both profiles of a man, without the spectator being obliged to walk round it as a statue. He painted "a warrior, who, having his back turned towards the spectator, stood looking at himself in a fountain, in whose limpid waters his full front figure was reflected. At the left of the warrior was suspended his suit of polished steel armor, in which was mirrored, with exact fidelity, the whole of his left side. At the right was painted a looking-glass, which reflected that side;" and thus he won the wager. So I would fain represent some truths as roundly and solidly as a statue, or as completely and in all their relations as Barbarelli his warrior,—so that you may see round them.

May 5. I succeed best when I *recur* to my experience not too late, but within a day or two; when there is some distance, but enough of freshness.

June 15. The seringo sings now *at noon* on a post; has a light streak over eye.

How rapidly new flowers unfold! as if Nature would get through her work too soon. One has as much as he can do to observe how flowers successively unfold. It is a flowery revolution, to which but few attend. Hardly too much attention can be bestowed on flowers. We follow, we march after, the highest color; that is our flag, our standard, our "color." Flowers were made to be seen, not overlooked. Their bright colors imply eyes, spectators. There have been many flower men who have rambled the world over to see them. The flowers robbed from an Egyptian traveller were at length carefully boxed up and forwarded to Linnaeus, the man of flowers. The common, early cultivated red roses are certainly very handsome, so rich a color and so full of blossoms; you see why even blunderers have introduced them into their gardens.

June 19. It requires considerable skill in crossing a country to avoid the houses and too cultivated parts,—somewhat of the engineer's or gunner's skill,—so to pass a house, if you must go near it through high grass,—pass the enemy's lines where houses are thick,—as to make a hill or wood screen you,—to shut every window with an apple tree. For that route which most avoids the houses is not only the one in which you will be least molested, but it is by far the most agreeable.

June 25. 8.30 P.M.—To Conantum.

Moon half full. Fields dusky; the evening star and one other bright one near the moon. It is a cool but pretty still night. Methinks I am less thoughtful than I was last year at this time. The flute I now hear from the Depot Field does not find such caverns to echo and resound in in my mind,—no such answering depths. Our minds should echo at least as many times as a Mammoth Cave to every musical sound. It should awaken reflections in us. I hear not many crickets. Some children calling their kitten home by some endearing name. Now his day's work is done, the laborer plays his flute,—only possible at this hour. Contrasted with his work, what an accomplishment! Some drink and gamble. He plays some well-known march. But the music is not in the tune; it is in the sound. It does not proceed from the trading nor political world. He practices his ancient art. There are light, vaporous clouds overhead; dark, fuscous ones in the north. The trees are turned black. As candles are lit on earth, stars are lit in the heavens. I hear the bullfrog's trump from afar.

Now I turn down the Corner road. At this quiet hour the evening wind is heard to moan in the hollows of your face, mysterious, spirit-like, conversing with you. It can be heard now only. The whip-poor-will sings. I hear a laborer going home, coarsely singing to himself. Though he has scarcely had a thought all day, killing weeds, at this hour he sings or talks to himself. His humble, earthy contentment gets expression. It is kindred in its origin with the notes or music of many creatures. A more fit and natural expression of his mood, this humming, than conversation is wont to be. The fireflies appear to be flying, though they may be stationary on the grass stems, for their perch and the nearness of the ground are obscured by the darkness, and now you see one here and then another there, as if it were one in motion. Their light is singularly bright and glowing to proceed from a living creature. Nature loves variety in all things, and so she adds glow-worms to fireflies, though I have not noticed any this year. The great story of the night is the moon's adventures with the clouds. What innumerable encounters she has had with them! When I enter on the moonlit causeway, where the light is reflected from the glistening alder leaves, and their deep, dark, liquid shade beneath strictly bounds the firm damp road and narrows it, it seems like autumn. The rows of willows completely fence the way and appear to converge in perspective, as I had not noticed by day. The bull-frogs are of various tones. Some horse in a distant pasture whin-nies; dogs bark; there is that dull, dumping sound of frogs, as if a bubble containing the lifeless sultry air of day burst on the surface, a belching sound. When two or more bullfrogs trump together, it is a ten-pound-ten note. In Conant's meadow I hear the gurgling of unwearied water, the trill of a toad, and go through the cool, primordial liquid air that has settled there. As I sit on the great door-step, the loose clapboards on the old house rattle in the wind weirdly, and I seem to hear some wild mice running about on the floor, and sometimes a loud crack from some weary timber trying to change its position.

On Conantum-top, all white objects like stones are observed, and dark masses of foliage, at a distance even. How distant is day and its associations! The light, dry cladonia lichens on the brows of hills reflect the moonlight well, looking like rocks. The night wind comes cold and whispering, murmuring weirdly from distant mountain-tops. No need to climb the Andes or Himalayas, for brows of lowest hills are highest mountain-tops in cool moonlight nights. Is it a cuckoo's chuckling note I heard? Occasionally there is something enormous and mon-strous in the size and distance of objects. A rock, is it? or an elephant asleep? Are these trees on an upland or a lowland? Or do they skirt the brink of a sea-beach? When I get there, shall I look off over the sea? The whiteweed is the only obvious flower. I see the tops of the rye wave, and grain-fields are more interesting than by day. The water is dull-colored, hardly more bright than a rye-field. There is dew only in the low grounds. What were the firefly's light, if it were not for darkness? The one implies the other.

You may not suspect that the milk of the cocoanut which is imported from the other side of the world is mixed. So pure do some truths come to us, I trust.

What a mean and wretched creature is man! By and by some Dr. Morton may be filling your cranium with white mustard seed to learn its internal capacity. Of all ways invented to come at a knowledge of a living man, this seems to me the worst, as it is the most belated. You would learn more by once paring the toenails of the living subject. There is nothing out of which the spirit has more completely departed, and in which it has left fewer significant traces.

June 26. I have not put darkness, duskiness, enough into my night and moonlight walks. Every sentence should contain some twilight or night. At least the light in it should be the yellow or creamy light of the moon or the fine beams of stars, and not the white light of day. The peculiar dusky serenity of the sentences must not allow the reader to forget that it is evening or night, without my saying that it is dark. Otherwise he will, of course presume a daylight atmosphere.

July 2. Nature is reported not by him who goes forth consciously as an observer, but in the fullness of life. To such a one she rushes to make her report. To the full heart she is all but a figure of speech.

July 14. Trees have commonly two growths in the year, a spring and a fall growth, the latter sometimes equalling the former, and you can see where the first was checked whether by cold or drouth, and wonder what there was in the summer to produce this check, this blight. So it is with man; most have a spring growth only, and never get over this first check to their youthful hopes; but plants of hardier constitution, or perchance planted in a more genial soil, speedily recover themselves, and . . . they push forward again and have a vigorous fall growth which is equivalent to a new spring.

Aug. 3. The *Hypericum Sarothra* appears to be out.

12 M. At the east window.—A temperate noon. I hear a cricket creak in the shade; also the sound of a distant piano. The music reminds me of imagined heroic ages; it suggests such ideas of human life and the field which the earth affords as the few noblest passages of poetry. Those few interrupted strains which reach me through the trees suggest the same thoughts and aspirations that all melody, by whatever sense appreciated, has ever done. I am affected. What coloring variously fair and intense our life admits of! How a thought will mould and paint it! Impressed by some vague vision, as it were, elevated into a more glorious sphere of life, we no longer know this, we can deny its existence. We say we are enchanted, perhaps. But what I am impressed by is the fact that this enchantment is no delusion. So far as truth is concerned, it is a fact such as what we *call* our actual existence, but it is a far higher and more glorious fact. It is evidence of such a sphere, of such possibilities. It is its truth and reality that affect me. A thrumming of piano-strings beyond the gardens and through the elms. At length the melody steals into my being. I know not when it began to occupy me. By some fortunate coincidence of thought or circumstance I am attuned to the universe, I am fitted to hear, my being moves in a sphere of melody, my fancy and imagination are excited to an inconceivable degree. This is no longer the dull earth on which I stood. It is possible to live a grander life here; already the steed is stamping, the knights are prancing; already our thoughts bid a proud farewell to the so-called actual life and its humble glories. Now this is the verdict of a soul in health. But the soul diseased says that its own vision and life alone is true and sane. What a different aspect will courage put upon the face of things! This suggests what a perpetual flow of spirit would produce.

Sept. 13. Yesterday it rained all day, with considerable wind, which has strewn the ground with apples and peaches, and, all the country over, people are busy picking up the windfalls. More leaves also have fallen. Rain has as much to do with it as wind. Rode round through Lincoln and a part of Weston and Wayland. The barberries, now red and reddening, begin to show. Asters, various shades of blue, and especially the smaller kinds of *dense-flowering white ones*, are more than ever by the roadsides. The great bidens in the sun in brooks affects me as the rose of the fall, the most *flavid* product of the water and the sun. They are low suns in the brook. The golden glow of autumn concentrated, more golden than the sun. How surely this yellow comes out along the brooks when you have applied the chemical test of autumn air to it! It yellows along the brook. The earth wears different colors or liveries at different seasons. If I come by at this season, a golden blaze will salute me here from a thousand suns.

How earnestly and rapidly each creature, each flower, is fulfilling its part while its day lasts! Nature never lost a day, nor a moment. As the planet in its orbit and around its axis, so do the seasons, so does time, revolve, with a rapidity inconceivable. In the moment, in the aeon, well employed, time ever advances with this rapidity. To an idler the man employed is terribly rapid. He that is not behind his time is swift. The immortals are swift. Clear the track! The plant that waited a whole year, and then blossomed the instant it was ready and the earth was ready for it, without the conception of delay, was rapid. To the conscience of the idle man, the stillness of a placid September day sounds like the din and whirl of a factory. Only employment can still this din in the air. . . .

I must walk more with free senses. It is as bad to *study* stars and clouds as flowers and stones. I must let my senses wander as my thoughts, my eyes see without looking. Carlyle said that how to observe was to look, but I say that it is rather to see, and the more you look the less you will observe. I have the habit of attention to such excess that my senses get no rest, but suffer from a constant strain. Be not preoccupied with looking. Go not to the object; let it come to you. When I have found myself looking down and confining my gaze to the flowers, I have thought it might be well to get into the habit of observing the clouds as a corrective; but no! that study would be just as bad.

What I need is not to look at all, but a true sauntering of the eye.

Sept. 16. Thursday. 8 A.M.—To Fair Haven Pond. . . .

What makes this such a day for hawks? There are eight or ten in sight from the Cliffs, large and small, one or more with a white rump. I detected the transit of the first by his shadow on the rock, and I look toward the sun for him. Though he is made light beneath to conceal him, his shadow betrays him. A hawk must get out of the wood, must get above it, where he can sail. It is narrow dodging for him amid the boughs. He cannot be a hawk there, but only perch gloomily. Now I see a large one—perchance an eagle, I say to myself!—down in the valley, circling and circling, higher and wider. This way he comes. How beautiful does he repose on the air, in the moment when he is directly over you, and you see the form and texture of his wings!

Dec. 28. It is worth the while to apply what wisdom one has to the conduct of his life, surely. I find myself oftenest wise in little things and foolish in great ones. That I may accomplish some particular petty affair well, I live my whole life coarsely. A broad margin of leisure is as beautiful in a man's life as in a book. Haste makes waste, no less in life than in housekeeping. Keep the time, observe the hours of the universe, not of the cars. What are three-score years and ten hurriedly and coarsely lived to moments of divine leisure in which your life is coincident with the life of the universe? We live too fast and coarsely, just as we eat too fast, and do not know the true savor of our food. We consult our will and understanding and the expectation of of men, not our genius. I can impose upon myself tasks which will crush me for life and prevent all expansion, and this I am but too inclined to do.

One moment of life costs many hours, hours not of business but of preparation and invitation. Yet the man who does not betake himself at once and desperately to sawing is called a loafer, though he may be knocking at the doors of heaven all the while, which shall surely be opened to him. That aim in life is highest which requires the highest and finest discipline. How much, what infinite, leisure it requires, as of a lifetime, to appreciate a single phenomenon! You must camp down beside it as for life, having reached your land of promise, and give yourself wholly to it. It must stand for the whole world to you, symbolical of all things. The least partialness is your own defect of sight and cheapens the experience fatally. Unless the humming of a gnat is as the music of the spheres, and the music of the spheres is as the humming of a gnat, they are naught to me. It is not communications to serve for a history,—which are science,—but the great story itself, that cheers and satisfies us.

Jan. 3, 1853. I love Nature partly *because* she is not man, but a retreat from him. None of his institutions control or pervade her. There a different kind of right prevails. In her midst I can be glad with an entire gladness. If this world were all man, I could not stretch myself, I should lose all hope. He is constraint, she is freedom to me. He makes me wish for another world. She makes me content with this.

Jan. 21. I pine for a new world in the heavens as well as on the earth, and though it is some consolation to hear of the wilderness of stars and systems invisible to the naked eye, yet the sky does not make that impression of variety and wildness that even the forest does, as it ought. It makes an impression, rather, of simplicity and unchangeableness, as of eternal laws; this being the same constellation which the shepherds saw, and obedient still to the same law. It does not affect me as that unhandselled wilderness which the forest is. I seem to see it pierced with visual rays from a thousand observatories. It is more the domain of science than of poetry. But it is the stars as not known to science that I would know, the stars which the lonely traveller knows.

March 5. F. Brown showed me to-day some lesser redpolls which he shot yesterday. They turn out to be my falsely-called chestnut-frontleted bird of the winter. "*Linaria minor*, Ray. Lesser Redpoll Linnet. From Pennsylvania and New Jersey to

Maine, in winter; inland to Kentucky. Breeds in Maine, Nova Scotia, Newfoundland, Labrador, and the Fur Countries."— Audubon's Synopsis. They have a sharp bill, black legs and claws, and a bright-crimson crown or frontlet, in the male reaching to the base of the bill, with, in his case, a delicate rose or carmine on the breast and rump. Though this is described by Nuttall as an occasional visitor in the winter, it has been the prevailing bird here this winter. . . .

The secretary of the Association for the Advancement of Science requests me, as he probably has thousands of others, by a printed circular letter from Washington the other day, to fill the blank against certain questions, among which the most important one was what branch of science I was specially interested in, using the term science in the most comprehensive sense possible. Now, though I could state to a select few that department of human inquiry which engages me, and should be rejoiced at an opportunity to do so, I felt that it would be to make myself the laughing-stock of the scientific community to describe or attempt to describe to them that branch of science which specially interests me, inasmuch as they do not believe in a science which deals with the higher law. So I was obliged to speak to their condition and describe to them that poor part of me which alone they can understand. The fact is I am a mystic, a transcendentalist, and a natural philosopher to boot. Now I think of it, I should have told them at once that I was a transcendentalist. That would have been the shortest way of telling them that they would not understand my explanations.

How absurd that, though I probably stand as near to nature as any of them, and am by constitution as good an observer as most, yet a true account of my relation to nature should excite their ridicule only! If it had been the secretary of an association of which Plato or Aristotle was the president, I should not have hesitated to describe my studies at once and particularly.

March 21. I sit down by a wall to see if I can muse again. We become, as it were, pliant and ductile again to strange but memorable influences; we are led a little way by our genius. We are affected like the earth, and yield to the elemental tenderness; winter breaks up within us; the frost is coming out of me, and I am heaved like the road; accumulated masses of ice and snow dissolve, and thoughts like a freshet pour down unwonted channels. A strain of music comes to solace the traveller over earth's downs and dignify his chagrins, the petty men whom he meets are the shadows of grander to come. Roads lead elsewhither than to Carlisle and Sudbury. The earth is uninhabited but fair to inhabit, like the old Carlisle road. Is then the road so rough that it should be neglected? Not only narrow but rough is the way that leadeth to life everlasting. Our experience does not wear upon us. It is seen to be fabulous or symbolical, and the future is worth expecting. Encouraged, I set out once more to climb the mountain of the earth, for my steps are symbolical steps, and in all my walking I have not reached the top of the earth yet.

March 23. Evelyn and others wrote when the language was in a tender, nascent state and could be moulded to express the shades of meaning; when sesquipedalian words, long since cut and apparently dried and drawn to mill,—not yet to the dictionary lumber-yard,—put forth a fringe of green sprouts here and there along in the angles of their rugged bark, their very bulk insuring some sap remaining; some florid suckers they sustain at least. Which words, split into shingles and laths, will supply poets for ages to come.

Man cannot afford to be a naturalist, to look at Nature directly, but only with the side of his eye. He must look through and beyond her. To look at her is fatal as to look at the head of Medusa. It turns the man of science to stone. I feel that I am dissipated by so many observations. I should be the magnet in the midst of all this dust and filings. I knock the back of my hand against a rock, and as I smooth back the skin, I find myself prepared to study lichens there. I look upon man but as a fungus. I have almost a slight, dry headache as the result of all this observing. How to observe is how to behave. O for a little Lethe! To crown all, lichens, which are so thin, are described in the *dry* state, as they are most commonly, not most truly, seen. Truly, they are *dryly* described.

Apr. 7. 10 A.M.—If you make the least correct observation of nature this year, you will have occasion to repeat it with illustrations the next, and the season and life itself is prolonged.

Apr. 27. Haverhill.—The warbling vireo.

Talked with a fisherman at the Burrough [*sic*], who was cracking and eating walnuts on a post before his hut. He said he got twenty cents a stick for sawing marked logs, which were mostly owned at Lowell, but trees that fell in and whatever was not marked belonged to them. Much went by in the ice and could not be got. They haul it in and tie it. He called it Little Concord where I lived. They got some small stuff which came from that river, and said he knew the ice, it was blue (it is not) and was turned over by the falls. The Lawrence dam breaks up the ice so now that it will not be so likely to jam below and produce a freshet. Said a thousand dollars' damage was done by a recent freshet to the farm just above, at the great bend. The wind blowing on to the shore ate it away, trees and all. In the greatest freshet he could remember, methinks about ten years ago, the water came up to his window-sill. His family took refuge on the hillside. His barn was moved and tipped over, his well filled up, and it took him, with help, a day or more to clear a passage through the ice from his door to his well. His trees were all prostrated by the ice. This was apparently between twenty and thirty feet above the present level. Says the railroad bridge hurts the fishing by stopping the ice and wearing away and deepening the channel near the north shore, where they fish,—draw their seines. Call it sixty rods wide,—their seines being thirty rods long,—and twenty-five feet deep in the middle.

Interesting to me are their habits and conversation who live along the shores of a great river. The shore, here some seventy or eighty feet high, is broken by gullies, more or less sandy, where water has flowed down, and the cottages rise not more than one sixth or one seventh the way up.

May 31. Some incidents in my life have seemed far more allegorical than actual; they were so significant that they plainly
served no other use. That is, I have been more impressed by
their allegorical significance and fitness; they have been like
myths or passages in a myth, rather than mere incidents or
history which have to wait to become significant. Quite in
harmony with my subjective philosophy. This, for instance:
that, when I thought I knew the flowers so well, the beautiful
purple azalea or pinxter-flower should be shown me by the
hunter who found it. Such facts are lifted quite above the level
of the actual. They are all just such events as my imagination
prepares me for, no matter how incredible. Perfectly in keeping
with my life and characteristic. Ever and anon something will
occur which my philosophy has not dreamed of. The limits of
the actual are set some thoughts further off. That which had
seemed a rigid wall of vast thickness unexpectedly proves a thin
and undulating drapery. The boundaries of the actual are no
more fixed and rigid than the elasticity of our imaginations.
The fact that a rare and beautiful flower which we never saw,
perhaps never heard [of], for which therefore there was no place
in our thoughts, may at length be found in our immediate
neighborhood, is very suggestive.

P.M.—A change in the weather. It is comparatively cool
since last night, and the air is very clear accordingly; none of
that haze in it occasioned by the late heat. . . .

I am going in search of the *Azalea nudiflora.* Sophia brought
home a single flower without twig or leaf from Mrs. Brooks's
last evening. Mrs. Brooks, I find, has a large twig in a vase of
water, still pretty fresh, which she says George Melvin gave
to her son George. I called at his office. He says that Melvin
came in to Mr. Gourgas's office, where he and others were
sitting Saturday evening, with his arms full and gave each a
sprig, but he doesn't know where he got it. Somebody, I heard,
had seen it at Captain Jarvis's; so I went there. I found that
they had some still pretty fresh in the house. Melvin gave it to
them Saturday night, but they did not know where he got it. A
young man working at Stedman Buttrick's said it was a secret;

there was only one bush in the town; Melvin knew of it and Stedman knew; when asked, Melvin said he got it in the swamp, or from a bush, etc. The young man thought it grew on the Island across the river on the Wheeler farm. I went on to Melvin's house, though I did not expect to find him at home at this hour, so early in the afternoon. (Saw the woodsorrel out, a day or two perhaps, by the way.) At length I saw his dog by the door, and knew he was at home.

He was sitting in the shade, bareheaded, at his back door. He had a large pailful of the azalea recently plucked and in the shade behind his house, which he said he was going to carry to town at evening. He had also a sprig set out. He had been out all the forenoon and said he had got seven pickerel,—perhaps ten [?]. Apparently he had been drinking and was just getting over it. At first he was a little shy about telling me where the azalea grew, but I saw that I should get it out of him. He dilly-dallied a little; called to his neighbor Farmer, whom he called "Razor," to know if he could tell me where the flower grew. He called it, by the way, the "red honeysuckle." This was to prolong the time and make the most of his secret. I felt pretty sure the plant was to be found on Wheeler's land beyond the river, as the young man had said, for I had remembered how, some weeks before this, when I went up the Assabet after the yellow rocket, I saw Melvin, who had just crossed with his dog, and when I landed to pluck the rocket he appeared out of the woods, said he was after a fish-pole, and asked me the name of my flower. Didn't think it was very handsome,—"not so handsome as the honeysuckle, is it?" And now I knew it was his "red honeysuckle," and not the columbine, he meant. Well, I told him he had better tell me where it was; I was a botanist and ought to know. But he thought I couldn't possibly find it by his directions. I told him he'd better tell me and have the glory of it, for I should surely find it if he didn't; I'd got a clue to it, and shouldn't give it up. I should go over the river for it. I could smell it a good way, you know. He thought I could smell it half a mile, and he wondered that I hadn't stumbled on it, or Channing. Channing, he said, came close by it once, when it was in flower. He thought he'd surely find it then; but he didn't, and he said nothing to him.

He told me he found it about ten years ago, and he went to it every year. It blossomed at the old election time, and he thought it "the handsomest flower that grows." Yarrow just out.

In the meanwhile, Farmer, who was hoeing, came up to the wall, and we fell into a talk about Dodge's Brook, which runs through his farm. A man in Cambridge, he said, had recently written to Mr. Monroe about it, but he didn't know why. All he knew about the brook was that he had seen it dry and then again, after a week of dry weather in which no rain fell, it would be full again, and either the writer or Monroe said there were only two such brooks in all North America. One of its sources—he thought the principal one—was in his land. We all went to it. It was in a meadow,—rather a dry one, once a swamp. He said it never ceased to flow at the head now, since he dug it out, and never froze there. He ran a pole down eight or nine feet into the mud to show me the depth. He had minnows there in a large deep pool, and cast an insect into the water, which they presently rose to and swallowed. Fifteen years ago he dug it out nine feet deep and found spruce logs as big as his leg, which the beavers had gnawed, with the marks of their teeth very distinct upon them; but they soon crumbled away on coming to the air. Melvin, meanwhile, was telling me of a pair of geese he had seen which were breeding in the Bedford Swamp. He had seen them within a day. Last year he got a large brood (11?) of black ducks there.

We went on down the brook,—Melvin and I and his dog,— and crossed the river in his boat, and he conducted me to where the *Azalea nudiflora* grew,—it was a little past its prime, perhaps, —and showed me how near Channing came. ("You won't tell him what I said; will you?" said he.) I offered to pay him for his trouble, but he wouldn't take anything. He had just as lief I'd know as not. He thought it first came out last Wednesday, on the 25th.

Azalea nudiflora,—purple azalea, pinxter-flower,—but Gray

and Bigelow say nothing about its *clamminess*. It is a conspic-
uously beautiful flowering shrub, with the sweet fragrance of the
common swamp-pink, but the flowers are larger and, in this
case, a fine lively rosey pink, not so clammy as the other, and,
being earlier, it is free from the insects which often infest and
spoil the first, though I find a very few little flies on them. With
a broader, somewhat downy pale-green leaf. Growing in the
shade of large wood, like the laurel. The flowers, being in naked
umbels, are so much the more conspicuous. (The *Viola debilis*
by the brook, near the azalea.) It is a flower with the fragrance
of the swamp[-pink], without its extreme clamminess and con-
sequent insects, and with a high and beautiful color and larger
segments to the corolla, with very much exserted stamens and
pistil. Eaton says the *nudiflora* is "not viscous;" names half a
dozen varieties and among them *A. partita* (flesh-colored flowers,
5-parted to the base), but then this is viscous. And it cannot be
his species *A. nitida*, with glabrous and shining and small leaves.
It must be an undescribed variety—a viscous one—of *A.
nudiflora*.

Melvin says the gray squirrel nests are made of leaves, the
the red squirrel of pine stuff. Jarvis tells me that Stedman
Buttrick once hired Melvin to work for him on condition that
he should not take his gun into the field, but he had known him
to do so when Buttrick was away and earn two or three dollars
with his game beside his day's work, but of course the last was
neglected.

There is a little danger of a frost to-night.

June 22. 5.30 P.M.—And then the rich warble of the blackbird
may still occasionally even at this season be heard. As I come
over the hill, I hear the wood thrush singing his evening lay.
This is the only bird whose note affects me like music, affects
the flow and tenor or my thought, my fancy and imagination.
It lifts and exhilarates me. It is inspiring. It is a medicative
draught to my soul. It is an elixir to my eyes and a fountain
of youth to all my senses. It changes all hours to an eternal
morning. It banishes all trivialness. It reinstates me in my

dominion, makes me the lord of creation, is chief musician of my court. This minstrel sings in a time, a heroic age, with which no event in the village can be contemporary. How can they be contemporary when only the latter is *temporary* at all? How can the infinite and eternal be contemporary with the finite and temporal? So there is something in the music of the cow-bell, something sweeter and more nutritious, than in the milk which the farmers drink. This thrush's song is a *ranz des vaches* to me. I long for wildness, a nature which I cannot put my foot through, woods where the wood thrush forever sings, where the hours are early morning ones, and there is dew on the grass, and the day is forever unproved, where I might have a fertile unknown for a soil about me. I would go after the cows, I would watch the flocks of Admetus there forever, only for my board and clothes. A New Hampshire everlasting and unfallen.

Aug. 11. Evening draws on while I am gathering bundles of pennyroyal on the further Conantum height. I find it amid the stubble mixed with blue-curls and, as fast as I get my hand full, tie it into a fragrant bundle. Evening draws on, smoothing the waters and lengthening the shadows, now half an hour or more before sundown. What constitutes the charm of this hour of the day? Is it the condensing of dews in the air just beginning, or the grateful increase of shadows in the landscape? Some fiat has gone forth and stilled the ripples of the lake; each sound and sight has acquired ineffable beauty. How agreeable, when the sun shines at this angle, to stand on one side and look down on flourishing sprout-lands or copses, where the cool shade is mingled in greater proportion than before with the light! Broad, shallow lakes of shadow stretch over the lower portions of the top of the woods. A thousand little cavities are filling with coolness. Hills and the least inequalities in the ground begin to cast an obvious shadow. The shadow of an elm stretches quite across the meadow. I see pigeons (?) in numbers fly up from the stubble. I hear some young bluebird's plaintive warble near me and some young hawks uttering a puling scream from time to time across the pond, to whom life is yet so novel. From far over the pond and woods I hear also a farmer calling loudly to his cows, in the clear still air, "Ker, ker, ker, ker."

What shall we name this season?—this very late afternoon, or very early evening, this severe and placid season of the day, most favorable for reflection, after the insufferable heats and the bustle of the day are over and before the dampness and twilight of evening! The serene hour, the Muses' hour, the season of reflection! It is commonly desecrated by being made tea-time. It begins perhaps with the very earliest condensation of moisture in the air, when the shadows of hills are first observed, and the breeze begins to go down, and birds begin again to sing. The pensive season. It is earlier than the "chaste eve" of the poet. Bats have not come forth. It is not twilight. There is no dew yet on the grass, and still less any early star in the heavens. It is the turning-point between afternoon and evening. The few sounds now heard, far or near, are delicious. It is not more dusky and obscure, but clearer than before. The clearing of the air by condensation of mists more than balances the increase of shadows. Chaste eve is merely *preparing* with "dewy finger" to draw o'er all "the gradual dusky veil." Not yet "the ploughman homeward plods his weary way," nor owls nor beetles are abroad. It is a season somewhat earlier than is celebrated by the poets. There is not such a sense of lateness and approaching night as they describe. I mean when the first emissaries of Evening come to smooth the lakes and streams. The poet arouses himself and collects his thoughts. He postpones tea indefinitely. Thought has taken her siesta. Each sound has a broad and deep relief of silence.

Sept. 1. Pickering says that "the missionaries (at the Hawaiian Islands) regarded as one main obstacle to improvement the extremely limited views of the natives in respect to style of living; 'a little fish and a little poi, and they were content.' " But this is putting the cart before the horse, the real obstacle being their limited views in respect to the object of living. A philosopher has equally limited views in their sense, but then he is not content with material comforts, nor is it, perhaps, quite necessary that he first be glutted with them in order to become wise. "A native, I was assured, 'could be supported for less than two cents a day.' " (They had adopted the use of coin.)

The savage lives simply through ignorance and idleness or laziness, but the philosopher lives simply through wisdom. In the case of the savage, the accompaniment of simplicity is idleness with its attendant vices, but in the case of the philosopher, it is the highest employment and development. The fact for the savage, and for the mass of mankind, is that it is better to plant, weave, and build than do nothing or worse; but the fact for the philosopher, or a nation loving wisdom, is that it is most important to cultivate the highest faculties and spend as little time as possible in planting, weaving, building, etc. It depends upon the height of your standard, and no doubt through manual labor as a police men are educated up to a certain level. The simple style is bad for the savage because he does worse than to obtain the luxuries of life; it is good for the philosopher because he does better than to work for them. The question is whether you can bear freedom. At present the vast majority of men, whether black or white, require the discipline of labor which enslaves them for their good. If the Irishman did not shovel all day, he would get drunk and quarrel. But the philosopher does not require the same discipline; if he shovelled all day, we should receive no elevating suggestions from him.

What a literary fame is that of Aesop,—an Aesopian fame! Pickering says: "A little to the west of Celebes, the literature of the Malay nation contains a translation of the Fables of Aesop; who, according to the unsatisfactory accounts we have of him, was one of the earliest of the Greek writers. And further, the fact may be noted, that the Aesopian style of composition is still in vogue at Madagascar. (See Ellis's Madagascar.)" A fame on its way round eastward with the Malay race to this western continent! A fame that travels round the world from west to east. P. gives California to the Malay race!

There are two kinds of simplicity,—one that is akin to foolishness, the other to wisdom. The philosopher's style of living is only outwardly simple, but inwardly complex. The savage's style is both outwardly and inwardly simple. A simpleton can perform many mechanical labors, but is not capable of profound thought. It was their limited view, not in respect to *style*, but to the *object* of living. A man who has equally limited views with respect to the end of living will not be helped by the most complex and refined style of living. It is not the tub that makes Diogenes, the Jove-born, but Diogenes the tub.

Oct. 22. Yesterday, toward night, gave Sophia and mother a sail as far as the Battle-Ground. One-eyed John Goodwin, the fisherman, was loading into a hand-cart and conveying home the piles of driftwood which of late he had collected with his boat. It was a beautiful evening, and a clear amber sunset lit up all the eastern shores; and that man's employment, so simple and direct,—though he is regarded by most as a vicious character,—whose whole motive was so easy to fathom,—thus to obtain his winter's wood,—charmed me unspeakably. So much do we love actions that are simple. They are all poetic. We, too, would fain be so employed. So unlike the pursuits of most men, so artificial or complicated. Consider how the broker collects his winter's wood, what sport he makes of it, what is his boat and hand-cart! Postponing instant life, he makes haste to Boston in the cars, and there deals in stocks, not quite relishing his employment,—and so earns the money with which he buys his fuel. And when, by chance, I meet him about this indirect and complicated business, I am not struck with the beauty of his employment. It does not harmonize with the sunset. How much more the former consults his genius, some genius at any rate! Now I should love to get my fuel so,—I have got some so, —but though I may be glad to have it, I do not love to get it in any other way less simple and direct. For if I buy one necessary of life, I cheat myself to some extent, I deprive myself of the pleasure, the inexpressible joy, which is the unfailing reward of satisfying any want of our nature simply and truly. . . .

Goodwin is a most constant fisherman. He must well know the taste of pickerel by this time. He will fish, I would not venture to say how many days in succession. When I can remember to have seen him fishing almost daily for some time, if it rains, I am surprised on looking out to see him slowly wending his way to the river in his oilcloth coat, with his basket and pole. I saw him the other day fishing in the middle of the stream, the day after I had seen him fishing on the shore, while by a kind of magic I sailed by him; and he said he was catching minnow for bait in the winter. When I was twenty rods off, he held up a pickerel that weighed two and a half pounds, which he had forgot to show me before, and the next morning, as he afterward told me, he caught one that weighed three pounds. If it is ever necessary to appoint a committee on fish-ponds and pickerel, let him be one of them. Surely he is tenacious of life, hard to scale.

Oct. 26. It is surprising how any reminiscence of a different season of the year affects us. When I meet with any such in my Journal, it affects me as poetry, and I appreciate that other season and that particular phenomenon more than at the time. The world so seen is all one spring, and full of beauty. You only need to make a faithful record of an average summer day's experience and summer mood, and read it in the winter, and it will carry you back to more than that summer day alone could show. Only the rarest flower, the purest melody, of the season thus comes down to us.

Oct. 28. For a year or two past, my *publisher*, falsely so called, has been writing from time to time to ask what disposition should be made of the copies of "A Week on the Concord and Merrimack Rivers" still on hand, and at last suggesting that he had use for the room they occupied in his cellar. So I had them all sent to me here, and they have arrived to-day by express, filling the man's wagon,—706 copies out of an edition of 1,000 which I bought of Munroe four years ago and have been ever since paying for, and have not quite paid for yet. The wares are sent to me at last, and I have an opportunity to examine my purchase. They are something more substantial than fame, as my back knows, which has borne them up two

flights of stairs to a place similar to that to which they trace
their origin. Of the remaining two hundred and ninety and odd,
seventy-five were given away, the rest sold. I have now a library
of nearly nine hundred volumes, over seven hundred of which
I wrote myself. Is it not well that the author should behold the
fruits of his labor? My works are piled up on one side of my
chamber half as high as my head, my *opera omnia*. This is
authorship; these are the work of my brain. There was just one
piece of good luck in the venture. The unbound were tied up
by the printer four years ago in stout paper wrappers, and
inscribed,—

H. D. Thoreau's
Concord River
50 cops.

So Munroe had only to cross out "River" and write "Mass."
and deliver them to the expressman at once. I can see now what
I write for, the result of my labors.

Nevertheless, in spite of this result, sitting beside the inert
mass of my works, I take up my pen to-night to record what
thought or experience I may have had, with as much satisfaction as ever. Indeed, I believe that this result is more inspiring
and better for me than if a thousand had bought my wares. It
affects my privacy less and leaves me freer.

Nov. 12. I cannot but regard it as a kindness in those who have
the steering of me that, by the want of pecuniary wealth, I have
been nailed down to this my native region so long and steadily,
and made to study and love this spot of earth more and more.
What would signify in comparison a thin and diffused love and
knowledge of the whole earth instead, got by wandering? The
traveller's is but a barren and comfortless condition. Wealth
will not buy a man a home in nature—house nor farm there.
The man of business does not by his business earn a residence in
nature, but is denaturalized rather. What is a farm, house and
land, office or shop, but a settlement in nature under the most
favorable conditions? It is insignificant, and a merely negative
good fortune, to be provided with thick garments against cold

and wet, an unprofitable, weak and defensive condition, compared with being able to extract some exhilaration, some warmth even, out of cold and wet themselves, and to clothe them with our sympathy. The rich man buys woollens and furs, and sits naked and shivering still in spirit, besieged by cold and wet. But the poor Lord of Creation, cold and wet he makes to warm him, and be his garments.

Nov. 15. P.M.—After having some business dealings with men, I am occasionally chagrined, and feel as if I had done some wrong, and it is hard to forget the ugly circumstance. I see that such intercourse long continued would make one thoroughly prosaic, hard, and coarse. But the longest intercourse with Nature, though in her rudest moods, does not thus harden and make coarse. A hard, insensible man whom we liken to a rock is indeed much harder than a rock. From hard, coarse, insensible men with whom I have no sympathy, I go to commune with the rocks, whose hearts are comparatively soft.

I was the other night elected a curator of our Lyceum, but was obliged to decline, because I did not know where to find good lecturers enough to make a course for the winter. We commonly think that we cannot have a good journal in New England, because we have not enough writers of ability; but we do not suspect likewise that we have not good lecturers enough to make a Lyceum.

The tall wool-grass, with its stately heads, still stands above and is reflected in the smooth water.

Together with the barberry, I dug up a brake root by chance. This, too, should have gone into the witches' caldron. It is large and black, almost like a cinder without, and within curiously black and white in parallel fibres, with a sort of mildewiness as if it were rotting; yet fresh shoots are ready for the spring with a cottony point.

Goodwin says he killed a mink the other day on a small *white pine tree*. Some years ago, about this season, he dug out fifteen muskrats in one nest in the ground at Goose Pond. He says the white rabbit does not run to his hole, but the gray one does.

This evening at sundown, when I was on the water, I heard come booming up the river what I suppose was the sound of cannon fired in Lowell to celebrate the Whig victory, the voting down the new Constitution. Perchance no one else in Concord heard them, and it is remarkable that I heard them, who was only interested in the natural phenomenon of sound borne far over water. The river is now so full and so high over the meadows, and at that hour was so smooth withal, that perchance the waves of sound flowed over the smooth surface of the water with less obstruction and further than in any other direction.

I also noticed this afternoon that, before the water generally was smoothed, those parts of the inundated meadow where spires of grass rose thinly above the surface were already quite smooth and glossy, so effectually did they break and dissipate the wavelets. A multitude of fine grass stems were a sufficient breakwater to render the surface smooth.

This afternoon has wanted no condition to make it a gossamer day, it seems to me, but a calm atmosphere. Plainly the spiders cannot be abroad on the water unless it is smooth.

Nov. 20. I once came near speculating in cranberries. Being put to it to raise the wind to pay for "A Week on the Concord and Merrimack Rivers," and having occasion to go to New York to peddle some pencils which I had made, as I passed through Boston I went to Quincy Market and inquired the price of cranberries. The dealers took me down cellar, asked if I wanted wet or dry, and showed me them. I gave them to understand that I might want an indefinite quantity. It made a slight sensation among them and for aught I know raised the price of the berry for a time. I then visited various New York packets and was told what would be the freight, on deck and in the hold, and one skipper was very anxious for my freight. When I got to New York, I again visited the markets as a purchaser, and "the best of Eastern Cranberries" were offered me by the barrel at a cheaper rate than I could buy them in Boston. I was obliged to manufacture a thousand dollars' worth of pencils and slowly dispose of and finally sacrifice them, in order to pay an assumed debt of a hundred dollars.

Dec. 22. Surveying the last three days. They have not yielded much that I am aware of. . . . It is remarkable how unprofitable it is for the most part to talk with farmers. They commonly stand on their good behavior and attempt to moralize or philosophize in a serious conversation. Sportsmen and loafers are better company. For society a man must not be too *good* or well-disposed, to spoil his natural disposition. The bad are frequently good enough to let you see how bad they are, but the good as frequently endeavor [to] get between you and themselves.

I have dined out five times and tea'd once within a week. Four times there was tea on the dinner-table, always meat, but once baked beans, always pie, but no puddings. I suspect tea has taken the place of cider with farmers. I am reminded of Haydon the painter's experiences when he went about painting the nobility. I go about the houses of the farmers and squires in like manner. This is my portrait-painting,—when I would fain be employed on higher subjects. I have offered myself much more earnestly as a lecturer than a surveyor. Yet I do not get any employment as a lecturer; was not invited to lecture once last winter, and only once (without pay) this winter. But I can get surveying enough, which a hundred others in this county can do as well as I, though it is not boasting much to say that a hundred others in New England cannot lecture as well as I on my themes. But they who do not make the highest demand on you shall rue it. It is because they make a low demand on themselves. All the while that they use only your humbler faculties, your higher unemployed faculties, like an invisible cimetar, are cutting them in twain. Woe be to the generation that lets any higher faculty in its midst go unemployed! That is to deny God and know him not, and he, accordingly, will know not of them.

Dec. 27. I wish that I could buy at the shops some kind of india-rubber that would rub out at once all that in my writing which it now costs me so many perusals, so many months if not years, and so much reluctance, to erase.

Jan. 1, 1854. As there is contention among the fishermen who shall be the first to reach the pond as soon as the ice will bear, in spite of the cold, as the hunters are forward to take the field as soon as the first snow has fallen, so the observer, or he who would make the most of his life for discipline, must be abroad early and late, in spite of cold and wet, in pursuit of nobler game, whose traces are then most distinct. A life which, pursued, does not earth itself, does not burrow downward but upward, which takes not to the trees but to the heavens as its home, which the hunter pursues with winged thoughts and aspirations,—these the dogs that tree it,—rallying his pack with the bugle notes of undying faith, and returns with some worthier trophy than a fox's tail, a life which we seek, not to destroy it, but to save our own. Is the great snow of use to the hunter only, and not to the saint, or him who is earnestly building up a life? Do the Indian and hunter only need snow-shoes, while the saint sits indoors in embroidered slippers?

The Indians might have imagined a large snow bunting to be the genius of the storm.

Jan. 19. Varro, having enumerated certain writers on agriculture, says accidentally [*sic*] that they wrote *soluta ratione*, i.e. in prose. This suggests the difference between the looseness of prose and the precision of poetry. A perfect expression requires a particular rhythm or measure for which no other can be substituted. The prosaic is always a loose expression.

Feb. 5. That sand foliage! It convinces me that Nature is still in her youth,—that florid fact about which mythology merely mutters,—that the very soil can fabulate as well as you or I. It stretches forth its baby fingers on every side. Fresh curls spring forth from its bald brow. There is nothing inorganic. This earth is not, then, a mere fragment of dead history, strata upon strata, like the leaves of a book, an object for a museum and an antiquarian, but living poetry, like the leaves of a tree,—not a fossil earth, but a living specimen. . . .

I fear only lest my expressions may not be extravagant enough,—may not wander far enough beyond the narrow limits of our ordinary insight and faith, so as to be adequate to the truth of which I have been convinced. I desire to speak somewhere without bounds, in order that I may attain to an expression in some degree adequate to truth of which I have been convinced. From a man in a waking moment, to men in their waking moments. Wandering toward the more distant boundaries of a wider pasture. Nothing is so truly bounded and obedient to law as music, yet nothing so surely breaks all petty and narrow bonds. Whenever I hear any music I fear that I may have spoken tamely and within bounds. And I am convinced that I cannot exaggerate enough even to lay the foundation of a true expression. As for books and the adequateness of their statements to the truth, they are as the tower of Babel to the sky.

Feb. 18. I read some of the speeches in Congress about the Nebraska Bill,—a thing the like of which I have not done for a year. What trifling upon a serious subject! while honest men are sawing wood for them outside. Your Congress halls have an ale-house odor,—a place for stale jokes and vulgar wit. It compels me to think of my fellow-creatures as apes and baboons. . . .

Feb. 19. I incline now to walk in swamps and on the river and ponds, where I cannot walk in the summer. . . .

The large moths apparently love the neighborhood of water, and are wont to suspend their cocoons over the edge of the meadow and river, places more or less inaccessible, to men at least. I saw a button-bush with what at first sight looked like the open pods of the locust or of the water asclepias attached. They were the light ash-colored cocoons of the *A. Promethea,* four or five, with the completely withered and faded leaves wrapped around them, and so artfully and admirably secured to the twigs by fine silk wound round the leaf-stalk and the twig,— which last add nothing to its strength, being deciduous, but aid its deception,—they are taken at a little distance for a few curled and withered leaves left on. Though the particular twigs on which you find some cocoons may never or very rarely retain any leaves,—the maple, for instance,—there are enough leaves left on other shrubs and trees to warrant their adopting this disguise. Yet it is startling to think that the inference has in this case been drawn by some mind that, as most other plants retain some leaves, the walker will suspect these also to. Each and all such disguises and other resources remind us that not some poor worm's instinct merely, as we call it, but the mind of the universe rather, which we share, has been intended upon each particular object. All the wit in the world was brought to bear on each case to secure its end. . . .

Much study a weariness of the flesh, eh? But did not they intend that we should read and ponder, who covered the whole earth with alphabets,—primers or bibles,—coarse or fine print? The very débris of the cliffs,—the stivers [?] of the rocks—are covered with geographic lichens: no surface is permitted to be bare long. As by an inevitable decree, we have come to times at last when our very waste paper is printed. Was not He who creates lichens the abettor of Cadmus when he invented letters? Types almost arrange themselves into words and sentences as dust arranges itself under the magnet. Print! it is a close-hugging lichen that forms on a favorable surface, which paper offers. The linen gets itself wrought into paper that the song of the shirt may be printed on it. Who placed us with eyes between a microscopic and a telescopic world?

There are so many rocks under the Grape-vine Cliff that apparently for this reason the chopper saws instead of cuts his trees into lengths. The wood fern (*Dryopteris marginalis?*) still green there. And are they not small saxifrages so perfectly green and fresh, as if just started in the crevices? I wait till sundown on Fair Haven to hear it boom, but am disappointed, though I hear much slight crackling. But, as for the previous cracking, it is so disruptive and produces such a commotion that it extends itself through snowdrifts six inches deep, and is even more distinct there than in bare ice, even to the sharpest angle of its forking. Saw an otter-track near Walden.

Feb. 20. P.M. Skating to Fair Haven Pond. Made a fire on the south side of the pond, using canoe birch bark and oak leaves for kindlings. It is best to lay down first some large damp wood on the ice for a foundation, since the success of a fire depends very much on the bed of coals it makes, and, if these are nearly quenched in the basin of melted ice, there is danger that it will go out. How much dry wood ready for the hunter, inviting flames, is to be found in every forest,—dry bark fibres and small dead twigs of the white pine and other trees, held up high and dry as if for this very purpose! The occasional loud snapping of the fire was exhilarating. I put on some hemlock boughs, and the rich salt crackling of its leaves was like mustard to the ears, —the firing of uncountable regiments. Dead trees love the fire.

We skated home in the dusk, with an odor of smoke in our clothes. It was pleasant to dash over the ice, feeling the inequalities which we could not see, now rising over considerable hillocks,—for it had settled on the meadows,—now descending into corresponding hollows.

March 1. In correcting my manuscripts, which I do with sufficient phlegm, I find that I invariably turn out much that is good along with the bad, which it is then impossible for me to distinguish—so much for keeping bad company; but after the lapse of time, having purified the main body and thus created a distinct standard for comparison, I can review the rejected sentences and easily detect those which deserve to be re-admitted.

March 28. P.M.—To White Pond.

Coldest day for a month or more,—severe as almost any in the winter. Saw this afternoon either a snipe or a woodcock; it appeared rather small for the last. Pond opening on the north-east. A flock of hyemalis drifting from a wood over a field incessantly for four or five minutes,—thousands of them, not-withstanding the cold. The fox-colored sparrow sings sweetly also. Saw a small slate-colored hawk, with wings transversely mottled beneath,—probably the sharp-shinned hawk.

Got first proof of "Walden."

March 31. In criticising your writing, trust your fine instinct. There are many things which we come very near questioning, but do not question. When I have sent off my manuscripts to the printer, certain objectionable sentences or expressions are sure to obtrude themselves on my attention with force, though I had not consciously suspected them before. My critical instinct then at once breaks the ice and comes to the surface.

April 8. I find that I can criticise my composition best when I stand at a little distance from it,—when I do not see it, for instance. I make a little chapter of contents which enables me to recall it page by page to my mind, and judge it more impartially when my manuscript is out of the way. The distraction of surveying enables me rapidly to take new points of view. A day or two surveying is equal to a journey.

April 10. I bought me a spy-glass some weeks since. I buy but few things, and those not till long after I begin to want them, so that when I do get them I am prepared to make a perfect use of them and extract their whole sweet.

April 11. A.M. Heard the clear, rather loud and rich warble of a purple finch and saw him on an elm. Wilson says they feed on the coverings of the blossoms. It is a distinct and peculiar note, not to be confounded with anything before it. I suspect that I heard one on the 1st of April, q. v.
  P.M. Surveying in Lincoln.

April 12. Wednesday. Waited at Lincoln depot an hour and a half. Heard the telegraph harp. I perceived distinctly that man melts at the sound of music, just like a rock exposed to a furnace heat. They need not have fabled that Orpheus moved the rocks and trees, for there is nothing more insensible than man; he sets the fashion to the rocks, and it is as surprising to see him melted, as when children see the lead begin to flow in a crucible. I observe that it is when I have been intently, and it may be laboriously, at work, and am somewhat listless or abandoned after it, reposing, that the muse visits me, and I see or hear beauty. It is from out the shadow of my toil that I look into the light. The music of the spheres is but another name for the Vulcanic force. May not such a record as this be kept on one page of the Book of Life: "A man was melted today."

June 16. The effect of a good government is to make life more valuable,—of a bad government, to make it less valuable. We can afford that railroad and all merely material stock should depreciate, for that only compels us to live more simply and economically; but suppose the value of life itself should be depreciated. Every man in New England capable of the sentiment of patriotism must have lived the last three weeks with the sense of having suffered a vast, indefinite loss. I had never respected this government, but I had foolishly thought that I might manage to live here, attending to my private affairs, and forget it. For my part, my old and worthiest pursuits have lost I cannot say how much of their attraction, and I feel that my investment in life here is worth many per cent. less since Massachusetts last deliberately and forcibly restored an innocent man, Anthony Burns, to slavery. I dwelt before in the illusion that my life passed somewhere only *between* heaven and hell, but now I cannot persuade myself that I do not dwell wholly within hell. . . .

I feel that, to some extent, the State has fatally interfered with my just and proper business. It has not merely interrupted me in my passage through Court Street on errands of trade, but it has, to some extent, interrrupted me and every man on his onward and upward path, on which he had trusted soon to leave Court Street far behind. I have found that hollow which I had relied on for solid. . . .

Art is as long as ever, but life is more interrupted and less available for a man's proper pursuits. It is time we had done referring to our ancestors. We have used up all our inherited freedom, like the young bird and the albumen in the egg. It is not an era of repose. If we would save our lives, we must fight for them.

The discovery is what manner of men your countrymen are.

They steadily worship mammon—and on the seventh day curse God with a tintamarre from one end of the *Union* to the other.

P.M.—To Baker Ditch *via* almshouse. . . .

There is a cool east wind,—and has been afternoons for several days,—which has produced a very thick haze or a fog. I find a tortoise egg on this peak at least sixty feet above the pond. There is a fine ripple and sparkle on the pond, seen through the mist. But what signifies the beauty of nature when men are base? We walk to lakes to see our serenity reflected in them. When we are not serene, we go not to them. Who can be serene in a country where both rulers and ruled are without principle? The remembrance of the baseness of politicians spoils my walks. My thoughts are murder to the State; I endeavor in vain to observe nature; my thoughts involuntarily go plotting against the State. I trust that all just men will conspire.

Aug. 2. 5 P.M. To Conantum on foot.

My attic chamber has compelled me to sit below with the family at evening for a month. I feel the necessity of deepening the stream of my life; I must cultivate privacy. It is very dissipating to be with people too much. As C. says, it takes the edge off a man's thoughts to have been much in society. I cannot spare my moonlight and my mountains for the best of man I am likely to get in exchange.

I am inclined now for a pensive evening walk. Methinks we think of spring mornings and autumn evenings. I go *via* Hubbard Path. Chelone, say two days, at Conant's meadow beyond Wheeler's. July has been to me a trivial month. It began hot and continued drying, then rained some toward the middle, bringing anticipations of the fall, and then was hot again about the 20th. It has been a month of haying, heat, low water, and weeds. Birds have grown up and flown more or less in small flocks, though I notice a new sparrow's nest and eggs and perhaps a catbird's eggs lately. The woodland quire has steadily diminished in volume. . . .

I sat on the Bittern Cliff as the still eve drew on. There was a man on Fair Haven furling his sail and bathing from his boat.

A boat on a river whose waters are smoothed, and a man disporting in it! How it harmonizes with the stillness and placidity of the evening! Who knows but he is a poet in his yet obscure but golden youth? Few else go alone into retired scenes without gun or fishing rod. He bathes in the middle of the pond while his boat slowly drifts away. As I go up the hill, surrounded by its shadow, while the sun is setting, I am soothed by the delicious stillness of the evening, save that on the hills the wind blows. I was surprised by the sound of my own voice. It is an atmosphere burdensome with thought. For the first time for a month, at least, I am reminded that thought is possible. The din of trivialness is silenced. I float over or through the deeps of silence. It is the first silence I have heard for a month. My life had been a River Platte, tinkling over its sands but useless for all great navigation, but now it suddenly became a fathomless ocean. It shelved off to unimagined depths.

I sit on rock on the hilltop, warm with the heat of the departed sun, in my thin summer clothes. . . .

The surface of the forest on the east of the river presents a singularly cool and wild appearance,—cool as a pot of green paint,—stretches of green light and shade, reminding me of some lonely mountainside. The nighthawk flies low, skimming over the ground now. How handsome lie the oats which have been cradled in long rows in the field, a quarter of a mile uninterruptedly! The thick stub ends, so evenly laid, are almost as rich a sight to me as the graceful tops. A few fireflies in the meadows. I am uncertain whether that so large and bright and high was a firefly or a shooting star. Shooting stars are but fireflies of the firmament. The crickets on the causeway make a *steady* creak, on the dry pasture-tops an *interrupted* one. I was compelled to stand to write where a soft, faint light from the western sky came in between two willows.

Fields today sends me a specimen copy of my "Walden." It is to be published on the 12th *inst.*

Aug. 7. Do you not feel the fruit of your spring and summer beginning to ripen, to harden its seed within you? Do not your thoughts begin to acquire consistence as well as flavor and ripeness? How can we expect a harvest of thought who have not had a seed-time of character? Already some of my small thoughts—fruit of my spring life—are ripe, like the berries which feed the first broods of birds; and other some are prematurely ripe and bright, like the lower leaves of the herbs which have felt the summer's drought.

IV

GOODWIN AND CO.

Sept. 4, 1854. 7.30. To Fair Haven Pond by boat.

Full moon; bats flying about; skaters and waterbugs (?) like sparks of fire on the surface between us and the moon. The high shore above the railroad bridge was very simple and grand, —first the bluish sky with the moon and a few brighter stars, then the near high level bank like a distant mountain ridge or a dark cloud in the eastern horizon, then its reflection in the water, making it double, and finally the glassy water and the sheen in one spot on the white lily pads. Some willows for relief in the distance on the right. It was Ossianic. . . .

A fine transparent mist. Lily Bay seemed as wide as a lake. You referred the shore back to the Clamshell Hills. The mere edge which a flat shore presents makes no distinct impression on the eye and, if seen at all, appears as the base of the distant hills. Commonly a slight mist yet more conceals it. The dim low shore, but a few rods distant, is seen as the base of the distant hills whose distance you know. The low shore, if not entirely concealed by the low mist, is seen against the distant hills and passes for their immediate base. For the same reason hills near the water appear much more steep than they are. We hear a faint metallic chip from a sparrow on the button-bushes or willows now and then. Rowse was struck by the simplicity of nature now,—the sky the greater part, then a little dab of earth, and after some water near you. Looking up the reach beyond Clamshell, the moon on our east quarter, its sheen was reflected for half a mile from the pads and the rippled water next them on that side, while the willows lined the shore in indistinct black masses like trees made with India ink (without distinct branches), and it looked like a sort of Broadway with the sun reflected from its pavements. Such willows might be made with soot or smoke merely, lumpish with fine edges. Meanwhile Fair Haven Hill, *seen blue through the transparent mist,* was as large and imposing as Wachusett, and we seemed to be approaching the *Highlands* of the river, a mountain pass, where the river had burst through mountains. A high mountain would be no more imposing.

Sept. 19. Thinking this afternoon of the prospect of my writing lectures and going abroad to read them the next winter, I realized how incomparably great the advantages of obscurity and poverty which I have enjoyed so long (and may still perhaps enjoy). I thought with what more than princely, with what poetical, leisure I had spent my years hitherto, without care or engagement, fancy-free. I have given myself up to nature; I have lived so many springs and summers and autumns and winters as if I had nothing else to do but *live* them, and imbibe whatever nutriment they had for me; I have spent a couple of years, for instance, with the flowers chiefly, having none other so binding engagement as to observe when they opened; I could have afforded to spend a whole fall observing the changing tints of the foliage. Ah, how I have thriven on solitude and poverty! I cannot overstate this advantage. I do not see how I could have enjoyed it, if the public had been expecting as much of me as there is danger now that they will. If I go abroad lecturing, how shall I ever recover the lost winter?

It has been my vacation, my season of growth and expansion, a prolonged youth.

Nov. 20. To Philadelphia. . . . 9 A.M., Boston to New York by express train, land route. . . . Started for Philadelphia from foot of Liberty Street at 6 P.M. *via* Newark, etc., etc., Bordentown, etc., etc., Camden Ferry, to Philadelphia, all in the dark. Saw only the glossy panelling of the cars reflected out into the dark, like the magnificent lit facade of a row of edifices reaching all the way to Philadelphia, except when we stopped and a lanthorn or two showed us a ragged boy and the dark buildings of some New Jersey town. Arrive at 10 P.M.; time, four hours from New York, thirteen from Boston, fifteen from Concord. Put up at Jones's Exchange Hotel, 77 Dock Street; lodgings thirty-seven and a half cents per night, meals separate; not to be named with French's in New York; next door to the fair of the Franklin Institute, then open, and over against the Exchange, in the neighborhood of the printing-offices.

Nov. 21. Looked from the cupola of the Statehouse, where the Declaration of Independence was declared. The best view of the city I got. Was interested in the squirrels, gray and black, in Independence and Washington Squares. Heard that they have, or have had, deer in Logan Square. The squirrels are fed, and live in boxes in the trees in the winter. Fine view from Fairmount water-works. The line of the hypothenuse of the gable end of Girard College was apparently deflected in the middle six inches or more, reminding me of the anecdote of the church of the Madeleine in Paris.

Was admitted into the building of the Academy of Natural Sciences by a Mr. Durand of the botanical department, Mr. Furness applying to him. The carpenters were still at work adding four stories (!) of galleries to the top. These four (Furness thought all of them, I am not sure but Durand referred to one side only) to be devoted to the birds. It is said to be the largest collection of birds in the world. They belonged to the son of Masséna (Prince of Essling?), and were sold at auction, and bought by a Yankee for $22,000, over all the crowned heads of Europe, and presented to the Academy. Other collections, also, are added to this. The Academy has received great donations. There is Morton's collection of crania, with (suppose a *cast* from) an Indian skull found in an Ohio mound; a polar bear killed by Dr. Kane; a male moose not so high as the female which we shot; a European elk (a skeleton) about seven feet high, with horns each about five feet long and *tremendously* heavy; grinders, etc., of the *Mastodon giganteum* from Barton County, Missouri; etc., etc. Zinzinger was named as of the geological department.

In Philadelphia and also New York an ornamental tree with

bunches of seed-vessels supplying the place of leaves now. I
suppose it the ailanthus, or Tree of Heaven. What were those
trees with long, black sickle-shaped pods? I did not see Stein-
hauser's Burd family at St. Stephen's Church. The American
Philosophical Society is described as a company of old women.

In the narrow market-houses in the middle of the streets, was
struck by the neat-looking women marketers with full cheeks.
Furness described a lotus identical with an Egyptian one as
found somewhere down the river below Philadelphia; also
spoke of a spotted chrysalis which he had also seen in Massachusetts. There was a mosquito about my head at night. Lodged at
the United States Hotel, opposite the Girard (formerly United
States) Bank.

Nov. 22. Left at 7.30 A.M. for New York, by boat to Tacony and
rail *via* Bristol, Trenton, Princeton (near by), New Brunswick,
Rahway, Newark, etc. Uninteresting, except the boat. The
country very level,—red sandstone (?) sand,—apparently all
New Jersey except the northern part. Saw wheat stubble and
winter wheat come up like rye. Was that Jamestownweed with
a prickly bur? Seen also in Connecticut. Many Dutch barns.
Just after leaving Newark, an extensive marsh, between the
railroad and the Kill, full of the *Arundo Phragmites*, I should say,
which had been burnt over.

Went to Crystal Palace; admired the houses on Fifth Avenue,
the specimens of coal at the Palace, one fifty feet thick as it was
cut from the mine, in the form of a square column, iron and
copper ore, etc. Saw sculptures and paintings innumerable, and
armor from the Tower of London, some of the Eighth Century.
Saw Greeley; Snow, the commercial editor of the *Tribune*;
Solon Robinson; Fry, the musical critic, etc.; and others.
Greeley carried me to the new operahouse where I heard Grisi
and her troupe. First, at Barnum's Museum, I saw the camelo-
pards, said to be one eighteen the other sixteen feet high. I
should say the highest stood about fifteen feet high at most
(twelve or thirteen ordinarily). The body was only about five
feet long. Why has it horns, but for ornament? Looked through

his diorama, and found the houses all over the world much alike. Greeley appeared to know and be known by everybody; was admitted free to the opera, and we were led by a page to various parts of the house at different times. Saw at Museum some large flakes of cutting arrowhead stone made into a sort of wide cleavers, also a hollow stone tube, probably from mounds.

Dec. 6. To Providence to lecture.

I see thick ice and boys skating all the way to Providence, but know not when it froze, I have been so busy writing my lecture; probably the night of the 4th.

In order to go to Blue Hill by Providence Railroad, stop at Readville Station (Dedham Low Plain once), eight miles; the hill apprently two miles east. Was struck with the Providence depot, its towers and great length of brick. Lectured in it. . . .

After lecturing twice this winter I feel that I am in danger of cheapening myself by trying to become a successful lecturer, i.e. to interest my audiences. I am disappointed to find that most that I am and value myself for is lost, or worse than lost, on my audience. I fail to get even the attention of the mass. I should suit them better if I suited myself less. I feel that the public demand an average man,—average thoughts and manners,—not originality, not even absolute excellence. You cannot interest them except as you are like them and sympathize with them. I would rather that my audience come to me than that I should go to them and so they be sifted; i.e. I would rather write books than lectures.

Jan. 5, 1855. R. W. E. told [of] Mr. Hill, his classmate, of Bangor, who was much interested in my "Walden," but relished it merely as a capital satire and joke, and even thought that the survey and map of the pond were not real, but a caricature of the Coast Surveys.

Jan. 9. What a strong and hearty but reckless, hit-or-miss style had some of the early writers of New England, like Josselyn and William Wood and others elsewhere in those days; as if they spoke with a relish, smacking their lips like a coach-whip, caring more to speak heartily than scientifically true. They are not to be caught napping by the wonders of Nature in a new country, and perhaps are often more ready to appreciate them than she is to exhibit them. They give you one piece of nature, at any rate, and that is themselves. (Cotton Mather, too, has a rich phrase.) They use a strong, coarse, homely speech which cannot always be found in the dictionary, nor sometimes be heard in polite society, but which brings you very near to the thing itself described. The strong new soil speaks through them. I have just been reading some in Wood's "New England's Prospect." He speaks a good word for New England, indeed will come very near lying for her, and when he doubts the justness of his praise, he brings it out not the less roundly; as who cares if it is not so? we love her not the less for all that. Certainly that generation stood nearer to nature, nearer to the facts, than this, and hence their books have more life in them.

Jan. 20. P.M. To Conantum and C. Miles place with Tappan.

There was a high wind last night, which relieved the trees of their burden almost entirely, but I may still see the drifts. The surface of the snow everywhere in the fields where it is hard blown, has a fine grain with low shelves, like a slate stone that does not split well. We cross the fields behind Hubbard's and suddenly slump into dry ditches concealed by the snow, up to the middle, and flounder out again. How new all things seem! Here is a broad, shallow pool in the fields, which yesterday was slosh, now converted into a soft, white, fleecy snow ice, like bread that has spewed out and baked outside the pan. It is like the beginning of the world. There is nothing hackneyed where a new snow can come and cover all the landscape. The snow lies chiefly behind the walls. It is surprising how much a straggling rail fence detains it, and it forms a broad, low swell beyond it, two or three rods wide, also just beyond the brow of a hill where it begins to slope to the south. You can tell by the ridges of the drifts on the south side of the walls which way the wind was. They all run from north to south; i.e. the common drift is divided into ridges or plaits in this direction, frequently down to the ground between; which separate drifts are of graceful outlines somewhat like fishes, with a sharp ridge or fin gracefully curved, both as you look from one side and down on them, their sides curving like waves about to break. The thin edge of some of these drifts at the wall end, where the air has come through the wall and made an eddy, are remarkably curved, like some shells, even thus, more than once round: I would not have believed it.

The world is not only new to the eye, but is still as at creation; every blade and leaf is hushed; not a bird or insect is heard; only, perchance, a faint tinkling sleigh-bell in the distance.

Feb. 3. I still recur in my mind to that skate of the 31st. I was thus enabled to get a bird's-eye view of the river,—to survey its length and breadth within a few hours, connect one part (one shore) with another in my mind, and realize what was going on upon it from end to end,—to know the whole as I ordinarily knew a few miles of it only. I connected the chestnut-tree house, near the shore in Wayland, with the chimney house in Billerica, Pelham's Pond with Nutting's Pond in Billerica. There is good skating from the mouth to Saxonville, measuring in a straight line some twenty-two miles, by the river say thirty now, Concord midway.

Feb. 5. In a journal it is important in a few words to describe the weather, or character of the day, as it affects our feelings. That which was so important at the time cannot be unimportant to remember.

March 10. I am not aware of growth in any plant yet, unless it be the further peeping out of willow catkins. They have crept out further from under their scales, and, looking closely into them, I detect a little redness along the twigs even now. You are always surprised by the sight of the first spring bird or insect; they seem premature, and there is no such evidence of spring as themselves, so that they literally *fetch* the year about. It is thus when I hear the first robin or bluebird, or, looking along the brooks, see the first water-bugs out circling. But you think, They have come, and Nature cannot recede. Thus, when on the 6th I saw the gyrinus at Second Division Brook, I saw no peculiarity in the water or the air to remind me of them, but today they are here and yesterday they were not.

Nov. 7. I find it good to be out this still, dark, mizzling after-noon; my walk or voyage is more suggestive and profitable than in bright weather. The view is contracted by the misty rain, the water is perfectly smooth, and the stillness is favorable to reflection. I am more open to impressions, more sensitive (not calloused or indurated by sun and wind), as if in a chamber still. My thoughts are concentrated; I am all compact. The solitude is real, too, for the weather keeps other men at home. This mist is like a roof and walls over and around, and I walk with a domestic feeling. The sound of a wagon going over an unseen bridge is louder than ever, and so of other sounds. I am *com-pelled* to look at near objects. All things have a soothing effect; the very clouds and mists brood over me. My power of observa-tion and comtemplation is much increased. My attention does not wander. The world and my life are simplified. What now of Europe and Asia?

Dec. 11. P.M. To Holden Swamp, Conantum. . . .
Standing there, though in this *bare* November landscape, I am reminded of the incredible phenomenon of small birds in winter,—that ere long, amid the cold powdery snow, as it were a fruit of the season, will come twittering a flock of delicate crimson-tinged birds, lesser redpolls, to sport and feed on the seeds and buds now just ripe for them on the sunny side of a wood, shaking down the powdery snow there in their cheerful social feeding, as if it were high midsummer to them. These crimson aerial creatures have wings which would bear them quickly to the regions of summer, but here is all the summer they want. What a rich contrast! tropical colors, crimson breasts, on cold white snow! Such etherealness, such delicacy in their forms, such ripeness in their colors, in this stern and barren season! It is as surprising as if you were to find a brilliant crimson flower which flourished amid snows. They greet the chopper and the

hunter in their furs. Their Maker gave them the last touch and launched them forth the day of the Great Snow. He made this bitter imprisoning cold before which man quails, but He made at the same time these warm and glowing creatures to twitter and be at home in it. He said not only, Let there be linnets in winter, but linnets of rich plumage and pleasing twitter, bearing summer in their natures. The snow will be three feet deep, the ice will be two feet thick, and last night, perchance, the mercury sank to thirty degrees below zero. All the fountains of nature seem to be sealed up. The traveller is frozen on his way. But under the edge of yonder birch wood will be a little flock of crimson-breasted lesser redpolls, busily feeding on the seeds of the birch and shaking down the powdery snow! As if a flower were created to be now in bloom, a peach to be now first fully ripe on its stem. I am struck by the perfect confidence and success of nature. There is no question about the existence of these delicate creatures, their adaptedness to their circumstances. There is superadded superfluous paintings and adornments, a crystalline, jewel-like health and soundness, like the colors reflected from ice-crystals. . . .

I saw this familiar—too *familiar*—fact at a different angle, and I was charmed and haunted by it. But I could only attain to be thrilled and enchanted, as by the sound of a strain of music dying away. I had seen into paradisaic regions, with their air and sky, and I was no longer wholly or merely a denizen of this vulgar earth. Yet had I hardly a foothold there. I was only sure that I was charmed, and no mistake. It is only necessary to behold thus the least fact or phenomenon, however familiar, from a point a hair's breadth aside from our habitual path or routine, to be overcome, enchanted by its beauty and significance. Only what we have touched and worn is trivial,—our scurf, repetition, tradition, conformity. To perceive freshly, with fresh senses, is to be inspired. Great winter itself looked like a precious gem, reflecting rainbow colors from one angle.

Dec. 13. This morning it is snowing, and the ground is whitened. The countless flakes, seen against the dark evergreens like a web that is woven in the air, impart a cheerful and busy aspect to nature. It is like a grain that is sown, or like leaves that have come to clothe the bare trees. Now, by 9 o'clock, it comes down in larger flakes, and I apprehend that it will soon stop. It does.

How pleasant a sense of preparedness for the winter,—plenty of wood in the shed and potatoes and apples, etc., in the cellar, and the house banked up! Now it will be a cheerful sight to see the snows descend and hear the blast howl.

Sanborn tells me that he was waked up a few nights ago in Boston, about midnight, by the sound of a flock of geese passing over the city, probably about the same night I heard them here. They go honking over cities where the arts flourish, waking the inhabitants; over State-houses and capitols, where legislatures sit; over harbors where fleets lie at anchor; mistaking the city, perhaps, for a swamp or the edge of a lake, about settling in it, not suspecting that greater geese than they have settled there.

Dec. 14. It began to snow again last evening, but soon ceased, and now it has turned out a fine winter morning, with half an inch of snow on the ground, the air full of mist, through which the smokes rise up perfectly straight; and the mist is frozen in minute leafets on the fences and trees and the needles of the pines, silvering them.

I stood by Bigelow the blacksmith's forge yesterday, and saw him repair an axe. He burned the handle out, then, with a chisel, cut off the red-hot edge even, there being some great gaps in it, and by hammering drew it out and shaped it anew,—all in a few minutes. It was interesting to see performed so simply and easily, by the aid of fire and a few rude tools, a work which would have surpassed the skill of a tribe of savages.

P.M. To Pink Azalea Woods.

The warm sun has quite melted the thin snow on the south sides of the hills, but I go to see the tracks of animals that have been out on the north sides. First getting over the wall under the walnut trees on the south brow of the hill, I see the broad tracks of squirrels, probably red, where they have ascended and descended the trees, and the empty shells of walnuts which they have gnawed left on the snow. The snow is so very shallow that the impression of their toes is the more distinctly seen. It imparts life to the landscape to see merely the squirrels' track in the snow at the base of the walnut tree. You almost realize a squirrel at every tree. The attractions of nature are thus condensed or multiplied. You see not merely bare trees and ground which you might suspect that a squirrel had left, but you have this unquestionable and significant evidence that a squirrel has been there since the snow fell,—as conclusive as if you had seen him.

A little further I heard the sound [of] a downy woodpecker tapping a pitch pine in a little grove, and saw him inclining to dodge behind the stem. He flitted from pine to pine before me. Frequently, when I pause to listen, I hear this sound in the orchards or streets. This was in one of these dense groves of young pitch pines.

Suddenly I heard the screwing mew and then the whir of a partridge on or beneath an old decaying apple tree which the pines had surrounded. There were several such, and another partridge burst away from one. They shoot off swift and steady, showing their dark-edge tails, almost like a cannon-ball. I saw one's track under an apple tree and where it had pecked a frozen-thawed apple.

Then I came upon a fox-track made last night, leading toward a farmhouse,—Wheeler's, where there are many hens, —running over the side of the hill parallel with Wheeler's new wall. He was dainty in the choice of his ground, for I observed that for a mile he had adhered to a narrow cow-path, in which the snow lay level, for smoothness. Sometimes he had cantered, and struck the snow with his foot between his tracks. Little does the farmer think of the danger which threatens his hens.

In a little hollow I see the sere gray pennyroyal rising above the snow, which, snuffed, reminds me of garrets full of herbs.

Now I hear, half a mile off, the hollow sound of wood-chopping, the work of short winter days begun, which is gradually laying bare and impoverishing our landscape. In two or three thicker woods which I have visited this season, I was driven away by this ominous sound.

Further over toward the river, I see the tracks of a deer mouse on a rock, which suddenly come to an end where apparently it had ascended a small pine by a twig which hung over it. Sometimes the mark of its tail was very distinct. Afterwards I saw in the pasture westward where many had run about in the night. In one place many had crossed the cow-path in which I was walking, in one trail, or the same one had come and gone many times. In the large hollows where rocks have been blasted, and on the sides of the river, I see irregular spaces of dark ice bare of snow, which was frozen after the snow ceased to fall. But this ice is rotten and mixed with snow. I am surprised to see the river frozen over for the most part with this thin and rotten snow ice, and the drooping or bent alders are already frozen into this slush, giving to the stream a very wintry aspect. I see some squirrel-tracks about a hole in a stump.

At the azalea meadow or swamp, the red tops of the osiers, which are very dense and of a uniform height, are quite attractive, in the absence of color at this season. Any brighter and warmer color catches our eye at this season. I see an elm there whose bark is worn quite smooth and white and bare of lichens, showing exactly the height at which the ice stood last winter.

Looking more closely at the light snow there near the swamp, I found that it was sprinkled all over (as with pellets of cotton) with regular star-shaped cottony flakes with six points, about an eighth of an inch in diameter and on an average a half an inch apart. It snowed geometry. . . .

I noticed this morning successive banks of frost on the windows, marked by their irregular waving edges, like the successive five, ten, and fifteen fathom lines which mark the depth of the shores on charts.

Thus by the snow I was made aware in this short walk of the recent presence there of squirrels, a fox, and countless mice, whose trail I had crossed, but none of which I saw, or probably should have seen before the snow fell. Also I saw this afternoon the track of one sparrow, probably a tree sparrow, which had run among the weeds in the road.

Dec. 26. In a true history or biography, of how little consequence those events of which so much is commonly made! For example, how difficult for a man to remember in what towns or houses he has lived, or when! Yet one of the first steps of his biographer will be to establish these facts, and he will thus give an undue importance to many of them. I find in my Journal that the most important events in my life, if recorded at all, are not dated.

Dec. 27. Recalled this evening, with the aid of Mother, the various houses (and towns) in which I have lived and some events of my life.

Born, July 12, 1817, in the

Minott House, on the Virginia Road, where Father occupied Grandmother's thirds, carrying on the farm. The Catherines the other half of the house. Bob Catherines and John threw up the turkeys. Lived there about eight months. Si Merriam next neighbor. Uncle David died when I was six weeks old. I was baptized in old M. H. by Dr. Ripley, when I was three months, and did not cry.

The *Red House,* where Grandmother lived, we the west side till October, 1818, hiring of Josiah Davis, agent for Woodwards. (There were Cousin Charles and Uncle C. more or less). According to day-book, Father hired of Proctor, October 16, 1818, and shop of *Spaulding, November 10, 1818.* Day-book first used by Grandfather, dated 1797. His part cut out and used by Father in Concord in 1808-9, and in Chelmsford, 1818-19-20-21.

Chelmsford, till March, 1821. (Last charge in Chelmsford about middle of March, 1821.) Aunt Sarah taught me to walk there when fourteen months old. Lived next the meeting-house, where they kept the powder in the garret. Father kept shop and painted signs, etc.

Pope's House, at South End in Boston, five or six (?) months, a ten-footer. Moved from Chelmsford through Concord, and may have tarried in Concord a little while. Day-book says, "Moved to Pinkney Street Sep. 10th 1821, on Monday."

Whitwell's House, Pinckney Street, Boston, to March, 1823 (?).

Brick House, Concord, to spring of 1826.

Davis's House (Next to S. Hoar's) to May 7th, 1827.

Shattuck House (Now William Monroe's) to spring of 1835. (Hollis Hall, Cambridge) (Hollis, Cambridge, 1833).

Aunt's House, to spring of 1837. At Brownson's while teaching (Hollis Hall, and Canton) in winter of 1835. Went to New York with Father, peddling, in 1836.

Parkman House, to fall of 1844. Was graduated in 1837 (?). (Hollis, Cambridge) Began the big Red Journal, October, 1837. Found first arrowheads, fall of 1837. Wrote a lecture (my first) on Society, March 14th, 1838, and read it before the Lyceum in the Mason's Hall, April 11th, 1838. Went to Maine for a school in May, 1838. Commenced school in the house in summer of 1838. Wrote an essay on Sound and Silence, December, 1838. Fall of 1839 up Merrimack to White Mountains.

"Aulus Persius Flaccus," first printed paper of consequence, February
10th, 1840. The Red Journal of 546
pages ended, June 1840. Journal of
396 pages ended January 31st, 1841.

(R. W. E.'s) Went to R. W. E.'s in spring of
1841 and stayed there to summer of
1843.

(William Emerson's, Went to Staten Island, June, 1843,
Staten Island.) and returned in December, 1843, or
to Thanksgiving. Made pencils in
1844.

Texas House, to August 29th, 1850. At Walden, July, 1845, to
(Walden) fall of 1847, then at R. W. E.'s to
(R. W. E.'s) fall of 1848, or while he was in
Europe.

Yellow House, reformed, till present.

Jan. 5. 1856. The thick snow now driving from the north and
lodging on my coat consists of those beautiful star crystals, not
cottony and chubby spokes, as on the 13th December, but thin
and partly transparent crystals. They are about a tenth of an
inch in diameter, perfect little wheels with six spokes without
a tire, or rather with six perfect little leafets, fern-like, with a
distinct straight and slender midrib, raying from the centre. . . .
How full of the creative genius is the air in which these are
generated! I should hardly admire more if real stars fell and
lodged on my coat. Nature is full of genius, full of the divinity;
so that not a snowflake escapes its fashioning hand. Nothing is
cheap and coarse, neither dewdrops nor snowflakes. Soon the
storm increases,—it was already very severe to face,—and the
snow comes finer, more white and powdery. Who knows but
this is the original form of all snowflakes, but that when I
observe these crystal stars falling around me they are but just
generated in the low mist next the earth? I am nearer to the
source of the snow, its primal, auroral, and golden hour or
infancy, but commonly the flakes reach us travel-worn and

agglomerated, comparatively without order or beauty, far down in their fall, like men in their advanced age. . . .

A divinity must have stirred within them before the crystals did thus shoot and set. Wheels of the storm chariots. The same law that shapes the earth-star shapes the snow-star. As surely as the petals of a flower are fixed, each of these countless snow-stars comes whirling to earth, pronouncing thus, with emphasis, the number six. Order, κόσμος.

On the Saskatchewan, when no man of science is there to behold, still down they come, and not the less fulfill their destiny, perchance melt at once on the Indian's face. What a world we live in! where myriads of these little disks, so beautiful to the most prying eye, are whirled down on every traveller's coat, the observant and the unobservant, and on the restless squirrel's fur, and on the far-stretching fields and forests, the wooded dells, and the mountain-tops. Far, far away from the haunts of man, they roll down some little slope, fall over and come to their bearings, and melt or lose their beauty in the mass, ready anon to swell some little rill with their contribution, and so, at last, the universal ocean from which they came. There they lie, like the wreck of chariot-wheels, after a battle in the skies. Meanwhile the meadow mouse shoves them aside in his gallery, the schoolboy casts them in his snowball, or the wood-man's sled glides smoothly over them, these glorious spangles, the sweeping of heaven's floor. And they all sing, melting as they sing of the mysteries of the number six,—six, six, six. He takes up the water of the sea in his hand, leaving the salt; He disperses it in mist through the skies; He recollects and sprinkles it like grain in six-rayed snowy stars over the earth, there to lie till He dissolves its bonds again.

Jan. 24. A journal is a record of experiences and growth, not a preserve of things well done or said. I am occasionally reminded of a statement which I have made in conversation and im-mediately forgotten, which would read much better than what I put in my journal. It is a ripe, dry fruit of long-past experience which falls from me easily, without giving pain or pleasure. The charm of the journal must consist in a certain greenness, though freshness, and not in maturity. Here I cannot afford to be remembering what I said or did, my scurf cast off, but what I am and aspire to become.

Feb. 28. How various are the talents of men! From the brook in which one lover of nature has never during all his lifetime detected anything larger than a minnow, another extracts a trout that weighs three pounds, or an otter four feet long. How much more game he will see who carries a gun, i.e. who goes to see it! Though you roam the woods all your days, you never will see by chance what he sees who goes on purpose to see it. One gets his living by shooting woodcocks; most never see one in their lives.

Feb. 29. Minott told me this afternoon of his catching a pickerel in the Mill Brook once,—before the pond was drawn off, when the brook had four or five times as much water as now,—which weighed four pounds. Says they stayed in it all winter in those days. This was near his land up the brook. He once also caught there, when fishing for pickerel, a trout which weighed three and a half pounds. He fell within two feet of the water, but [he] succeeded in tossing him higher up. When cutting peat thereabouts, he saw a stinkpot turtle in the water eating a frog which it had just caught. Speaks of seeing a mink swimming along a little [*sic*] in his beech wood-lot, and from time to time running along the shore; part way up an alder and down again.

He loves to recall his hunting days and adventures, and I willingly listen to the stories he has told me half a dozen times already. One day he saw about twenty black ducks on Goose Pond, and stole down on them, thinking to get a shot, but it chanced that a stray dog scared them up before he was ready. He stood on the point of the neck of land between the ponds, and watched them as they flew high toward Flint's Pond. As he looked, he saw one separate from the flock when they had got half-way to Flint's Pond, or half a mile, and return straight toward Goose Pond again. He thought he would await him, and give him a shot if he came near enough. As he flew pretty near and rather low, he fired, whereupon the duck rose right up high into the air, and he saw by his motions that he was wounded. Suddenly he dropped, by a slanting fall, into the point of a thick pine wood, and he heard him plainly strike the ground like a stone. He went there and searched for a long time, and was about giving it up, when at length he saw the duck standing, still alive and bleeding, by the side of a stump, and made out to kill him with a stick before he could reach the water.

He said he saw Emerson come home from lecturing the other day with his knitting-bag (lecture-bag) in his hand. He asked him if the lecturing business was as good as it used to be. Emerson said he didn't see but it was as good as ever; guessed the people would want lectures "as long as he or I lived."

Told again of the partridge hawk striking down a partridge which rose before him and flew across the run in the beech woods,—how suddenly he did it,—and he, hearing the fluttering of the partridge, came up and secured it, while the hawk kept out of gunshot.

March 11. Thermometer at 7 A.M. 6°, yet, the fire going out, Sophia's plants are frozen again. Dr. Bartlett's was −4°.

When it was proposed to me to go abroad, rub off some rust, and *better my condition* in a worldly sense, I fear lest my life will lose some of its homeliness. If these fields and streams and woods, the phenomena of nature here, and the simple occupations of the inhabitants should cease to interest and inspire me, no culture or wealth would atone for the loss. I fear the dissipation that travelling, going into society, even the best, the enjoyment of intellectual luxuries, imply. If Paris is much in your mind, if it is more and more to you, Concord is less and less, and yet it would be a wretched bargain to accept the proudest Paris in exchange for my native village. At best, Paris could only be a school in which to learn to live here, a stepping-stone to Concord, a school in which to fit for this university. I wish so to live ever as to derive my satisfactions and inspirations from the commonest events, every-day phenomena, so that what my senses hourly perceive, my daily walk, the conversation of my neighbors, may inspire me, and I may dream of no heaven but that which lies about me. . . .

In this sense I am not ambitious. I do not wish my native soil to become exhausted and run out through neglect. Only that travelling is good which reveals to me the value of home and enables me to enjoy it better.

March 23. . . . P.M.—To Walden.

The east side of the Deep Cut is nearly bare, as is the railroad itself, and, on the driest parts of the sandy slope, I go looking for *Cicindela*,—to see it run or fly amid the sere blackberry vines,—some life which the warmth of the dry sand under the spring sun has called forth; but I see none. I am reassured and reminded that I am the heir of eternal inheritances which are inalienable, when I feel the warmth reflected from this sunny bank, and see the yellow sand and the reddish subsoil, and hear some dried leaves rustle and the trickling of melting snow in some sluiceway. The eternity which I detect in Nature I predicate of myself also. How many springs I have had this same experience! I am encouraged, for I recognize this steady persistency and recovery of Nature as a quality of myself.

March 24. Monday. Very pleasant day. Thermometer 48° at noon. . . .

I am sometimes affected by the consideration that a man may spend the whole of his life after boyhood in accomplishing a particular design; as if he were put to a special and petty use, without taking time to look around him and appreciate the phenomenon of his existence. If so many purposes are thus necessarily left unaccomplished, perhaps unthought of, we are reminded of the transient interest we have *in this life.* Our interest in our country, in the spread of liberty, etc., strong and, as it were, innate as it is, cannot be as transient as our present existence here. It cannot be that all those patriots who die in the midst of their career have no further connection with the career of their country.

April 2. 8 A.M. To Lee's Cliff *via* railroad, Andromeda Ponds, and Well Meadow. I go early, while the crust is hard. . . .

Cross Fair Haven Pond to Lee's Cliff. The crowfoot and saxifrage seem remarkably backward; no growth as yet. But the catnep has grown even six inches, and perfumes the hillside when bruised. The columbine, with its purple leaves, has grown five inches, and one is flower-budded, apparently nearer to flower than anything there. *Turritis stricta* very forward, four inches high.

It is evident that it depends on the character of the season whether this flower or that is the most forward; whether there is more or less snow or cold or rain, etc. I am tempted to stretch myself on the bare ground above the Cliff, to feel its warmth in my back, and smell the earth and the dry leaves. I see and hear flies and bees about. A large buff-edged butterfly flutters by along the edge of the Cliff,—*Vanessa antiopa*. Though so little of the earth is bared, this frail creature has been warmed to life again. Here is the broken shell of one of those large white snails (*Helix albolabris*) on the top of the Cliff. It is like a horn with ample mouth wound on itself. I am rejoiced to find anything so pretty. I cannot but think it nobler, as it is rarer, to appreciate some beauty than to feel much sympathy with misfortune. The Powers are kinder to me when they permit me to enjoy this beauty than if they were to express any amount of compassion for me. I could never excuse them that.

April 3. Hosmer is overhauling a vast heap of manure in the rear of his barn, turning the ice within it up to the light; yet he asks despairingly what life is for, and says he does not expect to stay here long. But I have just come from reading Columella, who describes the same kind of spring work, in that to him new spring of the world, with hope, and I suggest to be brave and hopeful with nature. Human life may be transitory and full of trouble, but the perennial mind, whose survey extends from that spring to this, from Columella to Hosmer, is superior to change. I will identify myself with that which did not die with Columella and will not die with Hosmer.

April 7. Monday. Launched my boat, through three rods of ice on the riverside, half of which froze last night. The meadow is skimmed over, but by midforenoon it is melted.

P.M.—Up river in boat.

The first boats I have seen are out today, after muskrats, etc. Saw one this morning breaking its way far through the meadow, in the ice that had formed in the night. How independent they look who have come forth for a day's excursion! Melvin is out, and Goodwin, and another boat still. They can just row through the thinnest of the ice. The first boat on the meadows is exciting as the first flower or swallow. It is seen stealing along in the sun under the meadow's edge. One breaks the ice before it with a paddle, while the other pushes or paddles, and it grates and wears against the bows.

We see Goodwin skinning the muskrats he killed this forenoon on bank at Lee's Hill, leaving their red and mutilated carcasses behind. He says he saw a few geese go over the Great Meadows on the 6th. The half of the meadows next the river, or more, is covered with snow ice at the bottom, which from time to time rises up and floats off. . . . Before we get to Clamshell, see Melvin ahead scare up two black ducks, which make a wide circuit to avoid both him and us. . . . The open channel is now either over the river or on the upper side of the meadows next the woods and hills. Melvin floats slowly and quietly along the willows, watching for rats resting there, his white hound sitting still and grave in the prow, and every little while we hear his gun announcing the death of a rat or two. The dog looks on understandingly and makes no motion.

April 17. Was awakened in the night by a thunder and lightning shower and hail-storm—the old familiar burst and rumble, as if it had been rumbling somewhere else ever since I heard it last, and had not lost the knack.

April 28. Surveying the Tommy Wheeler farm.

Again, as so many times, I [am] reminded of the advantage to the poet, and philosopher, and naturalist, and whomso-ever, of pursuing from time to time some other business than his chosen one,—seeing with the side of the eye. The poet will so get visions which no deliberate abandonment can secure. The philosopher is so forced to recognize principles which long study might not detect. And the naturalist even will stumble upon some new and unexpected flower or animal.

Mr. Newton, with whom I rode, thought that there was a peculiar kind of sugar maple which he called the white; knew of a few in the middle of Framingham and said that there was one on our Common.

How promising a simple, unpretending, quiet, somewhat reserved man, whether among generals or scholars or farmers! How rare an equanimity and serenity which are an encouragement to all observers! Some youthfulness, some manliness, some goodness. Like Tarbell, a man apparently made a deacon on account of some goodness, and not on account of some hypocrisy and badness as usual.

Aug. 30. I have come out this afternoon a-cranberrying, chiefly to gather some of the small cranberry, *Vaccinium Oxycoccus,* which Emerson says is the common cranberry of the north of Europe. This was a small object, yet not to be postponed, on account of imminent frosts, i.e., if I would know this year the flavor of the European cranberry as compared with our larger kind. I thought I should like to have a dish of this sauce on the table at Thanksgiving of my own gathering. I could hardly make up my mind to come this way, it seemed so poor an object to spend the afternoon on. I kept foreseeing a lame conclusion,—how I should cross the Great Fields, look into Beck Stow's, and then retrace my steps no richer than before. In fact, I expected little of this walk, yet it did pass through the side of my mind that somehow, on this very account (my small expectation), it would turn out well, as also the advantage of having some purpose, however small, to be accomplished,—of letting your deliberate wisdom and foresight in the house to some extent direct and control your steps. If you would really take a position outside the street and daily life of men, you must have deliberately planned your course, you must have business which is not your neighbors' business, which they cannot understand. For only absorbing employment prevails, succeeds, takes up space, occupies territory, determines the future of individuals and states, drives Kansas out of your head, and actually and permanently occupies the only desirable and free Kansas against all border ruffians. The attitude of resistance is one of weakness, inasmuch as it only faces an emeny; it has its back to all that is truly attractive. You shall have your affairs, I will have mine. You will spend this afternoon in setting up your neighbor's stove, and be paid for it; I will spend it in gathering the few berries of the *Vaccinium Oxycoccus* which Nature produces here, before it is too late, and *be paid for it also* after another fashion. I have always reaped unexpected and incalculable advantages from carrying out at last, however tardily, any little enterprise which my genius suggested to me long ago as a thing to be done,—some step to be taken, however slight, out of the usual course. . . .

But a conscious and an unconscious life are good. Neither is good exclusively, for both have the same source. The wisely conscious life springs out of an unconscious suggestion. I have found my account in travelling in having prepared beforehand a list of questions which I would get answered, not trusting to my interest at the moment, and can then travel with the most profit. Indeed, it is by obeying the suggestions of a higher light within you that you escape from yourself and, in the transit, as it were see with the unworn sides of your eye, travel totally new paths. What is that pretended life that does not take up a claim, that does not occupy ground, that cannot build a causeway to its objects, that sits on a bank looking over a bog, singing its desires?

However, it was not with such blasting expectations as these that I entered the swamp. I saw bags of cranberries, just gathered and tied up, on the banks of Beck Stow's Swamp. They must have been raked out of the water, now so high, before they should rot. I left my shoes and stockings on the bank far off and waded barelegged through rigid andromeda and other bushes a long way, to the soft open sphagnous centre of the swamp.

Sept. 2. P.M.—To painted Cup Meadow. . . .

A few pigeons were seen a fortnight ago. I have noticed none in all walks, but G. Minott, whose mind runs on them so much, but whose age and infirmities confine him to his wood-shed on the hillside, saw a small flock a fortnight ago. I rarely pass at any season of the year but he asks if I have seen any pigeons. One man's mind running on pigeons, [he] will sit thus in the midst of a village, many of whose inhabitants never see nor dream of a pigeon except in the pot, and where even naturalists do not observe [them], and he, looking out with expectation and faith from morning till night, will surely see them.

I think we may detect that some sort of preparation and faint expectation preceded every discovery we have made. We blunder into no discovery but it will appear that we have prayed and disciplined ourselves for it. Some years ago I sought for Indian hemp (*Apocynum cannabinum*) hereabouts in vain, and concluded that it did not grow here. A month or two ago I read again, as many times before, that its blossoms were very small, scarcely a third as large as those of the common species, and for some unaccountable reason this distinction kept recurring to me, and I regarded the size of the flowers I saw, though I did not believe that it grew here; and in a day or two my eyes fell on [it] aye, in three different places, and different varieties of it. Also, a short time ago, I was satisfied that there was but one kind of sunflower (*divaricatus*) indigenous here. Hearing that one had found another kind, it occurred to me that I had seen a taller one than usual lately, but not so distinctly did I remember this as to name it to him or even fully remember it myself. (I rather remembered it afterwards.) But within that hour my genius conducted me to where I had seen the tall plants, and it was the other man's new kind. The next day I found a third kind, miles from there, and, a few days after, a fourth in another direction.

It commonly chances that I make my most interesting botanical discoveries when I [am] in a thrilled and expectant mood, perhaps wading in some remote swamp where I have just found something novel and feel more than usually remote from the town. Or some rare plant which for some reason has occupied a strangely prominent place in my thoughts for some time will present itself. My expectation ripens to discovery. I am prepared for strange things.

Oct. 1. Very heavy rain in the night; cooler now.

P.M. To Walden. . . .

It is cooler and windier, and I wear two thin coats. I do not perceive the poetic and dramatic capabilities of an anecdote or story which is told me, its significance, till some time afterwards. One of the qualities of a pregnant fact is that it does not surprise us, and we only perceive afterwards how interesting it is, and then must know all the particulars. We do not enjoy poetry fully unless we know it to be poetry.

Oct. 18. Men commonly exaggerate the theme. Some themes they think are significant and others insignificant. I feel that my life is very homely, my pleasures very cheap. Joy and sorrow, success and failure, grandeur and meanness, and indeed most words in the English language do not mean for me what they do for my neighbors. I see that my neighbors look with compassion on me, that they think it is a mean and unfortunate destiny which makes me to walk in these fields and woods so much and sail on this river alone. But so long as I find here the only real elysium, I cannot hesitate in my choice. My work is writing, and I do not hesitate, though I know that no subject is too trivial for me, tried by ordinary standards; for, ye fools, the theme is nothing, the life is everything. All that interests the reader is the depth and intensity of the life excited. We touch our subject but by a point which has no breadth, but the pyramid of our experience, or our interest in it, rests on us by a broader or narrower base. That is, man is all in all, Nature nothing, but as she draws him out and reflects him. Give me simple, cheap, and homely themes.

Oct. 21. A *very* warm Indian-summer day, too warm for a thick coat. It is remarkably hazy, too, but when I open the door I smell smoke, which may in part account for it. After being out awhile I do not perceive the smoke, only on first opening the door. It is so thick a blue haze that, when, going along in Thrush Alley Path, I look through the trees into Abel Brook's deep hollow, I cannot see across it to the woods beyond, though it is only a stone's throw. Like a deep blue lake at first glance.

Had a chat with Minott, sitting on a log by his door. . . .

Once, one Rice, who lived in Lincoln where Hayden does now, made a turkey-shooting, and he went to it with his English fowling-piece. He saw many on the road going to it. Saw Dakin [and] Jonas Minott (Captain Minott's son, who spent quite a fortune on shooting), one offering to take another down to the shooting for a mug of flip. They asked him what he was going to do with that little thing. You paid fourpence a shot at a live turkey only twenty rods off. Those who had rifles were not allowed to rest. Amos Baker was there (who was at Concord Fight). The turkey was a large white one. Minott rammed down his slug and, getting down behind a fence, rested on it while the rest laughed at him. He told Amos to look sharp and tell him where his ball struck, and fired. Amos said the ball struck just above the turkey. Others were firing in the meanwhile. Minott loaded and tried once more, and this time his ball cut off the turkey's neck, and it was his; worth a dollar, at least. You only had to draw blood to get the turkey. Another, a black one, was set up, and this time his ball struck the ground just this side the turkey, then scaled up and passed right through its body, lodging under the skin on the opposite side, and he cut it out.

Rice made his money chiefly by his liquor, etc. Some set up the turkeys they had gained: others "hustled" for liquor or for a supper; i.e. they would take sides and then, putting seven coppers in a hat, shake them up well and empty them, and the party that got the fewest heads after three casts paid for the supper.

M. says that, in all the time he lived at Baker's, in fact in all his life, he never went to market.

Dec. 1. P.M. By path around Walden.

With this little snow of the 29th *ult.* there is yet pretty good sledding, for it lies solid.

I see the old pale-faced farmer out again on his sled now for the five-thousandth time,—Cyrus Hubbard, a man of a certain New England probity and worth, immortal and natural, like a natural product, like the sweetness of a nut, like the toughness of hickory. He, too, is a redeemer for me. How superior actually to the faith he professes! He is not an office-seeker. What an institution, what a revelation is a man! We are wont foolishly to think that the creed which a man professes is more significant than the fact he is. It matters not how hard the conditions seemed, how mean the world, for a man is a prevalent force and a new law himself. He is a system whose law is to be observed. The old farmer condescends to countenance still this nature and order of things. It is a great encouragement that an honest man makes this world his abode. He rides on the sled drawn by oxen, world-wise, yet comparatively so young, as if they had seen scores of winters. The farmer spoke to me, I can swear, clean, cold, moderate as the snow. He does not melt the snow where he treads. Yet what a faint impression that encounter may make on me after all! Moderate, natural, true, as if he were made of earth, stone, wood, snow. I thus meet in this universe kindred of mine, composed of these elements. I see men like frogs; their peeping I partially understand.

Dec. 2. P.M.

Saw Melvin's lank bluish-white black-spotted hound, and Melvin with his gun near, going home at eve. He follows hunting, praise be to him, as regularly in our tame fields as the farmers follow farming. Persistent Genius! How I respect him and thank him for him! [sic] I trust the Lord will provide us with another Melvin when he is gone. How good in him to follow his own bent, and not continue at the Sabbath-school all his days! What a wealth he thus becomes in the neighborhood! Few know how to take the census. I thank my stars for Melvin. I think of him with gratitude when I am going to sleep, grateful that he exists,—that Melvin who is such a trial to his mother. Yet he is agreeable to me as a tinge of russet on the hillside. I would fain give thanks morning and evening for my blessings. Awkward, gawky, loose-hung, dragging his legs after him. He is my contemporary and neighbor. He is one tribe, I am another, and we are not at war.

Dec. 6. When I speak of the otter to our oldest village doctor, who should be *ex officio* our naturalist, he is greatly surprised, not knowing that such an animal is found in these parts, and I have to remind him that the Pilgrims sent home many otter skins in the first vessels that returned, together with beaver, mink, and black fox skins, and 1156 pounds of otter skins in the years 1631-36, which brought fourteen or fifteen shillings a pound, also 12,530 pounds of beaver skin. *Vide* Bradford's History. . . .

Where I crossed the river on the roughish white ice, there were coarse ripple-marks two or three feet apart and convex to the south or up-stream, extending quite across, and many spots of black ice a foot wide, more or less in the midst of the white, where probably was water yesterday. The water, apparently, had been blown southerly on to the ice already formed, and hence the ripple-marks.

In many places the otters appeared to have gone floundering along in the sloshy ice and water.

On all sides, in swamps and about their edges and in the woods, the bare shrubs are sprinkled with buds, more or less noticeable and pretty, their little gemmae or gems, their most vital and attractive parts now, almost all the greenness and color left, greens and salads for the birds and rabbits. Our eyes go searching along the stems for what is most vivacious and characteristic, the concentrated summer gone into winter quarters. For we are hunters pursuing the summer on snow-shoes and skates, all winter long. There is really but one season in our hearts.

What variety of pinweeds, clear brown seedy plants, give to the fields, which are yet but shallowly covered with snow! You were not aware before how extensive these grainfields. Not till the snow comes are the beauty and variety and richness of vegetation ever fully revealed. Some plants are now seen more simply and distinctly and to advantage. The pinweeds, etc., have been for the most part confounded with the russet or brown earth beneath them, being seen against a background of the same color, but now, being seen against a pure white background, they are as distinct as if held up to the sky.

Some plants seen, then, in their prime or perfection, when supporting an icy burden in their empty chalices.

Dec. 7. Sunday. P.M.—Take my first skate to Fair Haven Pond.

It takes my feet a few moments to get used to the skates. I see the track of one skater who has preceded me this morning. This is the first skating. I keep mostly to the smooth ice about a rod wide next the shore commonly, where there was an overflow a day or two ago. There is not the slightest overflow today, and yet it is warm (thermometer at 25° at 4.30 P.M.). It must be that the river is falling. Now I go shaking over hobbly places, now shoot over a bridge of ice only a foot wide between the water and the shore at a bend,—Hubbard Bath,—always so at first there. Now I suddenly see the trembling surface of water where I thought were black spots of ice only around me. The river is rather low, so that I cannot keep the river above the Clamshell Bend. I am confined to a very narrow edging of ice in the meadow, gliding with unexpected ease through withered sedge, but slipping sometimes on a twig; again taking to the snow to reach the next ice, but this rests my feet; straddling the bare black willows, winding between the button-bushes, and following narrow threadings of ice amid the sedge, which bring me out to clear fields unexpectedly. Occasionally I am obliged to take a few strokes over black and thin-looking ice, where the neighboring bank is springy, and am slow to acquire confidence in it, but, returning, how bold I am! Where the meadow seemed only sedge and snow, I find a complete ice connection.

At Cardinal Shore, as usual, there is a great crescent of hobbly ice, where two or three days ago, the northwest wind drove the waves back up-stream and broke up the edge of the ice. This crescent is eight or ten rods wide and twice as many long, and consists of cakes of ice from a few inches to half a dozen feet in diameter, with each a raised edge all around, where apparently the floating sludge has been caught and accumulated.

(Occasionally the raised edge is six inches high!) This is mottled black and white, and is not yet safe. It is like skating over so many rails, or the edges of saws. Now I glide over a field of white air-cells close to the surface, with coverings no thicker than egg-shells, cutting through with a sharp crackling sound. There are many of those singular spider-shaped dark places amid the white ice, where the surface water has run through some days ago.

As I enter on Fair Haven Pond, I see already three pickerel-fishers retreating from it, drawing a sled through the Baker Farm, and see where they have been fishing, by the shining chips of ice about the holes. Others were here even yesterday, as it appears. The pond must have been frozen by the 4th at least. Some fisherman or other is ready with his reels and bait as soon as the ice will bear, whether it be Saturday or Sunday. Theirs, too, is a sort of devotion, though it be called hard names by the preacher, who perhaps could not endure the cold and wet any day. Perhaps he dines off their pickerel on Monday at the hotel. The ice appears to be but three or four inches thick.

That grand old poem called Winter is round again without any connivance of mine. As I sit under Lee's Cliff, where the snow is melted, amid sere pennyroyal and frost-bitten catnep, I look over my shoulder upon an arctic scene. I see with surprise the pond a dumb white surface of ice speckled with snow, just as so many winters before, where so lately were lapsing waves or smooth reflecting water. I see the holes which the pickerel-fisher has made, and I see him, too, retreating over the hills, drawing his sled behind him. The water is already skimmed over again there. I hear, too, the familiar belching voice of the pond. It seemed as if winter had come without any interval since mid-summer, and I was prepared to see it flit away by the time I again looked over my shoulder. It was as if I had dreamed it. But I see that the farmers have had time to gather their harvest as usual, and the seasons have revolved as slowly as in the first autumn of my life. The winters come now as fast as snowflakes. It is wonderful that old men do not lose their reckoning. It was summer, and now again it is winter. Nature

loves this rhyme so well that she never tires of repeating it. So
sweet and wholesome is the winter, so simple and moderate, so
satisfactory and perfect, that her children will never weary of it.
What a poem! an epic in blank verse, enriched with a million
tinkling rhymes. It is solid beauty. It has been subjected to the
vicissitudes of millions of years of the gods, and not a single
superfluous ornament remains. The severest and coldest of the
immortal critics have shot their arrows at and pruned it till it
cannot be amended.

Dec. 11. Minott tells me that his and his sister's wood-lot together contains about ten acres and has, with a very slight ex-
ception at one time, supplied all their fuel for thirty years, and
he thinks would constantly continue to do so. They keep one
fire all the time, and two some of the time, and burn about eight
cords in a year. He knows his wood-lot and what grows in it as
well as an ordinary farmer does his corn-field, for he has cut his
own wood till within two or three years; knows the history of
every stump on it and the age of every sapling; knows how many
beech trees and black birches there are there, as another knows
his pear or cherry trees. He complains that the choppers make
a very long carf nowadays, doing most of the cutting on one
side, to avoid changing hands so much. It is more economical,
as well as more poetical, to have a woodlot and cut and get out
your own wood from year to year than to buy it at your door.
Minott may say to his trees; "Submit to my axe. I cut your
father on this very spot." How many sweet passages there must
have been in his life there, chopping all alone in the short winter
days! How many rabbits, partridges, foxes he saw! A rill runs
through the lot, where he quenched his thirst, and several times
he has laid it bare. At last rheumatism has made him a prisoner,
and he is compelled to let a stranger, a vandal, it may be, go
into his lot with an axe. It is fit that he should be buried there.

Dec. 15, has dried up almost all the water in the road. It still
blows hard at 2 P.M., but it is not cold.

   3 P.M.—To Walden. . . .

   I still recall to mind that characteristic winter eve of
December 9th; the cold, dry, and wholesome diet my mind and

senses necessarily fed on,—oak leaves, bleached and withered weeds that rose above the snow, the now dark green of the pines, and perchance the faint metallic chip of a single tree sparrow; the hushed stillness of the wood at sundown, aye, all the winter day; the short boreal twilight; the smooth serenity and the reflections of the pond, still alone free from ice; the melodious hooting of the owl, heard at the same time with the yet more distant whistle of a locomotive, more aboriginal, and perchance more enduring here than that, heard above the voices of all the wise men of Concord, as if they were not (how little he is Anglicized!); the last strokes of the woodchopper, who presently bends his steps homeward; the gilded bar of cloud across the apparent outlet of the pond, conducting my thoughts into the eternal west; the deepening horizon glow; and the hasty walk homeward to enjoy the long winter evening. The hooting of the owl! That is a sound which my red predecessors heard here more than a thousand years ago. It rings far and wide, occupying the spaces rightfully,—grand, primeval, aboriginal sound. There is no whisper in it of the Buckleys, the Flints, the Hosmers who recently squatted here, nor of the first parish, nor of Concord Fight, nor of the last town meeting.

Dec. 23. If the writer would interest readers, he must report so much life, using a certain satisfaction always as a *point d'appui.* However mean and limited, it must be a genuine and contented life that he speaks out of. They must have the essence or oil of himself, tried out of the fat of his experience and joy.

P.M. Surveying for Cyrus Jarvis.

Dec. 28. Walden completely frozen over again last night. Goodwin & Co. are fishing there today. Ice about four inches thick, occasionally sunk by the snow beneath the water. They have had but poor luck. One middling-sized pickerel and one large yellow perch only, since 9 or 10 A.M. It is now nearly sundown. The perch is very full of spawn. How handsome, with its broad dark transverse bars, sharp narrow triangles, broadest on the back!

The men are standing or sitting about a smoky fire of damp dead wood, near by the spot where many a fisherman has sat before, and I draw near, hoping to hear a fish story. One says Louis Menan, the French Canadian who lives in Lincoln, fed his ducks on the fresh-water clams which he got at Fair Haven Pond. He saw him open the shells, and the ducks snapped them up out of the shells very fast. . . .

Since the snow of the 23rd, the days seem considerably lengthened, owing to the increased light after sundown.

The fishermen sit by their damp fire of rotten pine wood, so wet and chilly that even smoke in their eyes is a kind of comfort. There they sit, ever and anon scanning their reels to see if any have fallen, and, if not catching many fish, still getting what they went for, though they may not be aware of it, i.e. a wilder experience than the town affords.

There lies a pickerel or perch on the ice, waving a fin or lifting its gills from time to time, gasping its life away.

I thrive best on solitude. If I have had a companion only one day in a week, unless it were one or two I could name, I find that the value of the week to me has been seriously affected. It dissipates my days, and often it takes me another week to get over it. As the Esquimaux of Smith's Strait in North Greenland laughed when Kane warned them of their utter extermination, cut off as they were by ice on all sides from their race, unless they attempted in season to cross the glacier southward, so do I laugh when you tell me of the danger of impoverishing myself by isolation. It is here that the walrus and the seal and the white bear, and the eider ducks and auks on which I batten, most abound.

Jan. 4, 1857. After spending four or five days surveying and drawing a plan incessantly, I especially feel the necessity of putting myself in communication with nature again, to recover my tone, to withdraw out of the wearying and unprofitable world of affairs. The things I have been doing have but a fleeting and accidental importance, however much men are immersed in them, and yield very little valuable fruit. I would

fain have been wading through the woods and fields and conversing with the sane snow. Having waded in the very shallowest stream of time, I would now bathe my temples in eternity.
I wish again to participate in the serenity of nature, to share the
happiness of the river and the woods. I thus from time to time
break off my connection with eternal truths and go with the
shallow stream of human affairs, grinding at the mill of the
Philistines; but when my task is done, with never-failing confidence I devote myself to the infinite again. It would be sweet
to deal with men more, I can imagine, but where dwell they?
Not in the fields which I traverse.

Jan. 5. A cold cutting northwest wind.

Jan. 6. Still colder and perhaps windier. The river is now for the
most part covered with snow again, which has blown from the
meadows and been held by the water which has oozed out. I
slump through snow into that water for twenty rods together,
which is not frozen though the thermometer says $-8°$. I think
that the bright-yellow wood of the barberry, which I have
occasion to break in my surveying, is the most interesting and
remarkable for its color of any. When I get home after that
slumping walk on the river, I find that the slush has balled and
frozen on my boots two or three inches thick, and can only be
thawed off by the fire, it is so solid.

I frequently have occasion in surveying to note the position or
bearing of the edge of a wood, which I describe as edge of wood.
In such a way apparently the name Edgewood originated.

Beatton, the old Scotch storekeeper, used to say of one
Deacon (Joe?) Brown, a grandfather of the milkman, who used
to dine at his house on Sundays and praise his wife's dinners but
yet prevented her being admitted to the church, that his was
like a "coo's (cow's) tongue, rough one side and smooth the
other."

A man asked me the other night whether such and such
persons were not as happy as anybody, being conscious, as I
perceived, of much unhappiness himself and not aspiring to
much more than an animal content. "Why!" said I, speaking

to his condition, "the stones are happy, Concord River is happy, and I am happy too. When I took up a fragment of a walnut-shell this morning, I saw by its very grain and composition, its form and color, etc., that it was made for happiness. The most brutish and inanimate objects that are made suggest an ever-lasting and thorough satisfaction; they are the homes of content. Wood, earth, mould, etc., exist for joy. Do you think that Concord River would have continued to flow these millions of years by Clamshell Hill and round Hunt's Island, if it had not been happy,—if it had been miserable in its channel, tired of existence, and cursing its maker and the hour that it sprang?"

Jan. 7. P.M.—To Walden down railroad and return over cliffs....

I go through the woods toward the Cliffs along the side of the Well Meadow Field....

In the street and in society I am almost invariably cheap and dissipated, my life is unspeakably mean. No amount of gold or respectability would in the least redeem it,—dining with the Governor or a member of Congress!! But alone in distant woods or fields, in unpretending sprout-lands or pastures tracked by rabbits, even in a bleak and, to most, cheerless day, like this, when a villager would be thinking of his inn, I come to myself, I once more feel myself grandly related, and that cold and solitude are friends of mine. I suppose that this value, in my case, is equivalent to what others get by churchgoing and prayer. I come to my solitary woodland walk as the homesick go home. I thus dispose of the superfluous and see things as they are grand and beautiful. I have told many that I walk every day about half the daylight, but I think they do not believe it. I wish to get the Concord, the Massachusetts, the America, out of my head and be sane a part of every day. If there are missionaries for the heathen, why not send them to me? I wish to know something; I wish to be made better. I wish to forget, a considerable part of every day, all mean, narrow, trivial men (and this requires usually to forego and forget all personal relations so long), and therefore I come out to these solitudes, where the problem of existence is simplified. I get away a mile or two from the town into the stillness and solitude of nature, with rocks, trees, weeds, snow about me. I enter some glade in the woods, perchance, where a few weeds and dry leaves alone lift themselves above the surface of the snow, and it is as if I had come to an open window. I see out and around myself. Our *skylights* are thus far away from the ordinary resorts of men. I am not satisfied with ordinary windows. I must have a true *skylight*. My true skylight is on the outside of the village. I am not thus expanded, recreated, enlightened, when I meet a company of men. It chances that the sociable, the town and county, or the farmers' club does not prove a skylight to me. I do not invariably find myself translated under those circumstances. They bore me. The man I meet with is not often so instructive as the silence he breaks. This stillness, solitude, wildness of nature is a kind of thoroughwort, or boneset, to my intellect. This is what I go out to seek. It is as if I always met in those places some grand serene, immortal, infinitely encouraging, though invisible, companion, and walked with him. There at last my nerves are steadied, my senses and my mind do their office. I am aware that most of my neighbors would think it a hardship to be compelled to linger here one hour, especially this bleak day, and yet I receive this sweet and ineffable compensation for it. It is the most agreeable thing I do. Truly, my coins are uncurrent with them.

Jan. 11. There was wit and even poetry in the negro's answer to the man who tried to persuade him that the slaves would not be obliged to work in heaven. "Oh, you g'way, Massa. I know better. If dere's no work for cullud folks up dar, dey'll *make* some fur 'em, and if dere's nuffin better to do, dey'll make em *shub de clouds along.* You can't fool this chile, Massa."

Feb. 8. Hayden senior (sixty-eight years old) tells me that he has been at work regularly with his team almost every day this winter, in spite of snow and cold. Even that cold Friday, about a fortnight ago, he did not go to a fire from early morning till night. As the thermometer, even at 12.45 P.M. was at

−9°, with a very violent wind from the northwest, this was as bad as an ordinary arctic day. He was hauling logs to a mill, and persevered in making his paths through the drifts, he alone breaking the road. However, he froze his ears that Friday. Says he never knew it so cold as the past month. He has a fine elm directly behind his house, divided into many limbs near the ground. It is a question which is the most valuable, this tree or the house. In hot summer days it shades the whole house. He is going to build a shed around it, inclosing the main portion of the trunk.

Feb. 18. I am excited by this wonderful air and go listening for the note of the bluebird or other comer. The very grain of the air seems to have undergone a change and is ready to split into the form of the bluebird's warble. Methinks if it were visible, or I could cast up some fine dust which would betray it, it would take a corresponding shape. The bluebird does not come till the air consents and his wedge will enter easily. The air over these fields is a foundry full of moulds for casting bluebirds' warbles. Any sound uttered now would take that form, not of the harsh, vibrating, rending scream of the jay, but a softer, flowing, curling warble, like a purling stream or the lobes of flowing sand and clay.

Feb. 20. I wish that there was in every town, in some place accessible to the traveller, instead [of] or beside the common directories, etc., a list of the worthies of the town, i.e. of those who are *worth* seeing.

March 8. P.M. To Hill.

When I cut a white pine twig the crystalline sap instantly exudes. How long has it been thus?

Get a glimpse of a hawk, the first of the season. The tree sparrows sing a little on this still sheltered and sunny side of the hill, but not elsewhere. A partridge goes off from amid the pitch pines. It lifts each wing so high above its back and flaps so low, and withal so rapidly, that they present the appearance of a broad wheel, almost a revolving sphere, as it whirs off like a cannon-ball shot from a gun.

Minott told me again the reason why the bushes were coming in so fast in the river meadows. Now that the mower takes nothing stronger than molasses and water, he darsn't meddle with anything bigger than a pipe-stem.

March 11. I see and talk with Rice, sawing off the ends of clapboards which he has planed, to make them square, for an addition to his house. He has got a fire in his shop, and plays at house-building there. His life is poetic. He does the work himself. He combines several qualities and talents rarely combined. Though he owns houses in the city, whose repair he attends to, finds tenants for them, and collects the rent, he also has his Sudbury farm and bean-fields. Though he lived in a city, he would still be natural and related to primitive nature around him. Though he owned all Beacon Street, you might find that his mittens were made of the skin of a woodchuck that had ravaged his bean-field, which he had cured. I noticed a woodchuck's skin tacked up to the inside of his shop. He said it had fatted on his beans, and William had killed [it] and expected to get another to make a pair of mittens of, one not being quite large enough. It was excellent for mittens. You could hardly wear it out.

Spoke of the cuckoo, which was afraid of the birds, was easily beaten; would dive right into the middle of a poplar, then come out on to some bare twig and look round for a nest to rob of young or eggs. Had noticed a pigeon woodpecker go repeatedly in a straight line from his nest in an apple tree to a distant brook-side in a meadow, dive down there, and in a few minutes return.

March 17. These days, beginning with the 14th, more spring-like. Last night it rained a little carrying off nearly all the little snow that remained, but this morning it is fair, and I hear the note of the woodpecker on the elms (that early note) and the bluebird again. Launch my boat.

No mortal is alert enough to be present at the first dawn of the spring, but he will presently discover some evidence that vegetation had awaked some days at least before. Early as I have looked this year, perhaps the first unquestionable growth of an indigenous plant detected was the fine tips of grass blades which the frost had killed, floating pale and flaccid, though still attached to their stems, spotting the pools like a slight fall or flurry of dull-colored snowflakes. After a few mild and sunny days, even in February, the grass in still muddy pools or ditches sheltered by the surrounding banks, which reflect the heat upon it, ventures to lift the points of its green phalanx into the mild and flattering atmosphere, advances rapidly from the saffron even to the rosy tints of morning. But the following night comes the frost, which, with rude and ruthless hand, sweeps the surface of the pool, and the advancing morning pales into the dim light of earliest dawn. I thus detect the first approach of spring by finding here and there its scouts and vanguard which have been slain by the rear-guard of retreating winter.

March 18. 9 A.M.—Up Assabet.

A still and warm but overcast morning, threatening rain. I now again hear the song sparrow's tinkle along the riverside, probably to be heard for a day or two, and a robin, which also has been heard a day or two. The ground is almost completely bare, and but little ice forms at night along the riverside.

I meet Goodwin paddling up the still, dark river on his first voyage to Fair Haven for the season, looking for muskrats and from time to time picking driftwood—logs and boards, etc.—out of the water and laying it up to dry on the bank, to eke out his wood-pile with. He says that the frost is not out so that he can lay wall, and so he thought he['d] go and see what there was at Fair Haven. Says that when you hear a woodpecker's *rat-tat-tat-tat-tat* on a dead tree it is a sign of rain. While Emerson sits writing [in] his study this still, overcast, moist day, Goodwin is paddling up the still, dark river. Emerson burns twenty-five cords of wood and fourteen (?) tons of coal; Goodwin perhaps a cord and a half, much of which he picks out of the river. He says he'd rather have a boat leak some for fishing. I hear the report of his gun from time to time for an hour, heralding the death of a muskrat and reverberating far down the river.

March 24. P.M.—Paddle up Assabet. . . .

If you are describing any occurrence, or a man, make two or more distinct reports at different times. Though you may think you have said all, you will tomorrow remember a whole new class of facts which perhaps interested most of all at the time, but did not present themselves to be reported. If we have recently met and talked with a man, and would report our experience, we commonly make a very partial report at first, failing to seize the most significant, picturesque, and dramatic points; we describe only what we have had time to digest and dispose of in our minds, without being conscious that there were other things really more novel and interesting to us, which will not fail to recur to us and impress us suitably at last.

March 27. I would fain make two reports in my Journal, first the incidents and observations of today; and by tomorrow I review the same and record what was omitted before, which will often be the most significant and poetic part. I do not know at first what it is that charms me. The men and things of today are wont to lie fairer and truer in tomorrow's memory.

March 28. Often I can give the truest and most interesting account of any adventure I have had after years have elapsed, for then I am not confused, only the most significant facts surviving in my memory. Indeed, all that continues to interest me after such a lapse of time is sure to be pertinent, and I may safely record all that I remember.

April 16. About a month ago, at the post office, Abel Brooks, who is pretty deaf, sidling up to me, observed in a loud voice which all could hear, "Let me see, your society is pretty large, ain't it?" "Oh, yes, large enough," said I, not knowing what he meant. "There's Stewart belongs to it, and Collier, he's one of them, and Emerson, and my boarder" (Pulsifer), "and Channing, I believe, I think he goes there." "You mean the *walkers*; don't you?" "Ye-es, I call you the Society. All go to the woods, don't you?" "Do you miss any of your wood?" I asked. "No, I hain't worried any yet. I believe you're a pretty clever set, as good as the average." etc., etc.

Telling Sanborn of this, he said that, when he first came to town and boarded at Holbrook's, he asked H. how many religious societies there were in town. H. said that there were three,—the Unitarian, the Orthodox, and the Walden Pond Society. I asked Sanborn with which Holbrook classed himself. He said he believes that he put himself with the last.

May 24. A.M. To Hill.

White ash, apparently yesterday, at Grape Shore but not at Conantum. What a singular appearance for some weeks its great masses of dark-purple anthers have made, fruit-like on the trees!

A very warm morning. Now the birds sing more than ever, methinks, now, when the leaves are fairly expanding, the first really warm summer days. The water on the meadows is perfectly smooth nearly all the day. At 3 P.M. the thermometer is at 88°. It soon gets to be quite hazy. Apple out. Heard one speak today of his sense of awe at the thought of God, and suggested to him that awe was the cause of the potato-rot. The same speaker dwelt on the sufferings of life, but my advice was to go about one's business, suggesting that no ecstasy was ever interrupted, nor its fruit blasted. As for completeness and roundness, to be sure, we are each like one of the laciniae of a lichen, a torn fragment, but not the less cheerfully we expand in a moist day and assume unexpected colors. We want no completeness but intensity of life. Hear the first cricket as I go through a warm hollow, bringing round the summer with his everlasting strain.

May 29. Fair Haven Lake, now, at 4.30 P.M. is perfectly smooth, reflecting the darker and glowing June clouds as it has not before. Fishes incessantly dimple it here and there, and I see afar, approaching steadily but diagonally toward the shore of the island, some creature on its surface, maybe a snake,—but my glass shows it to be a muskrat, leaving two long harrow-like ripples behind. Soon after, I see another, quite across the pond on the Baker Farm side, and even distinguish that to be a muskrat. The fishes, methinks, are busily breeding now. These things I see as I sit on the top of Lee's Cliff, looking into the light and dark eye of the lake. The heel of that summer-shower cloud, seen through the trees in the west, has extended further south and looks more threatening than ever. As I stand on the rocks, examining the blossoms of some forward black oaks which close overhang it, I think I hear the sound of flies against my hat. No, it is scattered raindrops, though the sky is perfectly clear above me, and the cloud from which they come is yet far on one side. I see through the tree-tops the thin vanguard of the storm scaling the celestial ramparts, like eager light infantry, or cavalry with spears advanced. But from the west a great, still, ash-colored cloud comes on. The drops fall thicker, and I seek a shelter under the Cliffs. I stand under a large projecting portion of the Cliff, where there is ample space above and around, and I can move about as perfectly protected as under a shed. To be sure, fragments of rock look as if they would fall, but I see no marks of recent ruin about me.

Soon I hear the low all-pervading hum of an approaching hummingbird circling above the rock, which afterward I mistake several times for the gruff voices of men approaching, unlike as these sounds are in some respects, and I perceive the resemblance even when I know better. Now I am sure it is a hummingbird, and now that it is two farmers approaching. But presently the hum becomes more sharp and thrilling, and the little fellow suddenly perches on an ash twig within a rod of me, and plumes himself while the rain is fairly beginning. He is quite out of proportion to the size of his perch. It does not acknowledge his weight.

I sit at my ease and look out from under my lichen-clad rocky roof, half-way up the Cliff, under freshly leafing ash and hickory trees on to the pond, while the rain is falling faster and faster, and I am rather glad of the rain, which affords me this experience. The rain has compelled me to find the cosiest and most homelike part of all the Cliff. The surface of the pond, though the rain dimples it all alike and I perceive no wind, is still divided into irregular darker and lighter spaces, with distinct boundaries, as it were *watered* all over. Even now that it rains very hard and the surface is all darkened, the boundaries of those spaces are not quite obliterated. The countless drops seem to spring again from its surface like stalagmites.

A mosquito, sole living inhabitant of this antrum, settles on my hand. I find here sheltered with me a sweetbriar growing in a cleft of the rock above my head, where perhaps some bird or squirrel planted it. Mulleins beneath. *Galium Aparine*, just begun to bloom, growing next the rock; and, in the earth-filled clefts, columbines, some of whose cornucopias strew the ground. *Ranunculus bulbosus* in bloom; saxifrage; and various ferns, as spleenwort, etc. Some of these plants are never rained on. I perceive the buttery-like scent of barberry bloom from over the rocks, and now and for some days the bunches of effete white ash anthers strew the ground.

It lights up a little, and the drops fall thinly again, and the birds begin to sing, but now I see a new shower coming up from the southwest, and the wind seems to have changed somewhat. Already I had heard the low mutterings of its thunder—for this is a thunder-shower—in the midst of the last. It seems to have shifted its quarters merely to attack me on a more exposed side of my castle. Two foes appear where I had expected none. But who can calculate the tactics of the storm? It is a first regular summer thunder-shower, preceded by a rush of wind, and I begin to doubt if my quarters will prove a sufficient shelter. I am fairly besieged and know not when I shall escape. I hear the still roar of the rushing storm at a distance, though no trees are seen to wave. And now the forked flashes descending to the earth succeed rapidly to the hollow roars above, and down comes the deluging rain. I hear the alarmed notes of birds flying to a shelter. The air at length is cool and chilly, the atmosphere is darkened, and I have forgotten the smooth pond and its reflections. The rock feels cold to my body, as if it were a different season of the year. I almost repent of having lingered here; think how far I should have got if I had started homeward. But then what a condition I should have been in! Who knows but the lightning will strike this cliff and topple the rocks down on me? The crashing thunder sounds like the overhauling of lumber on heaven's loft. And now, at last, after an hour of steady confinement the clouds grow thin again, and the birds begin to sing. They make haste to conclude the day with their regular evening songs (before the rain is fairly over) according to the program. The pepe on some pine tree top was heard almost in the midst of the storm. One or two bullfrogs trump. They care not how wet it is. Again I hear the still rushing, all-pervading roar of the withdrawing storm, when it is at least half a mile off, wholly beyond the pond, though no trees are seen to wave. It is simply the sound of the countless drops falling on the leaves and the ground. You were not aware what a sound the rain made. Several times I attempt to leave my shelter, but return to it. My first stepping abroad seems but a signal for the rain to commence again. Not till after an hour and a half do I escape. After all, my feet and legs are drenched by the wet grass.

May 30. Perhaps I could write meditations under a rock in a shower.

When first I had sheltered myself under the rock, I began at once to look out on the pond with new eyes, as from my house. I was at Lee's Cliff as I had never been there before, had taken up my residence there, as it were. Ordinarily we make haste away from all opportunities to be where we have instinctively endeavored to get. When the storm was over where I was, and only a few thin drops were falling around me, I plainly saw the rear of the rain withdrawing over the Lincoln woods south of the pond, and, above all, heard the grand rushing sound made by the rain falling on the freshly green forest, a very different sound when thus heard at a distance from what it is when we are in the midst of it. . . .

I sang "Tom Bowling" there in the midst of the rain, and the dampness seemed to be favorable to my voice.

July 2. P.M. To Gowing's Swamp.

Flannery says that there was a frost this morning in Moore's Swamp on the Bedford road, where he has potatoes. He observed something white on the potatoes about 3.30 A.M. and, stooping, breathed on and melted it. Minott says he has known a frost every month in the year, but at this season it would be a *black* frost, which bites harder than a white one.

The *Gaylussacia dumosa* var. *hirtella*, not yet quite in prime. This is commonly an inconspicuous bush, eight to twelve inches high, half prostrate over the sphagnum in which it grows, together with the andromedas, European cranberry, etc., etc., but sometimes twenty inches high quite on the edge of the swamp. It has a very large and peculiar bell-shaped flower, with prominent *ribs* and a rosaceous tinge, and is not to be mistaken for the edible huckleberry or blueberry blossom. . . .

Calla palustris (with its convolute point like the cultivated) at the south end of Gowing's Swamp. Having found this in one place, I now find it in another. Many an object is not seen though it falls within the range of our visual ray, because it does not come within the range of our intellectual ray, i.e., we are not looking for it. So, in the largest sense, we find only the world we look for.

July 3. Minott says that old Joe Merriam used to tell of his shooting black ducks in the Dam meadows and what luck he had. One day he had shot a couple of ducks and was bringing them home by the legs, when he came to a ditch. As he had his gun in the other hand, and the ditch was wide, he thought he would toss the ducks over before he jumped, but they had no sooner struck the ground than they picked themselves up and flew away, which discouraged him with respect to duck-shooting. . . .

[M.] once killed a black duck in Beck Stow's Swamp, but could not get it on account of the water. Somebody else got a boat and got it. Thus the ducks and geese will frequent a swamp where there is considerable water, in the spring.

Minott was sitting in his shed as usual, while his handsome pullets were perched on the wood within two feet of him, the rain having driven them to this shelter.

There always were poor and rich as now,—in that first year when our ancestors lived on pumpkins and raccoons, as now when flour is imported from the West.

Aug. 10. How meanly and miserably we live for the most part! We escape fate continually by the skin of our teeth, as the saying is. We are practically desperate. But as every man, in respect to material wealth, aims to become independent or wealthy, so, in respect to our spirits and imagination, we should have some spare capital and superfluous vigor, have some margin and leeway in which to move. What kind of gift is life unless we have spirits to enjoy it and taste its true flavor? if, in respect to spirits, we are to be forever cramped and in debt? In our ordinary estate we have not, so to speak, quite enough air to breathe, and this poverty qualifies our piety; but we should have more than enough and breathe it carelessly. Poverty is the rule. We should first of all be full of vigor like a strong horse, and beside have the free and adventurous spirit of his driver; i.e., we should have such a reserve of elasticity and strength that we may at any time be able to put ourselves at the top of our speed and go beyond our ordinary limits, just as the invalid hires a horse. Have the gods sent us into this world,—to this *muster,*— to do chores, hold horses, and the like, and not given us any spending money?

Sept. 30. Minott said he had seen a couple of pigeons go over at last, as he sat in his shed. At first he thought they were doves, but he soon saw that they were pigeons, they flew so straight and fast.

He says that that tall clock which still ticks in the corner belonged to old John Beatton, who died before he was born; thought it was two hundred years old!!! Some of the rest of the furniture came from the same source. His gun marked London was one that Beatton sent to England for, for a young man that lived with him. I read on John Beatton's tombstone near the powder-house that he died in 1776, aged seventy-four.

Oct. 3. Getting over the wall near Sam Barrett's the other day, I had gone a few rods in the road when I met Prescott Barrett, who observed, "Well you take a walk around the square sometimes." So little does he know of my habits. I go across lots over his grounds every three or four weeks, but I do not know that I ever walked round the square in my life.

How much more agreeable to sit in the midst of old furniture like Minott's clock and secretary and looking-glass, which have come down from other generations, than in [*sic*] that which was just brought from the cabinet-maker's and smells of varnish, like a coffin! To sit under the face of an old clock that has been ticking one hundred and fifty years,—there is something mortal, not to say immortal, about it! A clock that began to tick when Massachusetts was a province. Meanwhile John Beatton's heavy tombstone is cracked quite across and widely opened.

Oct. 14. Looking now toward the north side of the pond, I perceive that the reflection of the hillside seen from an opposite hill is not so broad as the hillside itself appears, owing to the different angle at which it is seen. The reflection exhibits such an aspect of the hill, *apparently*, as you would get if your eye were placed at that part of the surface of the pond where the reflection seems to be. In this instance, too, then, Nature avoids repeating herself. Not even reflections in still water are like their substances as seen by us. This, too, accounts for my seeing portions of the sky through the trees in reflections often when none appear in the substance. Is the reflection of a hillside, however, such an aspect of it as can be obtained by the eye directed to the hill itself from any single point of view? It plainly is not such a view as the eye would get looking upward from the immediate base of the hill or water's edge, for there the first rank of bushes on the lower part of the hill would conceal the upper. The reflection of the top appears to be such a view of it as I should get with my eye at the water's edge above the edge of the reflection; but would the lower part of the hill also appear from this point as it does in the reflection? Should I see as much of the under sides of the leaves there? If not, then the reflection is never a true copy or repetition of its substance, but a new composition, and this may be the source of its novelty and attractiveness, and of this nature, too, may be the charm of an echo. I doubt if you can ever get Nature to repeat herself exactly.

Oct. 20. I keep along the old Carlisle road. The leaves having mostly fallen, the country now seems deserted, and you feel further from home and more lonely. I see where squirrels, apparently, have gnawed the apples left in the road. The barberry bushes are now alive with, I should say, thousands of robins feeding on them. They must make a principal part of their food now. I see the yellowish election-cake fungi. Those large chocolate-colored ones have been burst some days (at least).

Warren Brown, who owns the Easterbrooks place, the west side the road, is picking barberries. Allows that the soil thereabouts is excellent for fruit, but it is so rocky that he has not patience to plow it. That is the reason this tract is not cultivated. The yellow birches are generally bare. The sassafras in Sted Buttrick's pasture near to E. Hubbard's Wood, nearly so; leaves all withered. Much or most of the fever-bush still green, though somewhat wrinkled.

There was Melvin, too, a-barberrying and nutting. He had got two baskets, one in each hand, and his game-bag, which hung from his neck, all full of nuts and barberries, and his mouth full of tobacco. Trust him to find where the nuts and berries grow. He is hunting all the year and he marks the bushes and the trees which are fullest, and when the time comes, for once leaves his gun, though not his dog, at home, and takes his basket to the spot. It is pleasanter to me to meet him with his gun or with his baskets than to meet some portly caterer for a family, basket on arm, at the stalls of Quincy Market. Better Melvin's pignuts than the others' shagbarks. It is to be observed that the best things are generally most abused, and so are not so much enjoyed as the worst. Shagbarks are eaten by epicures with diseased appetites; pignuts by the country boys who gather them. So fagots and rubbish yield more comfort than sound wood.

Melvin says he has caught partridges in his hands. If there's only one hole, knows they've not gone out. Sometimes shoots them through the snow.

What a wild and rich domain that Easterbrooks Country! Not a cultivated, hardly a cultivatable field in it, and yet it delights all natural persons, and feeds more still. Such great rocky and moist tracts, which daunt the farmer, are reckoned as unimproved land, and therefore worth but little; but think of the miles of huckleberries and of barberries, and of wild apples, so fair, both in flower and fruit, resorted to by men and beasts; Clark, Brown, Melvin, and the robins, these, at least, were attracted thither this afternoon. There are barberry bushes or clumps there, behind which I could actually pick two bushels of berries without being seen by you on the other side. And they are not a quarter picked at last, by all creatures together. I walk for two or three miles, and still the clumps of barberries, great sheaves with their wreaths of scarlet fruit, show themselves before me and on every side, seeming to issue from between the pines or other trees, as if it were they that were promenading there, not I.

That very dense and handsome maple and pine grove opposite the pond-hole on this old Carlisle road is Ebby Hubbard's. Melvin says there are those alive who remember mowing there. Hubbard loves to come with his axe in the fall or winter and trim up his woods. Melvin tells me that Skinner says he thinks he heard a wildcat scream in E. Hubbard's Wood, by the Close. It is worth the while to have a Skinner in the town; else we should not know that we had wildcats. They had better look out, or he will skin them, for that seems to have been the trade of his ancestors. How long Nature has manoeuvred to bring Skinner within earshot of that wildcat's scream! Saved Ebby's wood to be the scene of it! Ebby the *wood-saver*.

Melvin says that Sted sold the principal log of one of those pasture oaks to Garty for ten dollars and got several cords besides. What a mean bribe to take the life of so noble a tree!

Wesson is so gouty that he rarely comes out-of-doors, and is a spectacle in the street; but he loves to tell his old stories still! How, when he was stealing along to get a shot at his ducks, and was just upon them, a red squirrel sounded the alarm, *chickaree, chickaree, chickaree*, and off they went; but he turned his gun upon the squirrel to avenge himself.

It would seem as if men generally could better appreciate honesty of the John Beatton stamp, which gives you your due to a mill, than the generosity which habitually throws in the half-cent.

Oct. 21. Is not the poet bound to write his own biography? Is there any other work for him but a good journal? We do not wish to know how his imaginary hero, but how he, the actual hero, lived from day to day.

Oct. 29. I find when I have been building a fence or surveying a farm, or even collecting simples, that these were the true paths to perception and enjoyment. My being seems to have put forth new roots and to be more strongly planted. This is the true way to crack the nut of happiness.

Nov. 5. P.M. To the Dam Meadows.

But little corn is left in the field now, and that looks rather black. There is an abundance of cat-tail in the Dam Meadows.

Returning, talked with Minott. He told me how he and Harry Hooper used to go to Howard's meadow (Heywood's, by the railroad) when it was flowed and kill fishes through the ice. They would cut a long stick and go carefully over the ice when it was only a couple of inches thick, and when they saw a fish, strike the ice smartly, cracking it in all directions, right over him, and when he turned his belly, being stunned, would cut him out quickly before he came to. These were little fishes which he called "prods." He didn't know much more about them. They were somewhat like a small pout, but had different heads. They got so many once that he told Harry to cut a stick and string them and they'd give them to Zilpha as they went by. He has caught pickerel in the brook there which weighed two or three pounds.

He went to Bateman's Pond once in the winter to catch minnows with a net through the ice, but didn't get any. He went—rode—with Oliver Williams first into Acton and then round to this pond on this errand.

Minott was rather timid. One day early in the winter he had been over to Fair Haven Hill after a fox with John Wyman, but they didn't get him. The pond was frozen about two inches thick, but you could easily see the water through the ice, and when they came back, Wyman said he was going straight across because it was nearer, but Minott objected. But Wyman told him to follow; it was safe enough. Minott followed half a dozen rods and then decided that he wouldn't risk it and went back; he'd go ten miles round sooner than cross. "But," said Minott, "the fellow kept on and I'll be hanged if he didn't get safe across." . . .

Sometimes I would rather get a transient glimpse or side view of a thing than stand fronting to it,—as those polypodies. The object I caught a glimpse of as I went by haunts my thoughts a long time, is infinitely suggestive, and I do not care to front it and scrutinize it, for I know that the thing that really concerns me is not there, but in my relation to that. That is a mere reflecting surface. It is not the polypody in my pitcher or herbarium, or which I may possibly persuade to grow on a bank in my yard, or which is described in botanies, that interests me, but the one that I pass by in my walks a little distance off, when in the right mood. . . .

Start up a snipe feeding in a wet part of the Dam Meadows.

I think that the man of science makes this mistake, and the mass of mankind along with him: that you should coolly give your chief attention to the phenomenon which excites you as something independent on you, and not as it is related to you. The important fact is its effect on me. He thinks that I have no business to see anything else but just what he defines the rainbow to be, but I care not whether my vision of truth is a waking thought or dream remembered, whether it is seen in the light or in the dark. It is the subject of the vision, the truth alone, that concerns me. The Philosopher for whom rainbows, etc., can be explained away never saw them. With regard to such objects, I find that it is not they themselves (with which the men of science deal) that concern me; the point of interest is somewhere *between* me and them (i.e. the objects). . . .

Nov. 7. You will sometimes see a sudden wave flow along a puny ditch of a brook, inundating all its shores, when a musquash is making his escape beneath. He soon plunges into some hole in the bank under water, and all is still again.

P.M.—To Bateman's Pond with R. W. E. . . .

Minott adorns whatever part of nature he touches; whichever way he walks he transfigures the earth for me. If a common man speaks of Walden Pond to me, I see only a shallow, dull-colored body of water without reflections or peculiar color, but if Minott speaks of it, I see the green water and reflected hills at once, for he *has been* there. I hear the rustle of the leaves from woods which he goes through.

V

DISCOVERING SOMETHING OLD

Nov. 9, 1857. Surveying for Stedman Buttrick and Mr. Gordon.

Jacob Farmer says that he remembers well a particular bound (which is the subject of dispute between the above two men) from this circumstance: He, a boy, was sent, as the representative of his mother, to witness the placing of the bounds to her lot, and he remembers that, when they had fixed the stake and stones, old Mr. Nathan Barrett asked him if he had a knife about him, upon which he pulled out his knife and gave it to him. Mr. Barrett cut a birch switch and trimmed it in the presence of young Farmer, and then called out, "Boy, here's your knife," but as the boy saw that he was going to strike him when he reached his hand for the knife, he dodged into a bush which alone received the blow. And Mr. Barrett said that if it had not been for that, he would have got a blow which would have made him remember that bound as long as he lived, and explained to him that that was his design in striking him. He had before told his mother that since she could not go to the woods to see what bounds were set to her lot, she had better send Jacob as a representative of the family. This made Farmer the important witness in this case. He first, some years ago, saw Buttrick trimming up the trees, and told him he was on Gordon's land and pointed out this as the bound between them.

Nov. 20. We require that the reporter be very permanently planted before the facts which he observes, not a mere passer-by; hence the facts cannot be too homely. A man is worth most to himself and to others, whether as an observer, or poet, or neighbor, or friend, where he is most himself, most contented and at home. There his life is the most intense and he loses the fewest moments. Familiar and surrounding objects are the best symbols and illustrations of his life. If a man who has had deep experiences should endeavor to describe them in a book of travels, it would be to use the language of a wandering tribe instead of a universal language. The poet has made the best roots in his native soil of any man, and is the hardest to transplant. The man who is often thinking that it is better to be somewhere else than where he is excommunicates himself. If a man is rich and strong anywhere, it must be on his native soil. Here I have been these forty years learning the language of these fields that I may the better express myself. If I should travel to the prairies, I should much less understand them, and my past life would serve me but ill to describe them. Many a week here stands for more of life to me than the big trees of California would if I should go there. We only need travel enough to give our intellects an airing. In spite of Malthus and the rest, there will be plenty of room in this world, if every man will mind his own business. I have not heard of any planet running against another yet.

Nov. 25. It is surprising how much, from the habit of regarding writing as an accomplishment, is wasted on form. A very little information or wit is mixed up with a great deal of conventionalism in the style of expressing it, as with a sort of preponderating paste or vehicle. Some life is not simply expressed, but a long-winded speech is made, with an occasional attempt to put a little life into it.

Nov. 26. Minott's is a small, square, one-storied and unpainted house, with a hipped roof and at least one dormer-window, a third the way up the south side of a long hill which is some fifty feet high and extends east and west. A traveller of taste may go straight through the village without being detained a moment by any dwelling, either the form or surroundings being objectionable, but very few go by this house without being agreeably impressed, and many are therefore led to inquire who lives in it. Not that its form is so incomparable, nor even its weather-stained color, but chiefly, I think, because of its snug and picturesque position on the hillside, fairly lodged there, where all children like to be, and its perfect harmony with its surroundings and position. For if, preserving this form and color, it should be transplanted to the meadow below, nobody would notice it more than a schoolhouse which was lately of the same form. It is there because somebody was independent or bold enough to carry out the happy thought, of placing it high on the hillside. It is the locality, not the architecture, that takes us captive. There is exactly such a site, only of course less room on either side, between this house and the next westward, but few if any, even of the admiring travellers, have thought of this as a house-lot, or would be bold enough to place a cottage there.

Without side fences or gravelled walks or flowerplots, that simple sloping bank before it is pleasanter than any front yard, though many a visitor—and many times the master—has slipped and fallen on the steep path. From its position and exposure, it has shelter and warmth and dryness and prospect. He overlooks the road, the meadow and brook, and houses beyond, to the distant woods. The spring comes earlier to that dooryard than to any, and summer lingers longest there.

Jan. 6, 1858. The first snow-storm of much importance. By noon it *may be* six inches deep.

P.M. Up Railroad to North River.

The main stream, barely skimmed over with snow, which has sunk the thin ice and is saturated with water, is of a dull-brown color between the white fields. . . .

I walk amid the bare midribs of cinnamon ferns, with at most a terminal leafet, and here and there I see a little dark water at the bottom of a dimple in the snow, over which the snow has not yet been able to prevail.

I was feeling very cheap, nevertheless, reduced to make the most of dry dogwood berries. Very little evidence of God or man did I see just then, and life not as rich and inviting an enterprise as it should be, when my attention was caught by a snowflake on my coat-sleeve. It was one of those perfect, crystalline, star-shaped ones, six-rayed, like a flat wheel with six spokes, only the spokes were perfect little pine trees in shape, arranged around a central spangle. This little object, which, with many of its fellows, rested unmelting on my coat, so perfect and beautiful, reminded me that Nature had not lost her pristine vigor yet, and why should man lose heart? Sometimes the pines were worn and had lost their branches, and again it appeared as if several stars had impinged on one another at various angles, making a somewhat spherical mass. These little wheels came down like the wrecks of chariots from a battle waged in the sky. There were mingled with these starry flakes small down pellets also. This was at mid-afternoon, and it has not quite ceased snowing yet (at 10 P.M.) We are rained and snowed on with gems. I confess that I was a little encouraged, for I was beginning to believe that Nature was poor and mean, and I was now convinced that she turned off as good work as ever.

Jan. 25. Monday. A warm, moist day. Thermometer at 6.30 P.M. at 49°.

What a rich book might be made about buds, including, perhaps, sprouts!—the impregnable, vivacious willow catkins, but half asleep under the armor of their black scales, sleeping along the twigs; the birch and oak sprouts, and the rank and lusty dogwood sprouts; the round red buds of the blueberries; the small pointed red buds, close to the twig, of the paniceled andromeda; the large yellowish buds of the swamp-pink, etc. How healthy and vivacious must he be who would treat of these things!

You must love the crust of the earth on which you dwell more than the sweet crust of any bread or cake. You must be able to extract nutriment out of a sand-heap. You must have so good an appetite as this, else you will live in vain.

Jan. 26. A warm rain from time to time.

P.M.—To Clintonia Swamp down the brook.

When it rains it is like an April shower. The brook is quite open, and there is no snow on the banks or fields. From time to time I see a trout glance, and sometimes, in an adjoining ditch, quite a school of other fishes, but I see no tortoises. In a ditch I see very light-colored and pretty large lizards moving about, and I suspect I may even have heard a frog drop into the water once or twice. I like to sit still under my umbrella and meditate in the woods in this warm rain. . . .

This is a lichen day. The white lichens, partly encircling aspens and maples, look as if a painter had touched their trunks with his brush as he passed.

Jan. 27. Wednesday. P.M.—To Hill and beyond.

It is so mild and moist as I saunter along by the wall east of the Hill that I remember, or anticipate, one of those warm rain-storms in the spring, when the earth is just laid bare, the wind is south, and the cladonia lichens are swollen and lusty with moisture, your foot sinking into them and pressing the water out as from a sponge, and the sandy places also are drinking it in. You wander indefinitely in a beaded coat, wet to the skin of your legs, sit on moss-clad rocks and stumps, and hear the lisping of migrating sparrows flitting amid the shrub oaks, sit at a time, still, and have your thoughts. A rain which is as serene as fair weather, suggesting fairer weather than was ever seen. You could hug the clods that defile you. You feel the fertilizing influence of the rain in your mind. The part of you that is wettest is fullest of life, like the lichens. You discover evidences of immortality not known to divines. You cease to die. You detect some buds and sprouts of life. Every step in the old ryefield is on virgin soil.

And then the rain comes thicker and faster than before, thawing the remaining frost in the ground, detaining the migrating bird; and you turn your back to it, full of serene, contented thought, soothed by the steady dropping on the withered leaves, more at home for being abroad, more comfortable for being wet, sinking at each step deep into the thawing earth, gladly breaking through the gray rotting ice. The dullest sounds seem sweetly modulated by the air. You leave your tracks in fields of spring rye, scaring the fox-colored sparrows along the wood-sides. You cannot go home yet; you stay and sit in the rain. You glide along the distant wood-side, full of joy and expectation, seeing nothing but beauty, hearing nothing but music, as free as the fox-colored sparrow, seeing far ahead, a courageous knight [?], a great philosopher, not indebted to any academy or college for this expansion, but chiefly to the April rain, which descendeth on all alike; not encouraged by men in your walks, not by the divines nor the professors, and to the lawgiver an outlaw; not encouraged (even) when you are reminded of the government at Washington.

Time never passes so quickly and unaccountably as when I am engaged in composition, i.e. in writing down my thoughts. Clocks seem to have been put forward.

Jan. 28. Minott has a sharp ear for the note of any migrating bird. Though confined to his dooryard by the rheumatism, he commonly hears them sooner than the widest rambler. Maybe he listens all day for them, or they come and sing over his house, —report themselves to him and receive their season ticket. He is never at fault. If he says he heard such a bird, though sitting by his chimneyside, you may depend on it. He can swear through glass. He has not spoiled his ears by attending lectures and caucuses, etc. The other day the rumor went that a flock of geese had been seen flying north over Concord, midwinter as it was, by the almanac. I traced it to Minott, and yet I was compelled to doubt. I had it directly that he had heard them within a week. I saw him,—I made haste to him. His reputation was at stake. He said that he stood in his shed,—it was one of the late warm, muggy, April-like mornings,—when he heard one short but distinct *honk* of a goose. He went into the house, he took his cane, he exerted himself, or that sound imparted strength into him. Lame as he was, he went up on to the hill,— he had not done it for a year,—that he might hear all around. He saw nothing, but he heard the note again. It came from over the brook. It was a wild goose. He was sure of it. And hence the rumor spread and grew. He thought that the back of the winter was broken,—if it had any this year,—but he feared such a winter would kill him too.

I was silent; I reflected; I drew into my mind all its members, like the tortoise; I abandoned myself to unseen guides. Suddenly the truth flashed on me, and I remembered that within a week I had heard of a box at the tavern, which had come by railroad express, containing three wild geese and directed to his neighbor over the brook. The April-like morning had excited one so that he honked; and Minott's reputation acquired new lustre.

He has a propensity to tell stories which you have no ears to hear, which you cut short and return unfinished upon him.

March 18. 7 A.M.—By river.

Almost every bush has its song sparrow this morning, and their tinkling strains are heard on all sides. You see them just hopping under the bush or into some other covert, as you go by, turning with a jerk this way and that, or they flit away just above the ground, which they resemble. It is the prettiest strain I have heard yet. Melvin is already out in his boat for all day, with his white hound in the prow, bound up the river for musquash, etc., but the river is hardly high enough to drive them out.

P.M.—To Fair Haven Hill *via* Hubbard's Bath. . . .

When I get two thirds up the hill, I look round and am for the hundredth time surprised by the landscape of the river valley and the horizon with its distant blue scalloped rim. It is a spring landscape, and as impossible a fortnight ago as the song of birds. It is a deeper and warmer blue than in winter, methinks. The snow is off the mountains, which seem even to have come again like the birds. The undulating river is a bright-blue channel between sharp-edged shores of ice retained by the willows. The wind blows strong but warm from west by north, so that I have to hold my paper tight when I write this, making the copses creak and roar; but the sharp tinkle of a song sparrow is heard through it all. But ah! the needles of the pine, how they shine, as I look down over the Holden wood and westward! Every third tree is lit with the most subdued but clear ethereal light, as if it were the most delicate frostwork in a winter morning, reflecting no heat, but only light. And as they rock and wave in the strong wind, even a mile off, the light courses up and down there as over a field of grain; i.e., they are alternately light and dark, like looms above the forest, when the shuttle is thrown between the light woof and the dark web, weaving a light article,—spring goods for Nature to wear. At sight of this my spirit is like a lit tree. . . . Not only osiers but pine-needles, methinks, shine in the spring, and arrowheads and railroad rails, etc., etc. Anacreon noticed the same. Is it not the higher sun, and cleansed air, and greater animation of nature? There is a warmer red to the leaves of the shrub oak, and to the tail of the hawk circling over them.

May 6. Many are catching pouts this louring afternoon, in the little meadow by Walden. . . .

One man shall derive from the fisherman's story more than the fisher has got who tells it. The mass of men do not know how to cultivate the fields they traverse. The mass glean only a scanty pittance where the thinker reaps an abundant harvest. What is all your building, if you do not build with thoughts? No exercise implies more real manhood and vigor than joining thought to thought. How few men can tell what they have thought! I hardly know half a dozen who are not too lazy for this. They cannot get over some difficulty, and therefore they are on the long way round. You conquer fate by thought. If you think the fatal thought of men and institutions, you need never pull the trigger. The consequences of thinking inevitably follow. There is no more Herculean task than to think a thought about this life and then get it expressed.

June 2. 8.30 A.M.—Start for Monadnock.

Between Shirley Village and Lunenburg, I notice, in a meadow on the right hand, close to the railroad, the *Kalmia glauca* in bloom, as we are whirled past. The conductor says that he has it growing in his garden. Blake joins me at Fitchburg. Between Fitchburg and Troy saw an abundance of wild red cherry, now apparently in prime, in full bloom, especially in burnt lands and on hillsides, a small but cheerful lively white bloom.

Arrived at Troy Station at 11.5 and shouldered our knapsacks, steering northeast to the mountain, some four miles off,—its top. . . .

Almost without interruption we had the mountain in sight before us,—its sublime gray mass—that antique, brownish-gray, Ararat color. Probably these crests of the earth are for the most part of one color in all lands, that gray color of antiquity, which nature loves; color of unpainted wood, weather-stain, time-stain; not glaring nor gaudy; the color of all roofs, the color of things that endure, and the color that wears well; color of Egyptian ruins, of mummies and all antiquity; baked in the sun, done brown. Methought I saw the same color with which Ararat and Caucasus and all earth's brows are stained, which was mixed in antiquity and received a new coat every century; not scarlet, like the crest of the bragging cock, but that hard, enduring gray; a terrene sky-color; solidified air with a tinge of earth.

July 2. A.M.—Start for White Mountains in a private carriage with Edward Hoar. . . .

Spent the noon close by the old Dunstable graveyard, by a small stream north of it. Red lilies were abundantly in bloom in the burying-ground and by the river. Mr. Weld's monument is a large, thick, naturally flat rock, lying flat over the grave. Noticed the monument of Josiah Willard, Esq., "Captain of Fort Dummer." Died 1750, aged 58. . . .

Walked to and along the river and bathed in it. . . .

What a relief and expansion of my thoughts when I come out from that inland position by the graveyard to this broad river's shore! This vista was incredible there. Suddenly I see a broad reach of blue beneath, with its curves and headlands, liberating me from the more terrene earth. What a difference it makes whether I spend my four hours' nooning between the hills by yonder roadside, or on the brink of this fair river, within a quarter of a mile of that! Here the earth is fluid to my thought, the sky is reflected from beneath, and around yonder cape is the highway to other continents. This current allies me to all the world. Be careful to sit in an elevating and inspiring place. There my thoughts were confined and trivial, and I hid myself from the gaze of travellers. Here they are expanded and elevated, and I am charmed by the beautiful river-reach. It is equal to a different season and country and creates a different mood.... A river touching the back of a town is like a wing, it may be unused as yet, but ready to waft it over the world. With its rapid current it is a slightly fluttering wing. River towns are winged towns.

Aug. 6. I think that I speak impartially when I say that I have never met with a stream so suitable for boating and botanizing as the Concord, and fortunately nobody knows it. I know of reaches which a single country-seat would spoil beyond remedy, but there has not been any important change here since I can remember. The willows slumber along its shore, piled in light but low masses, even like the cumuli clouds above. We pass hay-makers in every meadow, who may think that we are idlers. But Nature takes care that every nook and crevice is explored by some one. While they look after the open meadows, we farm the tract between the river's brinks and behold the shores from that side. We, too, are harvesting an annual crop with our eyes, and think you Nature is not glad to display her beauty to us?

Aug. 9. The mind tastes but few flavors in the course of a year. We are visited by but few thoughts which are worth entertaining, and we chew the cud of these unceasingly. What ruminant spirits we are! I remember well the flavor of that rusk which I bought in New York two or three months ago and ate in the cars for my supper. A fellow-passenger, too, pretended to praise it, and yet, O man of little faith! he took a regular supper at Springfield. They cannot make such in Boston. The mere fragrance, rumor, and reminiscence of life is all that we get, for the most part. If I am visited by a thought, I chew that cud each successive morning, as long as there is any flavor in it. Until my keepers shake down some fresh fodder. Our genius is like a brush which only once in many months is freshly dipped into the paint-pot.

Aug. 16. P.M.—To Cardinal Ditch. . . .

Talked with Minott, who sits in his wood-shed, having, as I notice, several seats there for visitors,—one a block on the saw-horse, another a patchwork mat on a wheelbarrow, etc., etc.

His half-grown chickens, which roost overhead, perch on his shoulder or knee. According to him, the Holt is at the "diving ash," where is some of the deepest water in the river. He tells me some of his hunting stories again. He always lays a good deal of stress on the kind of gun he used, as if he had bought a new one every year, when probably he never had more than two or three in his life. In this case it was a "half-stocked" one, a little "cocking-piece," and whenever he finished his game he used the word "gavel," I think in this way, "gave him gavel," i.e. made him bite the dust, or settled him. Speaking of foxes he said: "As soon as the nights get to be cool, if you step outdoors at nine or ten o'clock when all is still, you'll hear them bark out on the flat behind the houses, half a mile off, or sometimes *whistle* through their noses. I can tell 'em. I know what that means. I know all about that. They are out after something to eat, I suppose." He used to love to hear the goldfinches sing on the hemp which grew near his gate.

At sunset paddled to Hill.

Goodwin has come again to fish, with three poles, hoping to catch some more of those large eels.

A blue heron, with its great undulating wings, prominent cutwater, and leisurely flight, goes over southwest, cutting off the bend of the river west of our house. Goodwin says he saw one two or three days ago, and also that he saw some black ducks. A muskrat is swimming up the stream, betrayed by two long diverging ripples, or ripple-lines, two or three rods long each, and enclosing about seventy-five degrees, methinks. The rat generally dives just before reaching the shore and is not seen again, probably entering some burrow in the bank.

Aug. 18. P.M. Last evening one of our neighbors, who has just completed a costly house and front yard, the most showy in the village, illuminated in honor of the Atlantic telegraph. I read in great letters before the house the sentence "Glory to God in the highest." But it seemed to me that that was not a sentiment to be illuminated, but to keep dark about. A simple and genuine sentiment of reverence would not emblazon these words as on a signboard in the streets. They were exploding countless crackers beneath it, and gay company, passing in and out, made it a kind of housewarming. I felt a kind of shame for [it], and was inclined to pass quickly by, the ideas of indecent exposure and cant being suggested. What is religion? That which is never spoken.

Aug. 23. The writer needs the suggestion and correction that a correspondent or companion is. I sometimes remember something which I have told another as worth telling to myself, i.e. writing in my Journal.

Channing, thinking of walks and life in the country, says, "You don't want to discover anything new, but to discover something old," i.e. be reminded that such things still are.

Aug. 26. P.M.—To Great Meadows. . . .
Two interesting tall purplish grasses appear to be the prevailing ones now in dry and sterile neglected fields and hillsides, —*Andropogon furcatus*, forked beard grass, and apparently *Andropogon scoparius*, purple wood grass, though the last appears to have three awns like an *Aristida*. The first is a very tall and slender-culmed grass, with four or five purple finger-like spikes, raying upward from the top. It is very abundant on the hillside behind Peter's. The other is also quite slender, two to three or four feet high, growing in tufts and somewhat curving, also commonly purple and with pretty purple stigmas like the last, and it has purple anthers. When out of bloom, its appressed spikes are recurving and have a whitish hairy or fuzzy look.

These are the prevailing conspicuous flowers where I walk this afternoon in dry ground. I have sympathy with them because they are despised by the farmer and occupy sterile and neglected soil. They also by their rich purple reflections or tinges seem to express the ripe-ness of the year. It is high-colored like ripe grapes, and expresses a maturity which the spring did not suggest. Only the August sun could have thus burnished these culms and leaves. The farmer has long since done his upland haying, and he will not deign to bring his scythe to where these slender wild grasses have at length flowered thinly. You often see the bare sand between them. I walk encouraged between the tufts of purple wood grass, over the sandy fields by the shrub oaks, glad to recognize these simple contemporaries. These two are almost the first grasses that I have learned to distinguish. . . .

Think what refuge there is for me before August is over, from college commencements and society that isolates me! I can skulk amid the tufts of purple wood grass on the borders of the Great Fields! Wherever I walk this afternoon the purple-fingered grass stands like a guideboard and points my thoughts to more poetic paths than they have lately travelled. . . .

Each humblest plant, or weed, as we call it, stands there to express some thought or mood of ours, and yet how long it stands in vain! I have walked these Great Fields so many Augusts and never yet distinctly recognized these purple companions that I have there. I have brushed against them and trampled them down, forsooth, and now at last they have, as it were, risen up and blessed me . . . I may say that I never saw them before, or can only recall a dim vision of them, and now wherever I go I hardly see anything else. It is the reign and presidence only of the andropogons. . . .

How hard one must work in order to acquire his language,— words by which to express himself! I have known a particular rush, for instance, for at least twenty years, but have ever been prevented from describing some [of] its peculiarities, because I did not know its name nor any one in the neighborhood who could tell me it. With the knowledge of the name comes a distincter recognition and knowledge of the thing. That shore is now more describable, and poetic even. My knowledge was cramped and confined before, and grew rusty because not used,—for it could not be used. My knowledge now becomes communicable and grows by communication. I can now learn what others know about the same thing.

Sept. 8. P.M.—To Owl Swamp. . . .

It is good policy to be stirring about your affairs, for the reward of activity and energy is that if you do not accomplish the object you had professed to yourself, you do accomplish something else. So, in my botanizing or natural history walks, it commonly turns out that, going for one thing, I get another thing. "Though man proposeth, God disposeth all."

Sept. 9. P.M.—To Waban Cliff. . . .

It requires a different intention of the eye in the same locality to see different plants, as, for example, *Juncaceae* and *Gramineae* even; i.e., I find that when I am looking for the former, I do not see the latter in their midst. How much more, then, it requires different intentions of the eye and of the mind to attend to different departments of knowledge! How differently the poet and the naturalist look at objects!

Oct. 16. P.M.—Sail up river. . . .

In the reflection the button-bushes and their balls appear against the sky, though the substance is seen against the meadow or distant woods and hills; i.e., they appear in the reflection as they would if viewed from that point on the surface from which they are reflected to my eye, so that it is as if I had another eye placed there to see for me. Hence, too, we are struck by the prevalence of sky or light in the reflection, and at twilight dream that the light has gone down into the bosom of the waters; for in the reflection the sky comes up to the very shore or edge and appears to extend under it, while, the substance being seen from a more elevated point, the actual horizon is perhaps many miles distant over the fields and hills. In the reflection you have an infinite number of eyes to see for you and report the aspect of things each from its point of view.

Oct. 18. P.M.—To Smith's chestnut grove and Saw Mill Brook.

The large sugar maples on the Common are now at the height of their beauty. . . .

Little did the fathers of the town anticipate this brilliant success when they caused to be imported from further in the country some straight poles with the tops cut off, which they called sugar maple trees,—and a neighboring merchant's clerk, as I remember, by way of jest planted beans about them. Yet these which were then jestingly called bean-poles are these days far the most beautiful objects noticeable in our streets. They are worth all and more than they have cost,—though one of the selectmen did take the cold which occasioned his death in setting them out,—if only because they have filled the open eyes of children with their rich color so unstintedly so many autumns. We will not ask them to yield us sugar in the spring, while they yield us so fair a prospect in the autumn. Wealth may be the inheritance of few in the houses, but it is equally distributed on the Common. All children alike can revel in this golden harvest. These trees, throughout the street, are at least equal to an annual festival and holiday, or a week of such,—not requiring any special police to keep the peace,—and poor indeed must be that New England village's October which has not the maple in its streets. This October festival costs no powder nor ringing of bells, but every tree is a liberty-pole on which a thousand bright flags are run up. Hundreds of children's eyes are steadily drinking in this color, and by these teachers even the truants are caught and educated the moment they step abroad. It is as if some cheap and innocent gala-day were celebrated in our town every autumn,—a week or two of such days.

What meant the fathers by establishing this *living* institution before the church,—this institution which needs no repairing nor repainting, which is continually "enlarged and repaired" by its growth? Surely trees should be set in our streets with a view to their October splendor. Do you not think it will make some odds to these children that they were brought up under the maples? . . .

No annual training or muster of soldiery, no celebration with its scarfs and banners, could import into the town a hundredth part of the annual splendor of our October. We have only to set the trees, or let them stand, and Nature will find the colored drapery,—flags of all her nations, some of whose private signals hardly the botanist can read. Let us have a good many maples and hickories and scarlet oaks, then, I say. Blaze away! Shall that dirty roll of bunting in the gun-house be all the colors a village can display? A village is not complete unless it has these trees to mark the season in it. They are as important as a town clock. Such a village will not be found to work well. It has a screw loose; an essential part is wanting. Let us have willows for spring, elms for summer, maples and walnuts and tupelos for autumn, evergreens for winter, and oaks for all seasons. . . . An avenue of elms as large as our largest, and three miles long, would seem to lead to some admirable place, though only Concord were at the end of it. . . .

As I come through Hubbard's Woods I see the wintergreen, conspicuous now above the freshly fallen white pine needles. Their shining green is suddenly revealed above the pale-brown ground. I hail its cool unwithering green, one of the humbler allies by whose aid we are to face the winter. . . .

Minott was sitting outside, as usual, and inquired if I saw any game in my walks these days; since, now that he cannot go abroad himself, he likes to hear from the woods. He tried to detain me to listen to some of his hunting-stories, especially about a slut that belonged to a neighbor by the name of Billings, which was excellent for squirrels, rabbits, and partridges, and would always follow him when he went out, though Billings was "plaguy mad about it;" however, he had only to go by Billings's to have the dog accompany him. B. afterward carried her up country and gave her away, the news of which almost broke Minott's heart.

Oct. 19. A remarkably warm day. I have not been more troubled by the heat this year, being a *little* more thickly clad than in summer. I walk in the middle of the street for air. The thermometer says 74° at 1 P.M. This must be Indian summer.

P.M.—Ride to Sam Barrett's mill.

Am pleased again to see the cobweb drapery of the mill. Each fine line hanging in festoons from the timbers overhead and on the sides, and on the discarded machinery lying about, is covered and greatly enlarged by a coating of meal, by which its curve is revealed, like the twigs under their ridges of snow in winter. It is like the tassels and tapestry of counterpane and dimity in a lady's bedchamber, and I pray that the cobwebs may not have been brushed away from the mills which I visit.

It is as if I were aboard a man-of-war, and this were the fine "rigging" of the mill, the sails being taken in. All things in the mill wear the same livery or drapery, down to the miller's hat and coat. I knew Barrett forty rods off in the cranberry meadow by the meal on his hat.

Oct. 22. I see Heavy Haynes fishing in his old gray boat, sinking the stern deep. It is remarkable that, of the four fishermen who most frequent this river,—Melvin, Goodwin, and the two Hayneses,—the last three have all been fishermen of the sea, have visited the Grand Banks, and are well acquainted with Cape Cod. These fishermen who sit thus alone from morning till night must be greater philosophers than the shoemakers.

Nov. 1. I leaned over a rail in the twilight on the Walden road, waiting for the evening mail to be distributed . . . I seemed to recognize the November evening as a familiar thing come round again, and yet I could hardly tell whether I had ever known it or only divined it. The November twilights just begun! . . . The long railroad causeway through the meadows west of me, the still twilight in which hardly a cricket was heard, the dark bank of clouds in the horizon long after sunset, the villagers crowding to the post-office, and the hastening home to supper by candle-light, had I not seen all this before! What new street was I to extract from it? Truly they mean that we shall learn our lesson well. Nature gets thumbed like an old spelling-book . . .

And yet there is no more tempting novelty than this new November. No going to Europe or another world is to be named with it. Give me the old familiar walk, post-office and all, with this ever new self, with this infinite expectation and faith, which does not know when it is beaten. We'll go nutting once more. We'll pluck the nut of the world, and crack it in the winter evenings. Theatres and all other sightseeing are puppet-shows in comparison. I will take another walk to the Cliff, another row on the river, another skate on the meadow, be out in the first snow, and associate with the winter birds. Here I am at home. In the bare and bleached crust of the earth I recognize my friend.

Nov. 4. A rainy day.

Called to C. from the outside of his house the other afternoon in the rain. At length he put his head out the attic window, and I inquired if he didn't want to take a walk, but he excused himself, saying that he had a cold. "But," added he, "you can take so much the longer walk. Double it."

On the 1st, when I stood on Poplar Hill, I saw a man, far off by the edge of the river, splitting billets off a stump. Suspecting who it was, I took out my glass, and beheld Goodwin, the one-eyed Ajax, in his short blue frock, short and square-bodied, as broad as for his height he can afford to be, getting his winter's wood; for this is one of the phenomena of the season. As surely as the ants which he disturbs go into winter quarters in the stump when the weather becomes cool, so does G. revisit the stumpy shores with his axe. As usual, his powder-flask peeped out from a pocket on his breast, his gun was slanted over a stump near by, and his boat lay a little further along. He had been at work laying wall still further off, and now, near the end of the day, betook himself to those pursuits which he loved better still. It would be no amusement to me to see a gentleman buy his winter wood. It is to see G. get his. I helped him tip over a stump or two. He said that the owner of the land had given him leave to get them out, but it seemed to me a condescension for him to ask any man's leave to grub up these stumps. The stumps to those who can use them, I say,—to those who will split them. He might as well ask leave of the farmer to shoot the musquash and the meadow-hen, or I might as well ask leave to look at the landscape. Near by were large hollows in the ground, now grassed over, where he had got out white oak stumps in previous years. But, strange to say, the town does not like to have him get his fuel in this way. They would rather the stumps would rot in the ground, or be floated down-stream to the sea. They have almost without dissent agreed on a different mode of living, with their division of labor. They would have him stick to laying wall, and buy corded wood for his fuel, as they do. He has drawn up an old bridge sleeper and cut his his name in it for security, and now he gets into his boat and pushes off in the twilight, saying he will go and see what Mr. Musquash is about. . . .

If, about the last of October, you ascend any hill in the outskirts of the town and look over the forest, you will see, amid the brown of other oaks, which are now withered, and the green of the pines, the bright-red tops or crescents of the scarlet oaks, very equally and thickly distributed on all sides, even to the horizon.Complete trees standing exposed on the edges of the forest, where you have never suspected them, or their tops only in the recesses of the forest surface, or perhaps towering above the surrounding trees, or reflecting a warm rose red from the very edge of the horizon in favorable lights. All this you will see, and much more, if you are prepared to see it,—if you *look* for it. . . . Objects are concealed from our view not so much because they are out of the course of our visual ray (continued) as because there is no intention of the mind and eye toward them. We do not realize how far and widely, or how near and narrowly, we are to look. The greater part of the phenomena of nature are for this reason concealed to us all our lives. Here, too, as in political economy, the supply answers to the demand. Nature does not cast pearls before swine. There is just as much beauty visible to us in the landscape as we are prepared to appreciate,—not a grain more. The actual objects which one person will see from a particular hilltop are just as different from those which another will see as the persons are different. The scarlet oak must, in a sense, be in your eye when you go forth. We cannot see anything until we are possessed with the idea of it, and then we can hardly see anything else. In my botanical rambles I find that first the idea, or image, of a plant occupies my thoughts, though it may at first seem very foreign to this locality, and for some weeks or months I go thinking of it and expecting it unconsciously, and at length I surely see it, and it is henceforth an actual neighbor of mine. This is the history of my finding a score or more of rare plants which I could name.

Nov. 7. My apple harvest! It is to glean after the husbandman and the cows, or to gather the crop of those wild trees far away on the edges of swamps which have escaped their notice. Now, when it is generally all fallen, if indeed any is left, though you would not suppose there were any on the first survey, nevertheless with experienced eyes I explore amid the clumps of alder (now bare) and in the crevices of the rocks full of leaves, and prying under the fallen and decaying ferns which, with apple and alder leaves, thickly strew the ground. From amid the leaves anywhere within the circumference of the tree, I draw forth the fruit, all wet and glossy, nibbled by rabbits and hollowed out by crickets, but still with the bloom on it and at least as ripe and well kept, if not better than those in barrels, while those which lay exposed are quite brown and rotten.

Nov. 8. Each phase of nature, while not invisible, is yet not too distinct and obtrusive. It is there to be found when we look for it, but not demanding our attention. It is like a silent but sympathizing companion in whose company we retain most of the advantages of solitude, with whom we can walk and talk, or be silent, naturally, without the necessity of talking in a strain foreign to the place.

Nov. 26. Walden is very low, compared with itself for some years. The bar between pond and Hubbard's pondhole is four feet wide, but the main bar is not *bare*. There is a shore at least six feet wide inside the alders at my old shore, and what is remarkable, I find that not only Goose Pond also has fallen correspondingly within a month, but even the smaller pond-holes only four or five rods over, such as Little Goose Pond, shallow as they are. I begin to suspect, therefore, that this rise and fall extending through a long series of years is not peculiar to the Walden system of ponds, but is true of ponds generally, and perhaps of rivers, though in their case it may be more difficult to detect. Even around Little Goose Pond the shore is laid bare for a space even wider than at Walden, it being less abrupt. The Pout's Nest, also, has lost ten feet on all sides.

Those pouts' nests which I discovered in the spring are high and dry six feet from the water. I overhauled one, ripping up the frozen roof with my hands. The roof was only three inches thick, then a cavity and a bottom of wet mud. In this mud I found two small frogs, one apparently a *Rana palustris* less than an inch long, the other apparently a young *R. pipiens* an inch and a half long. They were quite sluggish and had evidently gone into winter quarters there, but probably some mink would have got them.

The Pout's Nest was frozen just enough to bear, with two or three breathing-places left. The principal of these was a narrow opening about a rod long by eighteen inches wide within six feet of the southwest side of the pond-hole, and the immediately adjacent ice was darker and thinner than the rest, having formed quite recently. I observed that the water at this breathing-chink was all alive with pollywogs, mostly of large size, though some were small, which apparently had collected there chiefly, as the water-surface was steadily contracted, for the sake of the air (?). . . . There were also one or two frogs stirring among them. Here was evidently warmer water, probably a spring, and they had crowded to it. Looking more attentively, I detected also a great many minnows about one inch long either floating dead there or frozen into the ice,—at least fifty of them. They were shaped like bream, but had the transverse bars of perch. . . .

Examining those minnows by day, I find that they are one and one sixth inches long by two fifths of an inch wide (this my largest); in form like a bream; of a very pale golden like a perch, or more bluish. Have but one dorsal fin and, as near as I can count, rays, dorsal 19 (first, 9 stouter and stiff and more distinctly pointed, then 10 longer and flexible, whole fin about three times as long as average height), caudal 17 (?), anal 13 or 14, ventral 6, pectoral 10 (?). They have about seven transverse dusky bars like a perch (!). Yet, from their form and single dorsal fin, I think they are breams. Are they not a new species? Have young breams transverse bars?

Nov. 27. I got seventeen more of those little bream of yesterday. . . . They appear to be the young of the *Pomotis obesus*, described by Charles Girard to the Natural History Society in April, '54, obtained by Baird in Fresh water about Hingham and [in] Charles River in Holliston. . . .

How much more remote the newly discovered species seems to dwell than the old and familiar ones, though both inhabit the same pond! Where the *Pomotis obesus* swims must be a new country, unexplored by science. The seashore may be settled, but aborigines dwell unseen only thus far inland. This country is so new that species of fishes and birds and quadrupeds inhabit it which science has not yet detected. The water which such a fish swims in must still have a primitive forest decaying in it.

Nov. 28. A gray, overcast, still day, and more small birds—tree sparrows and chickadees—than usual about the house. There have been a very few fine snowflakes falling for many hours, and now, by 2 P.M., a regular snowstorm has commenced, fine flakes falling steadily, and rapidly whitening all the landscape. In half an hour the russet earth is painted white even to the horizon. Do we know of any other so silent and sudden a change?

I cannot now walk without leaving a track behind me; that is one peculiarity of winter walking. Anybody may follow my trail. I have walked, perhaps, a particular wild path along some swamp-side all summer, and thought to myself, I am the only villager that ever comes here. But I go out shortly after the first snow has fallen, and lo, here is the track of a sportsman and his dog in my secluded path, and probably he preceded me in the summer as well. Yet my hour is not his, and I may never meet him!

I asked Coombs the other night if he had been a-hunting lately. He said he had not been out but once this fall. He went out the other day with a companion, and they came near getting a fox. They broke his leg. He has evidently been looking forward to some such success all summer. Having done thus much, he can afford to sit awhile by the stove at the post-office. He is plotting now how to break his head.

Goodwin cannot be a very bad man, he is so cheery.

And all the years that I have known Walden these striped

breams have skulked in it without my knowledge! How many new thoughts, then, may I have?

Nov. 30. I cannot but see still in my mind's eye those little striped breams poised in Walden's glaucous water. They balance all the rest of the world in my estimation at present, for this is the bream that I have just found, and for the time I neglect all its brethren and am ready to kill the fatted calf on its account. For more than two centuries have men fished here and have not distinguished this permanent settler of the township. It is not like a new bird, a transient visitor that may not be seen again for years, but there it dwells and has dwelt permanently, who can tell how long? When my eyes first rested on Walden the striped bream was poised in it, though I did not see it, and when Tahatawan paddled his canoe there. How wild it makes the pond and the township to find a new fish in it! America renews her youth here. But in my account of this bream I cannot go a hair's breadth beyond the mere statement that it exists,—the miracle of its existence, my contemporary and neighbor, yet so different from me! I can only poise my thought there by its side and try to think like a bream for a moment. I can only think of precious jewels, of music, poetry, beauty, and the mystery of life. I only see the bream in its orbit, as I see a star, but I care not to measure its distance or weight. The bream, appreciated, floats in the pond as the centre of the system, another image of God. Its life no man can explain more than he can his own. I want you to perceive the mystery of the bream. I have a contemporary in Walden. It has fins where I have legs and arms. I have a friend among the fishes, at least a new acquaintance. Its character will interest me, I trust, not its clothes and anatomy. I do not want it to eat. Acquaintance with it is to make my life more rich and eventful. It is as if a poet or an anchorite had moved into the town, whom I can see from time to time and think of yet oftener. Perhaps there are a thousand of these striped bream which no one had thought of in that pond,—not their mere impressions in stone, but in the full tide of the bream life.

VI

THE MUSQUASH HUNTERS

Jan. 22, 1859. Many are out in boats, steering outside the ice of the river over the newly flooded meadows, shooting musquash. Cocks crow as in spring.

The energy and excitement of the musquash-hunter even, not despairing of life, but keeping the same rank and savage hold on it that his predecessors have for so many generations, while so many are sick and despairing, even this is inspiriting to me. Even these deeds of death are interesting as evidences of life, for life will still prevail in spite of all accidents. I have a certain faith that even musquash are immortal and not born to be killed by Melvin's double-B (?) shot. . . .

The musquash-hunter (last night), with his increased supply of powder and shot and boat turned up somewhere on the bank, now that the river is rapidly rising, dreaming of his exploits to-day in shooting musquash, of the greal pile of dead rats that will weigh down his boat before night, when he will return wet and weary and weather-beaten to his hut with an appetite for his supper and for much sluggish (punky) social intercourse with his fellows,—even he, dark, dull, and battered flint as he is, is an inspired man to his extent now, perhaps the most inspired by this freshet of any, and the Musketaquid Meadows cannot spare him. There are poets of all kinds and degrees, little known to each other. The Lake School is not the only or the principal one. They love various things. Some love beauty, and some love rum. Some go to Rome, and some go a-fishing, and are sent to the house of correction once a month. They keep up their fires by means unknown to me. I know not their comings and goings. How can I tell what violets they watch for? I know them wild and ready to risk all when their muse invites. The most sluggish will be up early enough then, and face any amount of wet and cold. I meet these gods of the river and woods with sparkling faces (like Apollo's) late from the house of correction, it may be carrying whatever mystic and forbidden bottles or other vessels concealed, while the dull regular priests are steering their parish rafts in a prose mood. What care I to see galleries full of representatives of heathen gods, when I can see natural living ones by an infinitely superior artist, without perspective tube?. . . .

I hear these guns going to-day, and I must confess they are to me a springlike and exhilarating sound, like the cock-crowing, though each one may report the death of a musquash. This, methinks, or the like of this, with whatever mixture of dross, is the real morning or evening hymn that goes up from these vales to-day, and which the stars echo. This is the best sort of glorifying of God and enjoying him that at all prevails here to-day, without any clarified butter or sacred ladles.

As a mother loves to see her child imbibe nourishment and expand, so God loves to see his children thrive on the nutriment he has furnished them. In the musquash-hunters I see the Almouchicois still pushing swiftly over the dark stream in their canoes. These aboriginal men cannot be repressed, but under some guise or other they survive and reappear continually. Just as simply as the crow picks up the worms which all over the fields have been washed out by the thaw, these men pick up the musquash that have been washed out the banks. And to serve such ends men plow and sail, and powder and shot are made, and the grocer exists to retail them, though he may think himself much more the deacon of some church.

Feb. 3. The writer must to some extent inspire himself. Most of his sentences may at first lie dead in his essay, but when all are arranged, some life and color will be reflected on them from the mature and successful lines; they will appear to pulsate with fresh life, and he will be enabled to eke out their slumbering sense, and make them worthy of their neighborhood. In his first essay on a given theme, he produces scarcely more than a frame and groundwork for his sentiment and poetry. Each clear thought that he attains to draws in its train many divided thoughts or perceptions. The writer has much to do even to create a theme for himself. Most that is first written on any subject is a mere groping after it, mere rubble-stone and foundation. It is only when many observations of different periods have been brought together that he begins to grasp his subject and can make one pertinent and just observation.

Feb. 20. In the composition it is the greatest art to find out as quickly as possible which are the best passages you have written, and tear the rest away to come at them. Even the poorest parts will be most effective when they serve these, as pediments to the column.

How much the writer lives and endures in coming before the public so often! A few years or books are with him equal to a long life of experience, suffering, etc. It is well if he does not become hardened. He learns how to bear contempt and to despise himself. He makes, as it were, *post-mortem* examinations of himself before he is dead. Such is art.

Feb. 25. P.M. Up river on ice. . . .

There are several men of whose comings and goings the town knows little. I mean the trappers. They may be seen coming from the woods and river, perhaps with nothing in their hands, and you do not suspect what they have been about. They go about their business in a stealthy manner for fear that any shall see where they set their traps,—for the fur trade still flourishes here. Every year they visit the out-of-the-way swamps and meadows and brooks to set or examine their traps for musquash or mink, and the owners of the land commonly know nothing of it. But, few as the trappers are here, it seems by Goodwin's accounts that they steal one another's traps.

All the criticism which I got on my lecture on Autumnal Tints at Worcester on the 22d was that I assumed that my audience had not seen so much of them as they had. But after reading it I am more than ever convinced that they have not seen much of them,—that there are few persons who do see much of nature.

Feb. 27. P.M.—To Cliffs. . . .

Health makes the poet, or sympathy with nature, a good appetite for his food, which is constantly renewing him, whetting his senses. Pay for your victuals, then, with poetry; give back life for life.

March 11. Find out as soon as possible what are the best things in your composition, and then shape the rest to fit them. The former will be the midrib and veins of the leaf.

There is always some accident in the best things, whether thoughts or expressions or deeds. The memorable thought, the happy expression, the admirable deed are only partly ours. The thought came to us because we were in a fit mood; also we were unconscious and did not know that we had said or done a good thing. We must walk consciously only part way toward our goal, and then leap in the dark to our success. What we do best or most perfectly is what we have most thoroughly learned by the longest practice, and at length it falls from us without our notice, as a leaf from a tree. It is the *last* time we shall do it,— our unconscious leavings.

March 28. P.M.—Paddle to the Bedford line.

It is now high time to look for arrowheads, etc. I spend many hours every spring gathering the crop which the melting snow and rain have washed bare. When, at length, some island in the meadow or some sandy field elsewhere has been plowed, perhaps for rye, in the fall, I take note of it, and do not fail to repair thither as soon as the earth begins to be dry in the spring. If the spot chances never to have been cultivated before, I am the first to gather a crop from it. The farmer little thinks that another reaps a harvest which is the fruit of his toil. As much ground is turned up in a day by the plow as Indian implements could not have turned over in a month, and my eyes rest on the evidences of an aboriginal life which passed here a thousand years ago perchance. Especially if the knolls in the meadows are washed by a freshet where they have been plowed the previous fall, the soil will be taken away lower down and the stones left,— the arrowheads, etc., and soapstone pottery amid them,—

somewhat as gold is washed in a dish or tom. I landed on two spots this afternoon and picked up a dozen arrowheads. It is one of the regular pursuits of the spring. As much as sportsmen go in pursuit of ducks, and gunners of musquash, and scholars of rare books, and travellers of adventures, and poets of ideas, and all men of money, I go in search of arrowheads when the proper season comes round again. So I help myself to live worthily, and loving my life as I should. It is a good collyrium to look on the bare earth,—to pore over it so much, getting strength to all your senses, like Antaeus. . . .

I have not decided whether I had better publish my experience in searching for arrowheads in three volumes, with plates and an index, or try to compress it into one. These durable implements seem to have been suggested to the Indian mechanic with a view to my entertainment in a succeeding period. After all the labor expended on it, the bolt may have been shot but once perchance, and the shaft which was devoted to it decayed, and there lay the arrowhead, sinking into the ground, awaiting me. They lie all over the hills with like expectation, and in due time the husbandman is sent, and, tempted by the promise of corn or rye, he plows the land and turns them up to my view. Many as I have found, methinks the last one gives me about the same delight that the first did. Some time or other, you would say, it had rained arrowheads, for they lie all over the surface of America. You may have your peculiar tastes. Certain localities in your town may seem from association unattractive and uninhabitable to you. You may wonder that the land bears any money value there, and pity some poor fellow who is said to survive in that neighborhood. But plow up a new field there, and you will find the omnipresent arrow-points strewn over it, and it will appear that the red man, with other tastes and associations, lived there too. No matter how far from the modern road or meeting-house, no matter how near. They lie in the meeting-house cellar, and they lie in the distant cow-pasture. And some collections which were made a century ago by the curious like myself have been dispersed again, and they are still as good as new. You cannot tell the third-hand ones (for they are all second-hand) from the others, such is their persistent out-of-door durability; for they were chiefly made to be lost. They are sown, like a grain that is slow to germinate, broadcast over the earth. Like the dragon's teeth which bore a crop of soldiers, these bear crops of philosophers and poets, and the same seed is just as good to plant again. It is a stone fruit. Each one yields me a thought. I come nearer to the maker of it than if I found his bones. His bones would not prove any wit that wielded them, such as this work of his bones does. It is humanity inscribed on the face of the earth, patent to my eyes as soon as the snow goes off, not hidden away in some crypt or grave or under a pyramid. No disgusting mummy, but a clean stone, the best symbol or letter that could have transmitted to me.

At every step I see it, and I can easily supply the "Tahatawan" or "Mantatuket" that might have been written if he had had a clerk. It is no single inscription on a particular rock, but a footprint—rather a mindprint—left everywhere, and altogether illegible. No vandals, however vandalic in their disposition, can be so industrious as to destroy them. . . .

They are not fossil bones, but, as it were, fossil thoughts, forever reminding me of the mind that shaped them. I would fain know that I am treading in the tracks of human game,—that I am on the trail of mind,—and these little reminders never fail to set me right. When I see these signs I know that the subtle spirits that made them are not far off, into whatever form transmuted.

April 3. Men's minds run so much on work and money that the mass instantly associate all literary labor with a pecuniary reward. They are mainly curious to know how much money the lecturer or author gets for his work. They think that the naturalist takes so much pains to collect plants or animals because he is paid for it. An Irishman who saw me in the fields making a minute in my note-book took it for granted that I was casting up my wages and actually inquired what they came to, as if he had never dreamed of any other use for writing. I might have quoted to him that the wages of sin is death, as the most pertinent answer. "What do you get for lecturing now?" I am occasionally asked. It is the more amusing since I only lecture about once a year out of my native town, often not at all; so that I might as well, if my objects were merely pecuniary, give up the business. Once, when I was walking on Staten Island, looking about me as usual, a man who saw me would not believe me when I told him that I was indeed from New England but was not looking at that region with a pecuniary view,—a view to speculation; and he offered me a handsome bonus if I would sell his farm for him.

Aug. 27. A little more rain last night. . . .

All our life, i.e. the living part of it, is a persistent dreaming awake. The boy does not camp in his father's yard. That would not be adventurous enough, there are too many sights and sounds to disturb the illusion; so he marches off twenty or thirty miles and there pitches his tent, where stranger inhabitants are tamely sleeping in their beds just like his father at home, and camps in *their* yard, perchance. But then he dreams uninterruptedly that he is anywhere but where he is.

I often see yarrow with a delicate pink tint, very distinct from the common pure-white ones.

What is often called poverty, but which is a simpler and truer relation to nature, gives a peculiar relish to life, just as to be kept short gives us an appetite for food.

Aug. 29. It is so cool a morning that for the first time I move into the entry to sit in the sun. But in this cooler weather I feel as if the fruit of my summer were hardening and maturing a little, acquiring color and flavor like the corn and other fruits in the field. When the very earliest ripe grapes begin to be scented in the cool nights, then, too, the first cooler airs of autumn begin to waft my sweetness on the desert airs of summer. Now, too, poets nib their pens afresh. I scent their first-fruits in the cool evening air of the year. By the coolness the experience of the summer is condensed and matured, whether our fruits be pumpkins or grapes. Man, too, ripens with the grapes and apples.

Sept. 16. Grasshoppers have been very abundant in dry fields for two or three weeks. Sophia walked through the Depot Field a fortnight ago, and when she got home picked fifty or sixty from her skirts,—for she wore hoops and crinoline. Would not this be a good way to clear a field of them,—to send a bevy of fashionably dressed ladies across a field and leave them to clean their skirts when they get home? It would supplant anything at the patent office, and the motive power is cheap.

I am invited to take some party of ladies or gentlemen on an excursion,—to walk or sail, or the like,—but by all kinds of evasions I omit it, and am thought to be rude and unaccommodating therefore. They do not consider that the wood-path and the boat are my studio, where I maintain a sacred solitude and cannot admit promiscuous company. I will see them occasionally in an evening or at the table, however. They do not think of taking a child away from its school to go a-huckleberrying with them. Why should not I, then, have my school and school hours to be respected? Ask me for a certain number of dollars if you will, but do not ask me for my afternoons.

Sept. 18. Dr. Bartlett handed me a paper to-day, desiring me to subscribe for a statue to Horace Mann. I declined, and said that I thought a man ought not any more to take up room in the world after he was dead. We shall lose one advantage of a man's dying if we are to have a statue of him forthwith. This is probably meant to be an opposition statue to that of Webster. At this rate they will crowd the streets with them. A man will have to add a clause to his will, "No statue to be made of me." It is very offensive to my imagination to see the dying stiffen into statues at this rate. We should wait till their bones begin to crumble—and then avoid too near a likeness to the living.

Sept. 24. P.M.—To Melvin's Preserve. . . .
I have many affairs to attend to, and feel hurried these days. Great works of art have endless leisure for a background, as the universe has space. Time stands still while they are created. The artist cannot be in [a] hurry. The earth moves round the sun with inconceivable rapidity, and yet the surface of the lake

is not ruffled by it. It is not by a compromise, it is not by a timid and feeble repentance, that a man will save his soul and *live*, at last. He has got to *conquer* a clear field, letting Repentance & Co. go. That's a well-meaning but weak firm that has assumed the debts of an old and worthless one. You are to fight in a field where no allowances will be made, no courteous bowing to one-handed knights. You are expected to do your duty, not in spite of everything but *one*, but in spite of *everything*. . . .

Going along this old Carlisle road,—road for walkers, for berry-pickers, and no more worldly travellers; road for Melvin and Clark, not for the sheriff nor butcher nor the baker's jingling cart; road where all wild things and fruits abound, where there are countless rocks to jar those who venture there in wagons; which no jockey, no wheelwright in his right mind, drives over, no little spidery gigs and Flying Childers; road which leads to and through a great but not famous garden, zoological and botanical garden, at whose *gate* you never arrive, —as I was going along there, I perceived the grateful scent of the dicksonia fern, now partly decayed, and it reminds me of all up-country with its springy mountainsides and unexhausted vigor. Is there any essence of dicksonia fern, I wonder? Surely that giant who, my neighbor expects, is to bound up the Alleghanies will have his handkerchief scented with that. In the lowest part of the road the dicksonia by the wall-sides is more than half frost-bitten and withered,—a sober Quaker-color, brown crape!—though not so tender or early [?] as the cinnamon fern; but soon I rise to where they are more yellow and green, and so my route is varied. On the higher places there are very handsome tufts of it, all yellowish outside and green within. The sweet fragrance of decay! When I wade through by narrow cow-paths, it is as if I had strayed into an ancient and decayed herb-garden. Proper for old ladies to scent their handkerchiefs with. Nature perfumes her garments with this essence now especially. She gives it to those who go a-barberry-ing and on dank autumnal walks. The essence of this as well as of new-mown hay, surely! The very scent of it, if you have a decayed frond in your chamber, will take you far up country in a twinkling. You would think you had gone after the cows there, or were lost on the mountains. It will make you as cool and well as a frog,—a wood frog, *Rana sylvatica*. It is the scent the earth yielded in the saurian period, before man was created and fell, before milk and water were invented, and the mints. Far wilder than they. *Rana sylvatica* passed judgment on it, or rather that peculiar-scented *Rana palustris*. It was in his reign it was introduced. That is the scent of the Silurian Period precisely, and a modern beau may scent his handkerchief with it. Before man had come and the plants that chiefly serve him. There were no Rosaceae nor mints then. So the earth smelled in the Silurian (?) Period, before man was created and any soil had been debauched with manure. The saurians had their handkerchiefs scented with it. For all the ages are represented still and you can smell them out.

A man must attend to Nature closely for many years to know when, as well as where, to look for his objects, since he must always anticipate her a little. Young men have not learned the phases of Nature; they do not know what constitutes a year, or that one year is like another. I would know when in the year to expect certain thoughts and moods, as the sportsman knows when to look for plover.

Though you may have sauntered near to heaven's gate, when at length you return toward the village you give up the enterprise a little, and you begin to fall into the old ruts of thought, like a regular roadster. Your thoughts very properly fail to report themselves to headquarters. Your thoughts turn toward night and the evening mail and become begrimed with dust, as if you were just going to put up at (with?) the tavern, or even come to make an exchange with a brother clergyman here on the morrow.

Oct. 15. Each town should have a park, or rather a primitive forest, of five hundred or a thousand acres, where a stick should never be cut for fuel, a common possession forever, for instruction and recreation. We hear of cow-commons and ministerial lots, but we want *men*-commons and lay lots, inalienable forever.

Let us keep the New World *new*, preserve all the advantages of living in the country. There is meadow and pasture and wood-lot for the town's poor. Why not a forest and huckleberry-field for the town's rich? All Walden Wood might have been pre-served for our park forever, with Walden in its midst, and the Easterbrooks Country, an unoccupied area of some four square miles, might have been our huckleberry-field. If any owners of these tracts are about to leave the world without natural heirs who need or deserve to be specially remembered, they will do wisely to abandon their possession to all, and not will them to some individual who perhaps has enough already. As some give to Harvard College or another institution, why might not another give a forest or huckleberry-field to Concord? A town is an institution which deserves to be remembered. We boast of our system of education, but why stop at schoolmasters and schoolhouses? We are all schoolmasters, and our schoolhouse is the universe. To attend chiefly to the desk or schoolhouse while we neglect the scenery in which it is placed is absurd. If we do not look out she shall find our fine schoolhouse standing in a cow-yard at last.

Oct. 16. Sunday. P.M.—For thirty years I have annually ob-served, about this time or earlier, the freshly erected winter lodges of the musquash along the riverside, reminding us that, if we have no gypsies, we have a more indigenous race of furry, quadru-pedal men maintaining their ground in our midst still. This may not be an annual phenomenon to you. It may not be in the Greenwich almanac or ephemeris, but it has an important place in my Kalendar. So surely as the sun appears to be in Libra or Scorpio, I see the conical winter lodges of the mus-quash rising above the withered pontederia and flags. There will be some reference to it, by way of parable or otherwise, in *my* New Testament. Surely, it is a defect in our Bible that it is not truly ours, but a Hebrew Bible. The most pertinent illustrations for us are to be drawn, not from Egypt or Babylonia, but from New England.

Talk about learning our *letters* and being *literate*! Why, the roots of *letters* are *things*. Natural objects and phenomena are the original symbols or types which express our thoughts and feelings, and yet American scholars, having little or no root in the soil, commonly strive with all their might to confine themselves to the imported symbols alone. All the true growth and experience, the living speech, they would fain reject as "Americanisms." It is the old error, which the church, the state, the school ever commit, choosing darkness rather than light, holding fast to the old and to tradition. A more intimate knowledge, a deeper experience, will surely originate a word. When I really know that our river pursues a serpentine course to the Merrimack, shall I continue to describe it by referring to some other river no older than itself which is like it, and call it a *meander*? It is no more *meandering* than the Meander is *musketaquidding*. As well sing of the nightingale here as the Meander. What if there were a tariff on words, on language, for the encouragement of home manufactures? Have we not the genius to coin our own? ...

For October, for instance, instead of making the sun enter the sign of the scorpion, I would much sooner make him enter a musquash-house. Astronomy is a fashionable study, patronized by princes, but not fungi. "Royal Astronomer." The snapping turtle, too, must find a place among the constellations, though it may have to supplant some doubtful characters already there. If there is no place for him overhead, he can serve us bravely underneath, supporting the earth. ...

Every rain exposes new arrowheads. We stop at Clamshell and dabble for a moment in the relics of a departed race.

Where we landed in front of Puffer's, found a jug which the haymakers had left in the bushes. Hid our boat there in a clump of willows, and though the ends stuck out, being a pale green and whitish, they were not visible or distinguishable at a little distance.

Oct. 19. What is the character of that calm which follows when the law and the slaveholder prevail! ...

Our foes are in our midst and all about us. Hardly a house

but is divided against itself. For our foe is the all but universal woodenness (both of head and heart), the want of vitality, of man,—the effect of vice,—whence are begotten fear and superstition and bigotry and persecution and slavery of all kinds. Mere figure-heads upon a hulk, with livers in the place of hearts. A church that can never have done with excommunicating Christ while it exists. Our plains were overrun the other day with a flock of adjutant-generals, as if a brood of cockerels had been let loose there, waiting to use their spurs in what sort of glorious cause, I ask. What more probable in the future, what more certain heretofore, than in grinding in the dust four hundred thousands of feeble and timid men, women, and children? The United States exclaims: "Here are four millions of human creatures which we have stolen. We have abolished among them the relations of father, mother, children, wife, and we mean to keep them in this condition. Will you, O Massachusetts, help us to do so?" And Massachusetts promptly answers, "Aye!" . . .

The momentary charge at Balaclava, in obedience to a blundering command,—proving what a perfect machine the soldier is—has been celebrated by a poet laureate; but the steady and for the most part successful charge against the legions of Slavery kept up for some years in Kansas by John Brown in obedience to an infinitely higher command is unsung, —as much more memorable than that as an intelligent and conscientious man is superior to a machine.

Oct. 21. The very fact that he had no rabble or troop of hirelings about him would alone distinguish him from ordinary heroes. His company was small indeed, because few could be found worthy to pass muster. He would have no rowdy or swaggerer, no profane swearer, for, as he said, he always found these men to fail at last. He would have only men of principle, and they are few. When it was observed that if he had had a chaplain his would have been a perfect Cromwellian company, he said that he would have had a chaplain if he could [have] found one who could perform that service suitably.

Each one who there laid down his life for the poor and oppressed was thus a picked man, culled out of many thousands, if not millions; a man of principle, of rare courage, and of devoted humanity; ready to lay down their lives any moment for the weak and enslaved. It may be doubted if there were any more their equals in all the land, for their leader scoured the land far and wide, seeking to swell his troop. These alone stood forward, prepared to step between the oppressor and the oppressed. Surely they were the very best men you could select to be hung. That was the greatest compliment this country could pay them. They were ripe for the gallows.

I regard this event as a touchstone designed to bring out with glaring distinctness the character of this government.

A man of Spartan habits, who at sixty has scruples about his diet at your table, must eat sparingly and fare hard, as becomes a soldier, he says, and one who is ever fitting himself for difficult enterprises.

A man of rare common sense and directness of speech, as of action; a Trancendentalist above all, a man of ideas and principles,—that was what distinguished him. Of unwavering purposes, not to be dissuaded but by an experience and wisdom greater than his own. Not yielding to a whim or transient impulse, but carrying out the purpose of a life.

He did not go to the college called Harvard; he was not fed on the pap that is there furnished. As he phrased it, "I know no more of grammar than one of your calves." But he went to the great university of the West, where he sedulously pursued the study of Liberty, for which he had early betrayed a fondness, and, having taken many degrees, he finally commenced the practice of Humanity, as you all know.

I see now that it was necessary that the bravest and humanest man in all the country should be hung. Perhaps he saw it himself. If any leniency were shown him, any compromise made with him, any treating with him at all, by the government, he might be suspected.

We needed to be thus assisted to see our government by the light of history. It needed to see itself.

Compare the platform of any or all of the political parties, which deem themselves sane, with the platform on which he lay and uttered these things!!

I foresee the time when the painter will paint that scene, the poet will sing it, the historian record it, and, with the Landing of the Pilgrims and the Declaration of Independence, it will be the ornament of some future national gallery, when the present form of slavery shall be no more. We shall then be at liberty to weep for John Brown. Then and not till then we will take our revenge.

I rejoice that I live in this age, that I was his contemporary.

Oct. 22. Think of him,—of his rare qualities!—such a man as it takes ages to make, and ages to understand; no mock hero, not the representative of any party. A man such as the sun may never rise upon again in this benighted land, to whose making went the costliest material, the finest adamant, the purest gold; sent to be the redeemer of those in captivity;—and the only use to which you can put him, after mature deliberation, is to hang him at the end of a rope. I need not describe him. He has stood where I now stand; you have all seen him. You who pretend to care for Christ crucified, consider what you are about to do to him who offered himself to be the savior of four millions of men!

I wish to correct the tone and some of the statements of the newspapers respecting the life and character and last action of John Brown. The newspapers seem to ignore, or perhaps they are really ignorant of, the fact that there are at least as many as one or two individuals to a town throughout the North who think much as I do about him and his enterprise. I do not hesitate to assert that they are an important and growing party.

I speak for the slave when I say that I prefer the philanthropy of John Brown to that philanthropy which neither shoots me nor liberates me.

Talk of failure and throwing his life away! he is not dead yet in any sense, and if he were dead he would still live. Were the battles of Black Jack and Ossawatomie and many encounters of less note useless and a failure? I think that it was he more than any other who made Kansas as free as she is, who taught the slaveholder that it was not safe for him to carry his slaves thither. None of the political parties have ever accomplished anything of the sort. It was he who taught Missouri that it was not profitable to hold slaves in that neighborhood. Was it a failure to deliver from bondage thirteen human beings and walk off with them by broad daylight, for weeks if not months, at a leisurely pace, through one State after another, for half the length of the North, conspicuous to all parties, with a price set upon his head, going into a courtroom on his way and telling what he had done? To face singly in his work of righteousness the whole power of this unrighteous government, and successfully too! Who has gained the most ground within five years,— Brown or the Slave Power? . . .

He is one of that class of whom we hear a great deal, but, for the most part, see nothing at all,—the Puritans. It is in vain to kill him. He died lately in the time of Cromwell, but he reappeared here. Why should he not? Some of the Puritan stock are said to have come over and settled in New England. They were a class that did something else than celebrate their forefathers' day and eat parched corn in remembrance of their ancestors. They were neither Democrats nor Republicans. They were men of simple habits, straightforward, prayerful; not thinking much of rulers who did not fear God, not making many compromises, or seeking after available candidates.

Nov. 12. There was a remarkable sunset, I think the 25th of October. The sunset sky reached quite from west to east, and it was the most varied in its forms and colors of any that I remember to have seen. At one time the clouds were most softly and delicately rippled, like the ripple-marks on sand. But it was hard for me to see its beauty then, when my mind was filled with Captain Brown. So great a wrong as his fate implied overshadowed all beauty in the world.

Dec. 8. Two hundred years ago is about as great an antiquity as we can comprehend or often have to deal with. It is nearly as

good as two thousand to our imaginations. It carries us back
to the days of aborigines and the Pilgrims; beyond the limits of
oral testimony, to history which begins already to be enamelled
with a gloss of fable, and we do not quite believe what we read;
to a strange style of writing and spelling and of expression; to
those ancestors whose names we do not know, and to whom we
are related only as we are to the race generally. It is the age of
our very oldest houses and cultivated trees. Nor is New England
very peculiar in this. In England also, a house two hundred
years old, especially if it be a wooden one, is pointed out as an
interesting relic of the past.

When we read the history of the world, centuries look cheap
to us and we find that we had doubted if the hundred years
preceding the life of Herodotus seemed as great an antiquity
to him as a hundred years does to us. We are inclined to think
of all Romans who lived within five hundred years B.C. as
contemporaries to each other. Yet Time moved at the same
deliberate pace then as now. Pliny the Elder, who died in the
79th year of the Christian era, speaking of the paper made of
papyrus which was then used,—how carefully it was made,—
says, *just as we might say*, as if it were something remarkable:
"There are, thus, ancient memorials in the handwriting of
Caius and Tiberius Gracchus, almost two hundred years old,
which I have seen in the possession of Pomponius Secundus the
poet, a very illustrious citizen. As for the handwriting of Cicero,
Augustus, and Virgil, we very often meet with it still." This too,
according to Pliny, was the age of the oldest wines. "In one
year the quality of all kinds of wine was peculiarly good. In the
consulship of Lucius Opimius, when Caius Gracchus, disturbing
the people with seditions, was killed, there was that bright and
serene weather (*ea caeli temperies fulsit*) which they call a *cooking*
(of the grape) by the heat of the sun. This was in the year of the
city 634. And some of those wines have lasted to this day, almost
two hundred years, now reduced to the appearance of candied
honey (*in speciem redacta mellis asperi*)."

How is it that what is actually present and transpiring is
commonly perceived by the common sense and understanding

only, is bare and bald, without halo or the blue enamel of intervening air? But let it be past or to come, and it is at once idealized. As the man dead is spiritualized, so the fact remembered is idealized. It is a deed ripe and with the bloom on it. It is not simply the understanding now, but the imagination, that takes cognizance of it. The imagination requires a long range. It is the faculty of the poet to see present things as if, in this sense, also past and future, as if distant or universally significant.

Dec. 16. A.M.—To Cambridge, where I read in Gerard's Herbal. His admirable though quaint descriptions are, to my mind, greatly superior to the modern more scientific ones. He describes not according to rule but to his natural delight in the plants. He brings them vividly before you, as one who has seen and delighted in them. It is almost as good as to see the plants themselves. It suggests that we cannot too often get rid of the barren assumption that is in our science. His leaves are leaves; his flowers, flowers; his fruit, fruit. They are green and colored and fragrant. It is a man's knowledge added to a child's delight. Modern botanical descriptions approach ever nearer to the dryness of an algebraic formula, as if $x+y$ were = to a love-letter. It is the keen joy and discrimination of the child who has just seen a flower for the first time and comes running in with it to its friends. How much better to describe your object in fresh English words rather than in these conventional Latinisms! He has really seen, and smelt, and tasted, and reports his sensations.

Dec. 25. Consider how the pickerel-fisher lives. G., whom I saw at Flint's Pond on the 22d, had been there all day, eaten all the dinner he had brought, and caught only four little fish, hardly enough for his supper, if he should cook them. His companion swore that he would not go a-fishing again for ten years. But G. said nothing of that sort. The next day I found him five miles from here on the other side of the town, with his lines set in the bay of the river off Ball's Hill. There, too, he had been tramping about from hole to hole,—this time alone,—and he had done a trifle better than the day before, for he caught three little fish and one great one. But instead of giving up here, he concluded to leave his lines in overnight,—since his bait would die if he took them off,—and return the next morning. The next was a bitter cold day, but I hear that Goodwin had some fish to dispose of. Probably not more than a dollar's worth, however....

How different are men and women, e.g. in respect to the adornment of their heads! Do you ever see an old or jammed bonnet on the head of a woman at a public meeting? But look at any assembly of men with their hats on; how large a proportion of the hats will be old, weatherbeaten, and indented, but I think so much the more picturesque and interesting! One farmer rides by my door in a hat which it does me good to see, there is so much character in it,—so much independence to begin with, and then affection for his old friends, etc., etc. I should not wonder if there were lichens on it. Think of painting a hero in a bran-new hat! The chief recommendation of the Kossuth hat is that it looks old to start with, and almost as good as new to end with. Indeed, it is generally conceded that a man does not look the worse for a somewhat dilapidated hat. But go to a lyceum and look at the bonnets and various other headgear of the women and girls,—who, by the way, keep their hats on, it being too dangerous and expensive to take them off!! Why every one looks as fragile as a butterfly's wings, having just come out of a bandbox,—as it will go into a bandbox again when the lyceum is over. Men wear their hats for use; women theirs for ornament. I have seen the greatest philosopher in the town with what the traders would call "a shocking bad hat" on, but the woman whose bonnet does not come up to the mark is at best a "bluestocking."

Jan. 5, 1860. P.M.—Via Turnpike to Smith's and back by Great Road.

How much the snow reveals! I see where the downy woodpecker has worked lately by the chips of bark and rotten wood scattered over the snow, though I rarely see him in the winter. Once to-day, however, I hear his sharp voice, even like a woodchuck's. Also I have occasionally seen where (probably) a flock of goldfinches in the morning had settled on a hemlock's top, by the snow strewn with scales, literally blackened or darkened with them for a rod. And now, about the hill in front of Smith's, I see where the quails have run along the roadside, and can count the number of the bevy better than if I saw them. Are they not peculiar in this, as compared with partridges,—that they run in company, while at this season I see but [one] or two partridges together?

A man receives only what he is ready to receive, whether physically of intellectually or morally, as animals conceive at certain seasons their kind only. We hear and apprehend only what we already half know. If there is something which does not concern me, which is out of my line, which by experience or by genius my attention is not drawn to, however novel and remarkable it may be, if it is spoken, we hear it not, if it is written, we read it not, or if we read it, it does not detain us. Every man thus *tracks himself* through life, in all his hearing and reading and observation and travelling. His observations make a chain. The phenomenon or fact that cannot in any wise be linked with the rest which he has observed, he does not observe. By and by we may be ready to receive what he cannot receive now. I find, for example, in Aristotle something about the spawning, etc., of the pout and perch, because I know something about it already and have my attention aroused; but I do not discover till very late that he has made other equally important observations on the spawning of other fishes, because I am not interested in those fishes.

Jan. 25. In keeping a journal of one's walks and thoughts it seems to be worth the while to record those phenomena which are most interesting to us at the time. Such is the weather. It makes a material difference whether it is foul or fair, affecting surely our mood and thoughts. . . .

When you think that your walk is profitless and a failure, and you can hardly persuade yourself not to return, it is on the point of being a success, for then you are in that subdued and knocking mood to which Nature never fails to open.

Feb. 2. I see where some meadow mouse—if not mole—just came to the surface of the snow enough to break it with his back for three or four inches, then put his head out and at once withdrew it.

We walked, as usual, on the fresh track of a fox, peculiarly pointed, and sometimes the mark of two toenails in front separate from the track of the foot in very thin snow. And as we were kindling a fire on the pond by the side of the island, we saw the fox himself at the inlet of the river. He was busily examining along the sides of the pond by the button-bushes and willows, smelling in the snow. Not appearing to regard us much, he slowly explored along the shore of the pond thus, half-way round it; at Pleasant Meadow, evidently looking for mice (or moles?) in the grass of the bank, smelling in the shallow snow there amid the stubble, often retracing his steps and pausing at particular spots. He was eagerly searching for food, intent on finding some mouse to help fill his empty stomach. He had a blackish tail and blackish feet. Looked lean and stood high. The tail peculiarly large for any creature to carry round. He stepped daintily about, softly, and is more to the manor born than a dog. It was a very arctic scene this cold day, and I suppose he would hardly have ventured out in a warm one.

The fox seems to get his living by industry and perseverance. He runs smelling for miles along the most favorable routes, especially the edge of rivers and ponds, until he smells the track of a mouse beneath the snow or the fresh track of a partridge, and then follows it till he comes upon his game. After exploring thus a great many quarters, after hours of fruitless search, he succeeds. There may be a dozen partridges resting in the snow within a square mile, and his work is simply to find them with the aid of his nose. Compared with the dog, he affects me as high-bred, unmixed. There is nothing of the mongrel in him. He belongs to a noble family which has seen its best days,—a younger son. Now and then he starts, and turns and doubles on his track, as if he heard or scented danger. (I watch him through my glass.) He does not mind us at the distance of only sixty rods. I have myself seen one place where a mouse came to the surface to-day in the snow. Probably he has smelt out many such galleries. Perhaps he seizes them *through* the snow.

I had a transient vision of one mouse this winter, and that the first for a number of years.

Feb. 12. In this cold, clear, rough air from the north-west we walk amid what simple surroundings! Surrounded by our thoughts or imaginary objects, living in our *ideas*, not one in a million ever sees the objects which are actually around him.

Above me is a cloudless blue sky; beneath, the sky-blue, i.e. sky-reflecting, ice with patches of snow scattered over it like mackerel clouds. At a distance in several directions I see the tawny earth streaked or spotted with white where the bank or hills and fields appear, or else the green-black evergreen forests, or the brown, or russet, or tawny deciduous woods, and here and there, where the agitated surface of the river is exposed, the blue-black water. That dark-eyed water, especially when I see it at right angles with the direction of the sun, is it not the first sign of spring? How its darkness contrasts with the general lightness of the winter! It has more life in it than any part of the earth's surface. It is where one of the arteries of the earth is palpable, visible.

Those are peculiar portions of the river which have thus always opened first,—been open latest and longest. In winter not only some creatures, but the very earth is partially dormant; vegetation ceases, and rivers, to some extent, cease to flow. Therefore, when I see the water exposed in midwinter, it is as if I saw a skunk or even a striped squirrel out. It is as if the woodchuck unrolled himself and snuffed the air to see if it were warm enough to be trusted.

It excites me to see early in the spring that black artery leaping once more through the snow-clad town. All is tumult and life there, not to mention the rails and cranberries that are drifting in it. Where this artery is shallowest, i.e. comes nearest to the surface and runs swiftest, there it shows itself soonest and you may see its pulse beat. These are the wrists, temples, of the earth, where I feel its pulse with my eye. The living waters, not the dead earth. It is as if the dormant earth opened its dark and liquid eye upon us. . . .

How unexpected is one season by another! Off Pleasant Meadow I walk amid the tops of bayonet rushes frozen in, as if the summer had been overtaken by the winter.

Returning just before sunset, I see the ice beginning to be green, and a rose-color to be reflected from the low snow-patches. I see the color from the snow first where there is some shade, as where the shadow of a maple falls afar over the ice and snow. From this is reflected a purple tinge when I see none elsewhere. Some shadow or twilight, then, is necessary, umbra mixed with the reflected sun. Off Holden Wood, where the low rays fall on the river from between the fringe of the wood, the snow-patches are not rose-color, but a very dark purple like a grape, and thus there are all degrees from pure white to black. When crossing Hubbard's broad meadow, the snow-patches are a most beautiful crystalline purple, like the petals of some flowers, or as if tinged with cranberry juice. It is quite a faery scene, surprising and wonderful, as if you walked amid those rosy and purple clouds that you see float in the evening sky. What need to visit the crimson cliffs of Beverly?

I thus find myself returning over a green sea, winding amid purple islets, and the low sedge of the meadow on one side is really a burning yellow.

The hunter may be said to invent his game, as Neptune did the horse, and Ceres corn.

It is twenty above at 5.30, when I get home.

I walk over a smooth green sea, or *aequor*, the sun just disappearing in the cloudless horizon, amid thousands of these flat isles as purple as the petal of a flower. It would not be more enchanting to walk amid the purple clouds of the sunset sky. And, by the way, this is but a sunset sky under our feet, produced by the same law, the same slanting rays and twilight. Here the clouds are these patches of snow or frozen vapor, and the ice is the greenish sky between them. Thus all of heaven is realized on earth. You have seen those purple fortunate isles in the sunset heavens, and that green and amber sky between them.

Would you believe that you could ever walk amid those isles? You can on many a winter evening. I have done so a hundred times. The ice is a solid crystalline sky under our feet.

Whatever aid is to be derived from the use of a scientific term, we can never begin to see anything as it is so long as we remember the scientific term which always our ignorance has imposed on it. Natural objects and phenomena are in this sense forever wild and unnamed by us.

Thus the sky and the earth sympathize, and are subject to the same laws, and in the horizon they, as it were, meet and are seen to be one.

I have walked in such a place and found it hard as marble.

Not only the earth but the heavens are made our footstool. That is what the phenomenon of ice means. The earth is annually inverted and we walk upon the sky. The ice reflects the blue of the sky. The waters become solid and make a sky below. The clouds grow heavy and fall to earth, and we walk on them. We live and walk on solidified fluids.

We have such a habit of looking away that we see not what is around us. How few are aware that in winter, when the earth is covered with snow and ice, the phenomenon of the sunset sky is double! The one is on the earth around us, the other in the horizon. These snow-clad hills answer to the rosy isles in the west. The winter is coming when I shall walk the sky. The ice is a solid sky on which we walk. It is the inverted year. There is an annual light in the darkness of the winter night. The shadows are blue, as the sky is forever blue. In winter we are purified and translated. The earth does not absorb our thoughts. It becomes a Valhalla.

Next above Good Fishing Bay and where the man was drowned, I pass Black Rock Shore, and over the Deep Causeway I come to Drifted Meadow.

North of the Warm Woodside (returning) is Bulrush Lagoon, —off Grindstone Meadow,—a good place for lilies; then Nut Meadow Mouth; Clamshell Bend, or Indian Bend; Sunset Reach, where the river flows nearly from west to east and is a fine sparkling scene from the hills eastward at sunset; then

Hubbard's Bathing-Place, and the swift place, and Lily Bay, or Willow Bay.

Feb. 13. The Scripture rule. "Unto him that hath shall be given," is true of composition. The more you have thought and written on a given theme, the more you can still write. Thought breeds thought. It grows under your hands.

Feb. 15. As in the expression of moral truths we admire any closeness to the physical fact which in all language is the symbol of the spiritual, so, finally, when natural objects are described, it is an advantage if words derived originally from nature, it is true, but which have been turned (*tropes*) from their primary signification to a moral sense, are used, i.e., if the object is personified. The one who loves and understands a thing the best will incline to use the personal pronouns in speaking of it. To him there is no *neuter* gender. Many of the words of the old naturalists were in this sense doubly tropes.

Feb. 17. We cannot spare the very lively and lifelike descriptions of some of the old naturalists. They sympathize with the creatures which they describe. Edward Topsell in his translation of Conrad Gesner, in 1607, called "The History of Four-footed Beasts," says of the antelopes that "they are bred in India and Syria, near the river Euphrates," and then—which enables you to realize the living creature and its habitat—he adds, "and delight much to drink of the cold water thereof." The beasts which most modern naturalists describe do not *delight* in anything, and their water is neither hot nor cold. Reading the above makes you want to go and drink of the Euphrates yourself, if it is warm weather. I do not know how much of his spirit he owes to Gesner, but he proceeds in his translation to say that "they have horns growing forth of the crown of their head, which are very long and sharp; so that Alexander affirmed they pierced through the shields of his soldiers, and fought with them very irefully; at which time his company slew as he travelled to India, eight thousand five hundred and fifty, which great slaughter may be the occasion why they are so rare and seldom seen to this day."

Now here *something* is described at any rate; it is a real account, whether of a real animal or not. You can plainly see the horns which "grew forth" from their crowns, and how well that word "irefully" describes a beast's fighting! And then for the number which Alexander's men slew "as he travelled to India,"—and what a travelling was that, my hearers!—eight thousand five hundred and fifty, just the number you would have guessed after the thousands were given, and [an] easy one to remember too. He goes on to say that "their horns are great and made like a saw, and they with them can cut asunder the branches of osier or small trees, whereby it cometh to pass that many times their necks are taken in the twists of the falling boughs, whereat the beast with repining cry, bewrayeth himself to the hunters, and so is taken." The artist too has done his part equally well, for you are presented with a drawing of the beast with serrated horns, the tail of a lion, a cheek tooth (canine?) as big as a boar's, a stout front, and an exceedingly "ireful" look, as if he were facing all Alexander's army.

Though some beasts are described in this book which have no existence as I can learn but in the imagination of the writers, they really have an existence there, which is saying not a little, for most of our modern authors have not imagined the actual beasts which they presume to describe. The very frontispiece is a figure of "the gorgon," which looks sufficiently like a hungry beast covered with scales, which you may have dreamed of, apparently just fallen on the track of you, the reader, and snuffing the odor with greediness.

These men had an adequate idea of a beast, or what a beast should be, a very *bellua* (the translator makes the word *bestia* to be "*a vastando*"); and they will describe and will draw you a cat with four strokes, more beastly or beast-like to look at than Mr. Ruskin's favorite artist draws a tiger. They had an adequate idea of the wildness of beasts and of men, and in their descriptions and drawings they did not always fail when they *surpassed* nature.

March 1. Rain all day, This will apparently take the frost out very much and still further settle the ways. . . .

I have thoughts, as I walk, on some subject that is running in my head, but all their pertinence seems gone before I can get home to set them down. The most valuable thoughts which I entertain are anything but what *I* thought. Nature abhors a vacuum, and if I can only walk with sufficient carelessness I am sure to be filled.

April 1. Sunday. Warm, with the thick haze still concealing the sun. . . .

The large *Rana fontinalis* sits enjoying the warmth on the muddy shore. I hear the first hylodes by chance, but no doubt they have been heard some time. Hear the hum of bees on the maples. Rye-fields look green. Pickerel dart, and probably have some time. The sweet-gale is almost in bloom; say next pleasant day.

The fruit a thinker bears is *sentences,*—statements or opinions. He seeks to affirm something as true. I am surprised that my affirmations or utterances come to me ready-made,—not fore-thought,—so that I occasionally awake in the night simply to let fall ripe a statement which I had never consciously considered before, and as surprising and novel and agreeable to me as anything can be. As if we only thought by sympathy with the universal mind, which thought while we were asleep. There is such a necessity [to] make a definite statement that our minds at length do it without our consciousness, just as we carry our food to our mouths. This occurred to me last night, but I was so surprised by the fact which I have just endeavored to report that I have entirely forgotten what the particular observation was.

Sept. 10. Lowell to Boston and Concord.

There was a frost this morning, as my host, who keeps a market, informed me.

Leaving Lowell at 7 A.M. in the cars, I observed and admired the dew on a fine grass in the meadows, which was almost as white and silvery as frost when the rays of the newly risen sun fell on it. Some of it *was* probably the frost of the morning melted. I saw that this phenomenon was confined to one species of grass, which grew in narrow curving lines and small patches along the edges of the meadows or lowest ground,—a grass with very fine stems and branches, which held the dew; in short, that it was what I had falsely called *Eragrostis capillaris*, but which is probably the *Sporobolus serotinus*, almost the only, if not the only, grass there in its prime. And thus this plant has its day. Owing to the number of its very fine branches, now in their prime, it holds the dew like a cobweb,—a clear drop at the end and lesser drops or beads all along the fine branches and stems. It grows on the higher parts of the meadows, where other herbage is thin, and is the less apt to be cut; and, seen toward the sun not long after sunrise, it is very conspicuous and bright a quarter of a mile off, like frostwork. Call it dew-grass. I find its *hyaline* seed.

Almost every plant, however humble, has thus its day, and sooner or later becomes the characteristic feature of some part of the landscape or other.

Oct. 17. The noblest trees and those which it took the longest to produce, and which are the longest-lived, as chestnuts, hickories (?), oaks, are the first to become extinct under our present system and the hardest to reproduce, and their place is taken by pines and birches, of feebler growth than the primitive pines and birches, for want of a change of soil.

There is many a tract now bearing a poor and decaying crop of birches, or perhaps of oaks, dying when a quarter grown and covered with fungi and excrescences, where two hundred years ago grew oaks or chestnuts of the largest size.

I look through a lot of young oaks twenty or twenty-five years old (Warren's, east of the Deep Cut, exclusively oak, the eastern part). There are plenty of little oaks from a few inches to a foot in height, but on examination I find fewer seedlings in proportion to the whole (i.e. manifestly seedlings) and they have much older and larger and poorer or more decayed roots than the oaks in dense pine woods. Oftenest they are shoots from the end of a horizontal twig running several feet under the leaves and leading to an old stump (?) under the surface. But I must examine again and further.

Oct. 18. What shall we say to that management that halts between two courses,—does neither this nor that, but botches both? I see many a pasture on which the pitch or white pines are spreading, where the bush-whack is from time to time used with a show of vigor, and I despair of my trees,—I say mine, for the farmer evidently does not mean they shall be his,—and yet this questionable work is so poorly done that those very fields grow steadily greener and more forest-like from year to year in spite of cows and bush-whack, till at length the farmer gives up the contest from sheer weariness, and finds himself the owner of a wood-lot. Now whether wood-lots or pastures are most profitable for him I will not undertake to say, but I am certain that a wood-lot and pasture combined is not profitable.

I see spatter-dock pads and pontederia in that little pool at south end of Beck Stow's. How did they get there? There is no stream in this case? It was perhaps rather reptiles and birds than fishes, then. Indeed we might as well ask how they got anywhere, for all the pools and fields have been stocked thus, and we are not to suppose as many new creations as pools. This suggests to inquire how any plant came where it is,—how, for instance, the pools which were stocked with lilies before we were born or this town was settled, and ages ago, were so stocked, as well as those which we dug. I think that we are warranted only in supposing that the former was stocked in the same way as the latter, and that there was not a sudden new creation,—at least since the first; yet I have no doubt that peculiarities more or less considerable have thus been gradually produced in the lilies thus planted in various pools, in consequence of their various conditions, though they all came originally from one seed.

We find ourselves in a world that is already planted, but is also still being planted as at first. We say of some plants that they grow in wet places and of others that they grow in desert places. The truth is that their seeds are scattered almost everywhere, but here only do they succeed. Unless you can show me the pool where the lily was created, I shall believe that the oldest fossil lilies which the geologist has detected (if this is found fossil) originated in that locality in a similar manner to these of Beck Stow's. We see thus how the fossil lilies which the geologist has detected are dispersed, as well as these which we carry in our hands to church.

The development theory implies a greater vital force in nature, because it is more flexible and accommodating, and equivalent to a sort of constant *new* creation.

Oct. 19. I examine that oak lot of Rice's next to the pine strip of the 16th. The oaks (at the southern end) are about a dozen years old. As I expected, I find the stumps of the pines which stood there before quite fresh and distinct, not much decayed, and I find by their rings that they were about forty years old when cut, while the pines which sprang from [them] are now about twenty-five or thirty. But further, and unexpectedly, I find the stumps, in great numbers, now much decayed, or an oak wood which stood there more than sixty years ago. They are mostly shells, the sap-wood rotted off and the inside turned to mould. Thus I distinguished four successions of trees.

Thus I can easily find in countless numbers in our forests, frequently in the third succession, the stumps of the oaks which were cut near the end of the last century. Perhaps I can recover thus generally the oak woods of the beginning of the last century, if the land has remained woodland. I have an advantage over the geologist, for I can not only detect the order of events but the time during which they elapsed, by counting the rings on the stumps. Thus you can unroll the rotten papyrus on which the history of the Concord forest is written.

It is easier far to recover the history of the trees which stood here a century of more ago than it is to recover the history of the men who walked beneath them. How much do we know— how little more can we know—of these two centuries of Concord life?

Nov. 22. You walk fast and far, and every apple left out is grateful to your invigorated taste. You enjoy not only the bracing coolness, but all the heat and sunlight that there is, reflected back to you from the earth. The sandy road itself, lit by the November sun, is beautiful. Shrub oaks and young oaks generally, and hazel bushes and other hardy shrubs, now more or less bare, are your companions, as if it were an iron age, yet in simplicity, innocence, and strength a golden one.

(Day before yesterday the rustling of the withered oak leaves in the wind reminded me of the similar sound produced by snow falling on them.)

It is glorious to consider how independent man is of all enervating luxuries; and the poorer he is in respect to them, the richer he is. Summer is gone with all its infinite wealth, and still nature is genial to man. Though he no longer bathes in the stream, or reclines on the bank, or plucks berries on the hills, still he beholds the same inaccessible beauty around him. What though he has no juice of the grape stored up for him in cellars; the air itself is wine of an older vintage, and far more sanely exhilarating, than any cellar affords. It is ever some gouty senior and not a blithe child that drinks, or cares for, that so famous wine. . . .

What though your hands are numb with cold, your sense of enjoyment is not benumbed. You cannot now find an apple but it is sweet to taste.

Simply to see to a distant horizon through a clear air,—the fine outline of a distant hill or a blue mountain-top through some new vista,—this is wealth enough for one afternoon.

We journeyed into the foreign land of Sudbury to see how the Sudbury men—the Hayneses, and the Puffers, and the Brighams—live. We traversed their pastures and their wood-lots, and were home again at night.

Nov. 23. Most of us are still related to our native fields as the navigator to undiscovered islands in the sea. We can any autumn discover a new fruit there which will surprise us by its beauty or sweetness. So long as I saw one or two kinds of berries in my walks whose names I did not know, the proportion of the unknown seemed indefinitely if not infinitely great.

Jan. 3, 1861. The third considerable snow-storm. . . .

What are the natural features which make a township

handsome? A river, with its waterfalls and meadows, a lake, a hill, a cliff or individual rocks, a forest, and ancient trees standing singly. Such things are beautiful; they have a high use which dollars and cents never represent. If the inhabitants of a town were wise, they would seek to preserve these things, though at a considerable expense; for such things educate far more than any hired teachers or preachers, or any at present recognized system of school education. I do not think him fit to be the founder of a state or even of a town who does not foresee the use of these things, but legislates chiefly for oxen, as it were.

Far the handsomest thing I saw in Boxboro was its noble oak wood. I doubt if there is a finer one in Massachusetts. Let her keep it a century longer, and men will make pilgrimages to it from all parts of the country; and yet it would be very like the rest of New England if Boxboro were ashamed of that woodland.

I have since heard, however, that she is contented to have that forest stand instead of the houses and farms that might supplant [it], because the land pays a much larger tax to the town now than it would then.

I said to myself, if the history of this town is written, the chief stress is probably laid on its parish and there is not a word about this forest in it.

It would be worth the while if in each town there were a committee appointed to see that the beauty of the town received no detriment. If we have the largest boulder in the county, then it should not belong to an individual, nor be made into door-steps.

As in many countries precious metals belong to the crown, so here more precious natural objects of rare beauty should belong to the public.

Not only the channel but one or both banks of every river should be a public highway. The only use of a river is not to float on it.

Think of a mountain-top in the township—even to the minds of the Indians a sacred place—only accessible through private grounds! a temple, as it were, which you cannot enter except by trespassing and at the risk of letting out or letting in

somebody's cattle! in fact the temple itself in this case private
property and standing in a man's cow-yard,—for such is
commonly the case!

New Hampshire courts have lately been deciding—as if it
was for them to decide—whether the top of Mt. Washington
belonged to A or to B; and, it being decided in favor of B, as I
hear, he went up one winter with the proper officer and took
formal possession of it. But I think that the top of Mt. Washington should not be private property; it should be left unappropriated for modesty and reverence's sake, or if only to suggest that
earth has higher uses than we put her to.

March 18. You can't read any genuine history—as that of
Herodotus or the Venerable Bede—without perceiving that our
interest depends not on the subject but on the man,—on the
manner in which he treats the subject and the importance he
gives it. A feeble writer and without genius must have what he
thinks a great theme, which we are already interested in
through the accounts of others, but a genius—a Shakespeare,
for instance—would make the history of his parish more
interesting than another's history of the world.

Nov. 3. After a violent easterly storm in the night, which clears
up at noon (November 3, 1861), I notice that the surface of the
railroad causeway, composed of gravel, is singularly marked, as
if stratified like some slate rocks, on their edges, so that I can
tell within a small fraction of a degree from what quarter the
rain came. These lines, as it were of stratification, are perfectly
parallel, and straight as a ruler, diagonally across the flat
surface of the causeway for its whole length. Behind each little
pebble, as a protecting boulder, an eighth or a tenth of an inch
in diameter, extends northwest a ridge of sand an inch or more,
which it has protected from being washed away, while the
heavy drops driven almost horizontally have washed out a
furrow on each side, and on all sides are these ridges, half an
inch apart and perfectly parallel.

All this is perfectly distinct to an observant eye, and yet could
easily pass unnoticed by most. Thus each wind is self-registering.

INDEX

Actual, the, 98
Actuality, 20
Admetus, 102. *See also* Apollo
Aeschylus, 3
Aesop, 104
Alcott, A. Bronson, 14
Antiquity, 8, 78, 210–11; colour of, 180
Apollo, 55, 57
Aristotle, 26, 95, 214
Arrowheads, 198–200
Artist, and indifference, 11
Author, aim of, 1
Azalea nudiflora, the search for, 98–101

Bacon, Francis, 12
Bartram, William, 57
Bible, the, in New England, 205
Blake, Harrison, 179
Blood, Perez, 39, 77
Books, 84
Brahe, Tycho, 39
Bravery, 6
Breams, 192–93, 193–94
Brown, John, 207–10
Buds, 175
Business, 57

Cable, the Atlantic, 182
Carew, Thomas, 17
Carlyle, Thomas, 14
Channing, William Ellery, 41, 74, 99, 100, 159, 183
Character, 119
Chaucer, Geoffrey, 9, 10, 26
Christ, 32, 63, 206, 209
Columella, 139
Composition, 3, 81, 177, 197, 198, 219. *See also* Writing
Concord, 31, 32, 33, 49, 224
Concord River, 181
Congress, 112
Conversation, 51–52
Craft, 69
Cromwell, Oliver, 207, 210
Crystals, snow, 134–35. *See also* Snowflakes
Cudworth, Ralph, 26

Daniel, Samuel, 18
Dante, 3
Darwin, Charles, 54
De Quincey, Thomas, 30, 64, 74
Donne, John, 18, 26
Douglas, Gavin, 8
Drummond, William, 17
Duty, 1

Earth, the, 175
Education, 22
Emerson, Ralph Waldo, 6, 14, 15, 76–77, 124, 137, 141, 158, 159, 171
Endymion, 69
Eternal, the, 102
Evelyn, John, 96
Evolution, 223–24
Experience, 46, 54, 214; returned to, 87; symbolical, 96
Expression; *see* Writing
Eye, intention of, 185. *See also* Seeing

Facts, 7, 73, 128; and poetry, 84
Fuller, Margaret, 76

Garrison, William Lloyd, 70
Genius, not dutiful, 1, 2
Gerard, John, 212
God, 8, 9, 11, 33, 62, 108, 128, 174, 194, 196
Gods, the, 11, 12, 165
Goodwin, John, 105, 106, 108, 140, 158, 182, 188, 193, 212–13; Goodwin & Co., 151–52; the one-eyed Ajax, 189
Government, 116, 117
Grasses, 183–84, 221–22
Gray, Thomas, quoted, 1

Happiness, 153–54
Herodotus, 227
Hindus, 19
Homer, 3, 83
Hosmer, Edmund, 79, 139
Hubbard, Cyrus, 146
Humboldt, Alexander von, 54
Hunters, 195–96

Iamblichus, 12
Ignorance, use of, 13; advantage of, 26
Imagination, 212

Immortality, 176
Indian, the, 6, 19–20, 22. *See also* Arrowheads
Integrity, 1
Intensity, 160

Journal, keeping a, 2, 10, 13; use of, 23, 25, 73,
    82, 83, 126, 132, 133, 134, 135–36, 159, 169,
    183, 214

Knowledge, 26, 40

Labour, manual, and style, 10, 11; use of, 115–16. *See.*
    also Task
Language, 205–06, 219; acquiring one's, 184
Lecturing, 121, 124, 197, 201
Leisure, 7, 8; and work, 13, 93, 94, 202
Lichens, 9, 96, 176
Life, 67, 195, 198; conduct of, 93; free of morality, 7;
    when serene, 3
Linnaeus, C., 87
Literature, and wildness, 22
Living, getting a, 29, 46–47
Lyceum, 108
Lydgate, John, 13

Maker, the; *see* God
Malthus, J. R., 173
Man, 33
Marlowe, Christopher, 17, 18
Mather, Cotton, 125
Melvin, George, 24, 98, 99, 100, 101, 140, 146–47, 167,
    178, 188
Men, affairs of, 65
Mill, Sam Barrett's, 187–88
Milton, John, 2, 26
Mind, the, 40, 53, 181; moods of, 62; the infinite, 85;
    the unconscious, 221
Minott, George, 71–73, 74–75, 136–37, 145, 150, 157,
    163, 164, 165, 169, 170, 171, 173, 177–78, 181–82,
    187
Moment, the, 82–83
Moonlight, walking by, 33–37, 41–45, 54–55, 57–60,
    68, 69, 88–90
Music, 112. *See also* Sounds
Myth, 98
Mythology, 27, 57

Naturalists, style of, 219–20

Nature, 8, 27, 58, 60, 63, 86, 87, 89, 90, 92, 108, 111, 134, 138, 166, 175, 188, 191, 204, 214; different from man, 94; silence of, 5

New York, 123–24

Observation, 54, 62–63, 92–93, 96, 97, 111, 127, 136, 143–44, 164, 172–73, 190, 197, 214. *See also* Reporting

Ossoli, Marquis of, 20

Past, the, 7, 200. *See also* Antiquity, Arrowheads

Peele, George, 17, 18

Perception, 169

Philadelphia, 121–23

Philosopher, the, 104

Plato, 12, 26, 95

Poet, the, 9, 62, 75, 84, 169, 173

Poetry, and uncommon sense, 13

Poverty, 121, 198, 201; of spirit, 165

Privacy, 117

Prose, 111

Puritanism, 210

Pythagoras, 12

Rain, walking in the, 176–77. *See also* Storm

Raleigh, Sir Walter, 17

Ray, visual, 164, 190

Reflection, 86, 120, 185; as composition, 166; of sky 217–18

Religion, 5, 63, 183; Hebrew, 19; Hindu, 19; Thoreau's impartiality in, 19

Reporter, the, 172

Reporting, on observation, 159

Repose, 40

Revision; *see* Writing

Rhyme, in nature, 86, 149–50

Riordan, Johnny, 78

River(s), 9, 22, 65, 85–86, 180–81; Concord, 181

Sauntering, 6

Scholar, 81

Science, 95; men of, 170

Seasons, record of, 106

Seeing, 5, 28, 29; with the side of the eye, 6, 96, 140. *See also* Eye, Observation

Senses, the, 38, 46

Sentences, 11, 73–74, 221; and character, 4

Serenity, 38

Shakespeare, William, 13, 26, 227; genius of, 17

Sidney, Sir Philip, 17

Sky, reflected, 217–18

Slave, a fugitive, 70–71

Slavery, 30–33, 116, 206–10

Snowflakes, 174–75. *See also* Crystals, snow

Society, 25, 63, 154–55; impermanence of, 21

Solitude, 154–55

Sounds, 4, 6, 8, 55, 56, 88, 91

Spenser, Edmund, 17, 26

Storm, a, 160–63

Style, 68; and manual labour, 10, 11; of naturalists, 219–20. *See also* Writing

Surveying, 76, 110, 115, 140, 152, 172

Talent, 1; and character, 12. *See also* Genius

Task, value of a, 184–85

Thoreau, Henry D., life of, 15–16, 24, 39, 107, 137–38; his nature, 9; houses lived in, 132–34; sense of himself, 23; trip to Monadnock, 179–80; discovers new species of fish in Walden, 192–94; *Walden*, 114, 118, 124; *A Week on the Concord and Merrimack Rivers*, 106–07. *See also* New York, Philadelphia, Lecturing, Surveying, Walking, Writing

Thoreau, Sophia, 105, 202

Thought, 7, 40, 61, 66, 68, 76, 82, 184, 219, 221; and matter, 19; style of, 11; transcription of, 1; unconscious, 221

Time, 12, 92; renovation of, 188; use of, 202. *See also* Past, the; Antiquity

Titian, 86

Towns and parks, 204–05, 225–26

Tragedy, Elizabethan, 17

Transcendentalist, Thoreau a, 95; John Brown a, 208

Trappers, 197

Trees, 185–87, 222–23, 224

Truth, vision of, 170

Unconscious, life, 142

Unconsciousness, 2

Verse, 13

View, a side, 170

Walden Pond, 171, 191, 193

Walking, 27, 47–51, 53–54, 75; by moonlight, 33–37, 41–45, 54–55, 57–60, 68, 69, 88–90; to return to the senses, 24

Weeds, 21–22

Wisdom, 2, 38, 104

Woodthrush, 101–02

Work, significant, 20–21; a means of preparation, 77.
See also Labour, Task, Surveying

Worthies, of the town, 156

Writer, the, 83, 124–25, 196–97

Writing, 6, 52, 64, 66, 73, 110–11, 112, 121, 144, 151,
173; homeliness in, 4; discipline of, 78–79; revision
of, 112, 115

A CATALOGUE OF SELECTED DOVER BOOKS
IN ALL FIELDS OF INTEREST

A CATALOGUE OF SELECTED DOVER
BOOKS IN ALL FIELDS OF INTEREST

CELESTIAL OBJECTS FOR COMMON TELESCOPES, T. W. Webb. The most used book in amateur astronomy: inestimable aid for locating and identifying nearly 4,000 celestial objects. Edited, updated by Margaret W. Mayall. 77 illustrations. Total of 645pp. 5⅜ x 8½.
20917-2, 20918-0 Pa., Two-vol. set $9.00

HISTORICAL STUDIES IN THE LANGUAGE OF CHEMISTRY, M. P. Crosland. The important part language has played in the development of chemistry from the symbolism of alchemy to the adoption of systematic nomenclature in 1892. ". . . wholeheartedly recommended,"—Science. 15 illustrations. 416pp. of text. 5⅝ x 8¼.
63702-6 Pa. $6.00

BURNHAM'S CELESTIAL HANDBOOK, Robert Burnham, Jr. Thorough, readable guide to the stars beyond our solar system. Exhaustive treatment, fully illustrated. Breakdown is alphabetical by constellation: Andromeda to Cetus in Vol. 1; Chamaeleon to Orion in Vol. 2; and Pavo to Vulpecula in Vol. 3. Hundreds of illustrations. Total of about 2000pp. 6⅛ x 9¼.
23567-X, 23568-8, 23673-0 Pa., Three-vol. set $27.85

THEORY OF WING SECTIONS: INCLUDING A SUMMARY OF AIR-FOIL DATA, Ira H. Abbott and A. E. von Doenhoff. Concise compilation of subatomic aerodynamic characteristics of modern NASA wing sections, plus description of theory. 350pp. of tables. 693pp. 5⅜ x 8½.
60586-8 Pa. $8.50

DE RE METALLICA, Georgius Agricola. Translated by Herbert C. Hoover and Lou H. Hoover. The famous Hoover translation of greatest treatise on technological chemistry, engineering, geology, mining of early modern times (1556). All 289 original woodcuts. 638pp. 6¾ x 11.
60006-8 Clothbd. $17.95

THE ORIGIN OF CONTINENTS AND OCEANS, Alfred Wegener. One of the most influential, most controversial books in science, the classic statement for continental drift. Full 1966 translation of Wegener's final (1929) version. 64 illustrations. 246pp. 5⅜ x 8½. 61708-4 Pa. $4.50

THE PRINCIPLES OF PSYCHOLOGY, William James. Famous long course complete, unabridged. Stream of thought, time perception, memory, experimental methods; great work decades ahead of its time. Still valid, useful; read in many classes. 94 figures. Total of 1391pp. 5⅜ x 8½.
20381-6, 20382-4 Pa., Two-vol. set $13.00

THE CURVES OF LIFE, Theodore A. Cook. Examination of shells, leaves, horns, human body, art, etc., in *"the* classic reference on how the golden ratio applies to spirals and helices in nature . . . ."—Martin Gardner. 426 illustrations. Total of 512pp. 5⅜ x 8½.   23701-X Pa. $5.95

AN ILLUSTRATED FLORA OF THE NORTHERN UNITED STATES AND CANADA, Nathaniel L. Britton, Addison Brown. Encyclopedic work covers 4666 species, ferns on up. Everything. Full botanical information, illustration for each. This earlier edition is preferred by many to more recent revisions. 1913 edition. Over 4000 illustrations, total of 2087pp. 6⅛ x 9¼.   22642-5, 22643-3, 22644-1 Pa., Three-vol. set $25.50

MANUAL OF THE GRASSES OF THE UNITED STATES, A. S. Hitchcock, U.S. Dept. of Agriculture. The basic study of American grasses, both indigenous and escapes, cultivated and wild. Over 1400 species. Full descriptions, information. Over 1100 maps, illustrations. Total of 1051pp. 5⅜ x 8½.   22717-0, 22718-9 Pa., Two-vol. set $15.00

THE CACTACEAE,, Nathaniel L. Britton, John N. Rose. Exhaustive, definitive. Every cactus in the world. Full botanical descriptions. Thorough statement of nomenclatures, habitat, detailed finding keys. The one book needed by every cactus enthusiast. Over 1275 illustrations. Total of 1080pp. 8 x 10¼.   21191-6, 21192-4 Clothbd., Two-vol. set $35.00

AMERICAN MEDICINAL PLANTS, Charles F. Millspaugh. Full descriptions, 180 plants covered: history; physical description; methods of preparation with all chemical constituents extracted; all claimed curative or adverse effects. 180 full-page plates. Classification table. 804pp. 6½ x 9¼.   23034-1 Pa. $12.95

A MODERN HERBAL, Margaret Grieve. Much the fullest, most exact, most useful compilation of herbal material. Gigantic alphabetical encyclopedia, from aconite to zedoary, gives botanical information, medical properties, folklore, economic uses, and much else. Indispensable to serious reader. 161 illustrations. 888pp. 6½ x 9¼. (Available in U.S. only)   22798-7, 22799-5 Pa., Two-vol. set $13.00

THE HERBAL or GENERAL HISTORY OF PLANTS, John Gerard. The 1633 edition revised and enlarged by Thomas Johnson. Containing almost 2850 plant descriptions and 2705 superb illustrations, Gerard's *Herbal* is a monumental work, the book all modern English herbals are derived from, the one herbal every serious enthusiast should have in its entirety. Original editions are worth perhaps $750. 1678pp. 8½ x 12¼.   23147-X Clothbd. $50.00

MANUAL OF THE TREES OF NORTH AMERICA, Charles S. Sargent. The basic survey of every native tree and tree-like shrub, 717 species in all. Extremely full descriptions, information on habitat, growth, locales, economics, etc. Necessary to every serious tree lover. Over 100 finding keys. 783 illustrations. Total of 986pp. 5⅜ x 8½.   20277-1, 20278-X Pa., Two-vol. set $11.00

PRINCIPLES OF ORCHESTRATION, Nikolay Rimsky-Korsakov. Great classical orchestrator provides fundamentals of tonal resonance, progression of parts, voice and orchestra, tutti effects, much else in major document. 330pp. of musical excerpts. 489pp. 6½ x 9¼.   21266-1 Pa. $7.50

TRISTAN UND ISOLDE, Richard Wagner. Full orchestral score with complete instrumentation. Do not confuse with piano reduction. Commentary by Felix Mottl, great Wagnerian conductor and scholar. Study score. 655pp. 8⅛ x 11.   22915-7 Pa. $13.95

REQUIEM IN FULL SCORE, Giuseppe Verdi. Immensely popular with choral groups and music lovers. Republication of edition published by C. F. Peters, Leipzig, n. d. German frontmaker in English translation. Glossary. Text in Latin. Study score. 204pp. 9⅜ x 12¼.
23682-X Pa. $6.00

COMPLETE CHAMBER MUSIC FOR STRINGS, Felix Mendelssohn. All of Mendelssohn's chamber music: Octet, 2 Quintets, 6 Quartets, and Four Pieces for String Quartet. (Nothing with piano is included). Complete works edition (1874-7). Study score. 283 pp. 9⅜ x 12¼.
23679-X Pa. $7.50

POPULAR SONGS OF NINETEENTH-CENTURY AMERICA, edited by Richard Jackson. 64 most important songs: "Old Oaken Bucket," "Arkansas Traveler," "Yellow Rose of Texas," etc. Authentic original sheet music, full introduction and commentaries. 290pp. 9 x 12.   23270-0 Pa. $7.95

COLLECTED PIANO WORKS, Scott Joplin. Edited by Vera Brodsky Lawrence. Practically all of Joplin's piano works—rags, two-steps, marches, waltzes, etc., 51 works in all. Extensive introduction by Rudi Blesh. Total of 345pp. 9 x 12.   23106-2 Pa. $14.95

BASIC PRINCIPLES OF CLASSICAL BALLET, Agrippina Vaganova. Great Russian theoretician, teacher explains methods for teaching classical ballet; incorporates best from French, Italian, Russian schools. 118 illustrations. 175pp. 5⅜ x 8½.   22036-2 Pa. $2.50

CHINESE CHARACTERS, L. Wieger. Rich analysis of 2300 characters according to traditional systems into primitives. Historical-semantic analysis to phonetics (Classical Mandarin) and radicals. 820pp. 6⅛ x 9¼.
21321-8 Pa. $10.00

EGYPTIAN LANGUAGE: EASY LESSONS IN EGYPTIAN HIERO-GLYPHICS, E. A. Wallis Budge. Foremost Egyptologist offers Egyptian grammar, explanation of hieroglyphics, many reading texts, dictionary of symbols. 246pp. 5 x 7½. (Available in U.S. only)
21394-3 Clothbd. $7.50

AN ETYMOLOGICAL DICTIONARY OF MODERN ENGLISH, Ernest Weekley. Richest, fullest work, by foremost British lexicographer. Detailed word histories. Inexhaustible. Do not confuse this with Concise Etymological Dictionary, which is abridged. Total of 856pp. 6½ x 9¼.
21873-2, 21874-0 Pa., Two-vol. set $12.00

A MAYA GRAMMAR, Alfred M. Tozzer. Practical, useful English-language grammar by the Harvard anthropologist who was one of the three greatest American scholars in the area of Maya culture. Phonetics, grammatical processes, syntax, more. 301pp. 5⅜ x 8½.   23465-7 Pa. $4.00

THE JOURNAL OF HENRY D. THOREAU, edited by Bradford Torrey, F. H. Allen. Complete reprinting of 14 volumes, 1837-61, over two million words; the sourcebooks for Walden, etc. Definitive. All original sketches, plus 75 photographs. Introduction by Walter Harding. Total of 1804pp. 8½ x 12¼.   20312-3, 20313-1 Clothbd., Two-vol. set $70.00

CLASSIC GHOST STORIES, Charles Dickens and others. 18 wonderful stories you've wanted to reread: "The Monkey's Paw," "The House and the Brain," "The Upper Berth," "The Signalman," "Dracula's Guest," "The Tapestried Chamber," etc. Dickens, Scott, Mary Shelley, Stoker, etc. 330pp. 5⅜ x 8½.   20735-8 Pa. $4.50

SEVEN SCIENCE FICTION NOVELS, H. G. Wells. Full novels. First Men in the Moon, Island of Dr. Moreau, War of the Worlds, Food of the Gods, Invisible Man, Time Machine, In the Days of the Comet. A basic science-fiction library. 1015pp. 5⅜ x 8½. (Available in U.S. only)
                20264-X Clothbd. $8.95

ARMADALE, Wilkie Collins. Third great mystery novel by the author of The Woman in White and The Moonstone. Ingeniously plotted narrative shows an exceptional command of character, incident and mood. Original magazine version with 40 illustrations. 597pp. 5⅜ x 8½.
                23429-0 Pa. $6.00

MASTERS OF MYSTERY, H. Douglas Thomson. The first book in English (1931) devoted to history and aesthetics of detective story. Poe, Doyle, LeFanu, Dickens, many others, up to 1930. New introduction and notes by E. F. Bleiler. 288pp. 5⅜ x 8½. (Available in U.S. only)
                23606-4 Pa. $4.00

FLATLAND, E. A. Abbott. Science-fiction classic explores life of 2-D being in 3-D world. Read also as introduction to thought about hyperspace. Introduction by Banesh Hoffmann. 16 illustrations. 103pp. 5⅜ x 8½.
                20001-9 Pa. $2.00

THREE SUPERNATURAL NOVELS OF THE VICTORIAN PERIOD, edited, with an introduction, by E. F. Bleiler. Reprinted complete and unabridged, three great classics of the supernatural: The Haunted Hotel by Wilkie Collins, The Haunted House at Latchford by Mrs. J. H. Riddell, and The Lost Stradivarius by J. Meade Falkner. 325pp. 5⅜ x 8½.
                22571-2 Pa. $4.00

AYESHA: THE RETURN OF "SHE," H. Rider Haggard. Virtuoso sequel featuring the great mythic creation, Ayesha, in an adventure that is fully as good as the first book, She. Original magazine version, with 47 original illustrations by Maurice Greiffenhagen. 189pp. 6½ x 9¼.
                23649-8 Pa. $3.50

SECOND PIATIGORSKY CUP, edited by Isaac Kashdan. One of the greatest tournament books ever produced in the English language. All 90 games of the 1966 tournament, annotated by players, most annotated by both players. Features Petrosian, Spassky, Fischer, Larsen, six others. 228pp. 5⅜ x 8½. 23572-6 Pa. $3.50

ENCYCLOPEDIA OF CARD TRICKS, revised and edited by Jean Hugard. How to perform over 600 card tricks, devised by the world's greatest magicians: impromptus, spelling tricks, key cards, using special packs, much, much more. Additional chapter on card technique. 66 illustrations. 402pp. 5⅜ x 8½. (Available in U.S. only) 21252-1 Pa. $4.95

MAGIC: STAGE ILLUSIONS, SPECIAL EFFECTS AND TRICK PHO-TOGRAPHY, Albert A. Hopkins, Henry R. Evans. One of the great classics; fullest, most authorative explanation of vanishing lady, levitations, scores of other great stage effects. Also small magic, automata, stunts. 446 illustrations. 556pp. 5⅜ x 8½. 23344-8 Pa. $6.95

THE SECRETS OF HOUDINI, J. C. Cannell. Classic study of Houdini's incredible magic, exposing closely-kept professional secrets and revealing, in general terms, the whole art of stage magic. 67 illustrations. 279pp. 5⅜ x 8½. 22913-0 Pa. $4.00

HOFFMANN'S MODERN MAGIC, Professor Hoffmann. One of the best, and best-known, magicians' manuals of the past century. Hundreds of tricks from card tricks and simple sleight of hand to elaborate illusions involving construction of complicated machinery. 332 illustrations. 563pp. 5⅜ x 8½. 23623-4 Pa. $6.00

MADAME PRUNIER'S FISH COOKERY BOOK, Mme. S. B. Prunier. More than 1000 recipes from world famous Prunier's of Paris and London, specially adapted here for American kitchen. Grilled tournedos with anchovy butter, Lobster a la Bordelaise, Prunier's prized desserts, more. Glossary. 340pp. 5⅜ x 8½. (Available in U.S. only) 22679-4 Pa. $3.00

FRENCH COUNTRY COOKING FOR AMERICANS, Louis Diat. 500 easy-to-make, authentic provincial recipes compiled by former head chef at New York's Fitz-Carlton Hotel: onion soup, lamb stew, potato pie, more. 309pp. 5⅜ x 8½. 23665-X Pa. $3.95

SAUCES, FRENCH AND FAMOUS, Louis Diat. Complete book gives over 200 specific recipes: bechamel, Bordelaise, hollandaise, Cumberland, apricot, etc. Author was one of this century's finest chefs, originator of vichyssoise and many other dishes. Index. 156pp. 5⅜ x 8. 23663-3 Pa. $2.75

TOLL HOUSE TRIED AND TRUE RECIPES, Ruth Graves Wakefield. Authentic recipes from the famous Mass. restaurant: popovers, veal and ham loaf, Toll House baked beans, chocolate cake crumb pudding, much more. Many helpful hints. Nearly 700 recipes. Index. 376pp. 5⅜ x 8½. 23560-2 Pa. $4.50

HOLLYWOOD GLAMOUR PORTRAITS, edited by John Kobal. 145 photos capture the stars from 1926-49, the high point in portrait photography. Gable, Harlow, Bogart, Bacall, Hedy Lamarr, Marlene Dietrich, Robert Montgomery, Marlon Brando, Veronica Lake; 94 stars in all. Full background on photographers, technical aspects, much more. Total of 160pp. 8⅜ x 11¼. 23352-9 Pa. $6.00

THE NEW YORK STAGE: FAMOUS PRODUCTIONS IN PHOTO- GRAPHS, edited by Stanley Appelbaum. 148 photographs from Museum of City of New York show 142 plays, 1883-1939. *Peter Pan, The Front Page, Dead End, Our Town,* O'Neill, hundreds of actors and actresses, etc. Full indexes. 154pp. 9½ x 10. 23241-7 Pa. $6.00

DIALOGUES CONCERNING TWO NEW SCIENCES, Galileo Galilei. Encompassing 30 years of experiment and thought, these dialogues deal with geometric demonstrations of fracture of solid bodies, cohesion, leverage, speed of light and sound, pendulums, falling bodies, accelerated motion, etc. 300pp. 5⅜ x 8½. 60099-8 Pa. $4.00

THE GREAT OPERA STARS IN HISTORIC PHOTOGRAPHS, edited by James Camner. 343 portraits from the 1850s to the 1940s: Tamburini, Mario, Caliapin, Jeritza, Melchior, Melba, Patti, Pinza, Schipa, Caruso, Farrar, Steber, Gobbi, and many more—270 performers in all. Index. 199pp. 8⅜ x 11¼. 23575-0 Pa. $7.50

J. S. BACH, Albert Schweitzer. Great full-length study of Bach, life, background to music, music, by foremost modern scholar. Ernest Newman translation. 650 musical examples. Total of 928pp. 5⅜ x 8½. (Available in U.S. only) 21631-4, 21632-2 Pa., Two-vol. set $11.00

COMPLETE PIANO SONATAS, Ludwig van Beethoven. All sonatas in the fine Schenker edition, with fingering, analytical material. One of best modern editions. Total of 615pp. 9 x 12. (Available in U.S. only) 23134-8, 23135-6 Pa., Two-vol. set $15.50

KEYBOARD MUSIC, J. S. Bach. Bach-Gesellschaft edition. For harpsichord, piano, other keyboard instruments. English Suites, French Suites, Six Partitas, Goldberg Variations, Two-Part Inventions, Three-Part Sinfonias. 312pp. 8⅛ x 11. (Available in U.S. only) 22360-4 Pa. $6.95

FOUR SYMPHONIES IN FULL SCORE, Franz Schubert. Schubert's four most popular symphonies: No. 4 in C Minor ("Tragic"); No. 5 in B-flat Major; No. 8 in B Minor ("Unfinished"); No. 9 in C Major ("Great"). Breitkopf & Hartel edition. Study score. 261pp. 9⅜ x 12¼. 23681-1 Pa. $6.50

THE AUTHENTIC GILBERT & SULLIVAN SONGBOOK, W. S. Gilbert, A. S. Sullivan. Largest selection available; 92 songs, uncut, original keys, in piano rendering approved by Sullivan. Favorites and lesser-known fine numbers. Edited with plot synopses by James Spero. 3 illustrations. 399pp. 9 x 12. 23482-7 Pa. $9.95

AMERICAN BIRD ENGRAVINGS, Alexander Wilson et al. All 76 plates. from Wilson's *American Ornithology* (1808-14), most important ornithological work before Audubon, plus 27 plates from the supplement (1825-33) by Charles Bonaparte. Over 250 birds portrayed. 8 plates also reproduced in full color. 111pp. 9⅜ x 12½.   23195-X Pa. $6.00

CRUICKSHANK'S PHOTOGRAPHS OF BIRDS OF AMERICA, Allan D. Cruickshank. Great ornithologist, photographer presents 177 closeups, groupings, panoramas, flightings, etc., of about 150 different birds. Expanded *Wings in the Wilderness*. Introduction by Helen G. Cruickshank. 191pp. 8¼ x 11.   23497-5 Pa. $6.00

AMERICAN WILDLIFE AND PLANTS, A. C. Martin, et al. Describes food habits of more than 1000 species of mammals, birds, fish. Special treatment of important food plants. Over 300 illustrations. 500pp. 5⅜ x 8½.
20793-5 Pa. $4.95

THE PEOPLE CALLED SHAKERS, Edward D. Andrews. Lifetime of research, definitive study of Shakers: origins, beliefs, practices, dances, social organization, furniture and crafts, impact on 19th-century USA, present heritage. Indispensable to student of American history, collector. 33 illustrations. 351pp. 5⅜ x 8½.   21081-2 Pa. $4.50

OLD NEW YORK IN EARLY PHOTOGRAPHS, Mary Black. New York City as it was in 1853-1901, through 196 wonderful photographs from N.-Y. Historical Society. Great Blizzard, Lincoln's funeral procession, great buildings. 228pp. 9 x 12.   22907-6 Pa. $8.95

MR. LINCOLN'S CAMERA MAN: MATHEW BRADY, Roy Meredith. Over 300 Brady photos reproduced directly from original negatives, photos. Jackson, Webster, Grant, Lee, Carnegie, Barnum; Lincoln; Battle Smoke, Death of Rebel Sniper, Atlanta Just After Capture. Lively commentary. 368pp. 8⅜ x 11¼.   23021-X Pa. $8.95

TRAVELS OF WILLIAM BARTRAM, William Bartram. From 1773-8, Bartram explored Northern Florida, Georgia, Carolinas, and reported on wild life, plants, Indians, early settlers. Basic account for period, entertaining reading. Edited by Mark Van Doren. 13 illustrations. 141pp. 5⅜ x 8½.   20013-2 Pa. $5.00

THE GENTLEMAN AND CABINET MAKER'S DIRECTOR, Thomas Chippendale. Full reprint, 1762 style book, most influential of all time; chairs, tables, sofas, mirrors, cabinets, etc. 200 plates, plus 24 photographs of surviving pieces. 249pp. 9⅞ x 12¾.   21601-2 Pa. $7.95

AMERICAN CARRIAGES, SLEIGHS, SULKIES AND CARTS, edited by Don H. Berkebile. 168 Victorian illustrations from catalogues, trade journals, fully captioned. Useful for artists. Author is Assoc. Curator, Div. of Transportation of Smithsonian Institution. 168pp. 8½ x 9½.
23328-6 Pa. $5.00

THE PHILOSOPHY OF HISTORY, Georg W. Hegel. Great classic of Western thought develops concept that history is not chance but a rational process, the evolution of freedom. 457pp. 5⅜ x 8½. 20112-0 Pa. $4.50

LANGUAGE, TRUTH AND LOGIC, Alfred J. Ayer. Famous, clear introduction to Vienna, Cambridge schools of Logical Positivism. Role of philosophy, elimination of metaphysics, nature of analysis, etc. 160pp. 5⅜ x 8½. (Available in U.S. only) 20010-8 Pa. $2.00

A PREFACE TO LOGIC, Morris R. Cohen. Great City College teacher in renowned, easily followed exposition of formal logic, probability, values, logic and world order and similar topics; no previous background needed. 209pp. 5⅜ x 8½. 23517-3 Pa. $3.50

REASON AND NATURE, Morris R. Cohen. Brilliant analysis of reason and its multitudinous ramifications by charismatic teacher. Interdisciplinary, synthesizing work widely praised when it first appeared in 1931. Second (1953) edition. Indexes. 496pp. 5⅜ x 8½. 23633-1 Pa. $6.50

AN ESSAY CONCERNING HUMAN UNDERSTANDING, John Locke. The only complete edition of enormously important classic, with authoritative editorial material by A. C. Fraser. Total of 1176pp. 5⅜ x 8½.
20530-4, 20531-2 Pa., Two-vol. set $16.00

HANDBOOK OF MATHEMATICAL FUNCTIONS WITH FORMULAS, GRAPHS, AND MATHEMATICAL TABLES, edited by Milton Abramowitz and Irene A. Stegun. Vast compendium: 29 sets of tables, some to as high as 20 places. 1,046pp. 8 x 10½. 61272-4 Pa. $14.95

MATHEMATICS FOR THE PHYSICAL SCIENCES, Herbert S. Wilf. Highly acclaimed work offers clear presentations of vector spaces and matrices, orthogonal functions, roots of polynomial equations, conformal mapping, calculus of variations, etc. Knowledge of theory of functions of real and complex variables is assumed. Exercises and solutions. Index. 284pp. 5⅝ x 8¼. 63635-6 Pa. $5.00

THE PRINCIPLE OF RELATIVITY, Albert Einstein et al. Eleven most important original papers on special and general theories. Seven by Einstein, two by Lorentz, one each by Minkowski and Weyl. All translated, unabridged. 216pp. 5⅜ x 8½. 60081-5 Pa. $3.50

THERMODYNAMICS, Enrico Fermi. A classic of modern science. Clear, organized treatment of systems, first and second laws, entropy, thermodynamic potentials, gaseous reactions, dilute solutions, entropy constant. No math beyond calculus required. Problems. 160pp. 5⅜ x 8½.
60361-X Pa. $3.00

ELEMENTARY MECHANICS OF FLUIDS, Hunter Rouse. Classic undergraduate text widely considered to be far better than many later books. Ranges from fluid velocity and acceleration to role of compressibility in fluid motion. Numerous examples, questions, problems. 224 illustrations. 376pp. 5⅝ x 8¼. 63699-2 Pa. $5.00

THE ANATOMY OF THE HORSE, George Stubbs. Often considered the great masterpiece of animal anatomy. Full reproduction of 1766 edition, plus prospectus; original text and modernized text. 36 plates. Introduction by Eleanor Garvey. 121pp. 11 x 14¾. 23402-9 Pa. $6.00

BRIDGMAN'S LIFE DRAWING, George B. Bridgman. More than 500 illustrative drawings and text teach you to abstract the body into its major masses, use light and shade, proportion; as well as specific areas of anatomy, of which Bridgman is master. 192pp. 6½ x 9¼. (Available in U.S. only) 22710-3 Pa. $3.50

ART NOUVEAU DESIGNS IN COLOR, Alphonse Mucha, Maurice Verneuil, Georges Auriol. Full-color reproduction of *Combinaisons ornementales* (c. 1900) by Art Nouveau masters. Floral, animal, geometric, interlacings, swashes—borders, frames, spots—all incredibly beautiful. 60 plates, hundreds of designs. 9⅜ x 8-1/16. 22885-1 Pa. $4.00

FULL-COLOR FLORAL DESIGNS IN THE ART NOUVEAU STYLE, E. A. Seguy. 166 motifs, on 40 plates, from *Les fleurs et leurs applications decoratives* (1902): borders, circular designs, repeats, allovers, "spots." All in authentic Art Nouveau colors. 48pp. 9⅜ x 12¼. 23439-8 Pa. $5.00

A DIDEROT PICTORIAL ENCYCLOPEDIA OF TRADES AND IN-DUSTRY, edited by Charles C. Gillispie. 485 most interesting plates from the great French Encyclopedia of the 18th century show hundreds of working figures, artifacts, process, land and cityscapes; glassmaking, paper-making, metal extraction, construction, weaving, making furniture, clothing, wigs, dozens of other activities. Plates fully explained. 920pp. 9 x 12. 22284-5, 22285-3 Clothbd., Two-vol. set $40.00

HANDBOOK OF EARLY ADVERTISING ART, Clarence P. Hornung. Largest collection of copyright-free early and antique advertising art ever compiled. Over 6,000 illustrations, from Franklin's time to the 1890's for special effects, novelty. Valuable source, almost inexhaustible.
Pictorial Volume. Agriculture, the zodiac, animals, autos, birds, Christmas, fire engines, flowers, trees, musical instruments, ships, games and sports, much more. Arranged by subject matter and use. 237 plates. 288pp. 9 x 12. 20122-8 Clothbd. $14.50

Typographical Volume. Roman and Gothic faces ranging from 10 point to 300 point, "Barnum," German and Old English faces, script, logotypes, scrolls and flourishes, 1115 ornamental initials, 67 complete alphabets, more. 310 plates. 320pp. 9 x 12. 20123-6 Clothbd. $15.00

CALLIGRAPHY (CALLIGRAPHIA LATINA), J. G. Schwandner. High point of 18th-century ornamental calligraphy. Very ornate initials, scrolls, borders, cherubs, birds, lettered examples. 172pp. 9 x 13. 20475-8 Pa. $7.00

THE COMPLETE BOOK OF DOLL MAKING AND COLLECTING, Catherine Christopher. Instructions, patterns for dozens of dolls, from rag doll on up to elaborate, historically accurate figures. Mould faces, sew clothing, make doll houses, etc. Also collecting information. Many illustrations. 288pp. 6 x 9. 22066-4 Pa. $4.50

THE DAGUERREOTYPE IN AMERICA, Beaumont Newhall. Wonderful portraits, 1850's townscapes, landscapes; full text plus 104 photographs. The basic book. Enlarged 1976 edition. 272pp. 8¼ x 11¼. 23322-7 Pa. $7.95

CRAFTSMAN HOMES, Gustav Stickley. 296 architectural drawings, floor plans, and photographs illustrate 40 different kinds of "Mission-style" homes from *The Craftsman* (1901-16), voice of American style of simplicity and organic harmony. Thorough coverage of Craftsman idea in text and picture, now collector's item. 224pp. 8⅛ x 11. 23791-5 Pa. $6.00

PEWTER-WORKING: INSTRUCTIONS AND PROJECTS, Burl N. Osborn. & Gordon O. Wilber. Introduction to pewter-working for amateur craftsman. History and characteristics of pewter; tools, materials, step-by-step instructions. Photos, line drawings, diagrams. Total of 160pp. 7⅞ x 10¾. 23786-9 Pa. $3.50

THE GREAT CHICAGO FIRE, edited by David Lowe. 10 dramatic, eyewitness accounts of the 1871 disaster, including one of the aftermath and rebuilding, plus 70 contemporary photographs and illustrations of the ruins—courthouse, Palmer House, Great Central Depot, etc. Introduction by David Lowe. 87pp. 8¼ x 11. 23771-0 Pa. $4.00

SILHOUETTES: A PICTORIAL ARCHIVE OF VARIED ILLUSTRATIONS, edited by Carol Belanger Grafton. Over 600 silhouettes from the 18th to 20th centuries include profiles and full figures of men and women, children, birds and animals, groups and scenes, nature, ships, an alphabet. Dozens of uses for commercial artists and craftspeople. 144pp. 8⅜ x 11¼. 23781-8 Pa. $4.50

ANIMALS: 1,419 COPYRIGHT-FREE ILLUSTRATIONS OF MAMMALS, BIRDS, FISH, INSECTS, ETC., edited by Jim Harter. Clear wood engravings present, in extremely lifelike poses, over 1,000 species of animals. One of the most extensive copyright-free pictorial sourcebooks of its kind. Captions. Index. 284pp. 9 x 12. 23766-4 Pa. $8.95

INDIAN DESIGNS FROM ANCIENT ECUADOR, Frederick W. Shaffer. 282 original designs by pre-Columbian Indians of Ecuador (500-1500 A.D.). Designs include people, mammals, birds, reptiles, fish, plants, heads, geometric designs. Use as is or alter for advertising, textiles, leathercraft, etc. Introduction. 95pp. 8¾ x 11¼. 23764-8 Pa. $3.50

SZIGETI ON THE VIOLIN, Joseph Szigeti. Genial, loosely structured tour by premier violinist, featuring a pleasant mixture of reminiscenes, insights into great music and musicians, innumerable tips for practicing violinists. 385 musical passages. 256pp. 5⅝ x 8¼. 23763-X Pa. $4.00

THE COMPLETE WOODCUTS OF ALBRECHT DURER, edited by Dr. W. Kurth. 346 in all: "Old Testament," "St. Jerome," "Passion," "Life of Virgin," Apocalypse," many others. Introduction by Campbell Dodgson. 285pp. 8½ x 12¼.   21097-9 Pa. $7.50

DRAWINGS OF ALBRECHT DURER, edited by Heinrich Wolfflin. 81 plates show development from youth to full style. Many favorites; many new. Introduction by Alfred Werner. 96pp. 8⅛ x 11.   22352-3 Pa. $5.00

THE HUMAN FIGURE, Albrecht Dürer. Experiments in various techniques—stereometric, progressive proportional, and others. Also life studies that rank among finest ever done. Complete reprinting of *Dresden Sketchbook*. 170 plates. 355pp. 8⅜ x 11¼.   21042-1 Pa. $7.95

OF THE JUST SHAPING OF LETTERS, Albrecht Dürer. Renaissance artist explains design of Roman majuscules by geometry, also Gothic lower and capitals. Grolier Club edition. 43pp. 7⅞ x 10¾   21306-4 Pa. $3.00

TEN BOOKS ON ARCHITECTURE, Vitruvius. The most important book ever written on architecture. Early Roman aesthetics, technology, classical orders, site selection, all other aspects. Stands behind everything since. Morgan translation. 331pp. 5⅜ x 8½.   20645-9 Pa. $4.50

THE FOUR BOOKS OF ARCHITECTURE, Andrea Palladio. 16th-century classic responsible for Palladian movement and style. Covers classical architectural remains, Renaissance revivals, classical orders, etc. 1738 Ware English edition. Introduction by A. Placzek. 216 plates. 110pp. of text. 9½ x 12¾.   21308-0 Pa. $10.00

HORIZONS, Norman Bel Geddes. Great industrialist stage designer, "father of streamlining," on application of aesthetics to transportation, amusement, architecture, etc. 1932 prophetic account; function, theory, specific projects. 222 illustrations. 312pp. 7⅞ x 10¾.   23514-9 Pa. $6.95

FRANK LLOYD WRIGHT'S FALLINGWATER, Donald Hoffmann. Full, illustrated story of conception and building of Wright's masterwork at Bear Run, Pa. 100 photographs of site, construction, and details of completed structure. 112pp. 9¼ x 10.   23671-4 Pa. $5.50

THE ELEMENTS OF DRAWING, John Ruskin. Timeless classic by great Viltorian; starts with basic ideas, works through more difficult. Many practical exercises. 48 illustrations. Introduction by Lawrence Campbell. 228pp. 5⅜ x 8½.   22730-8 Pa. $3.75

GIST OF ART, John Sloan. Greatest modern American teacher, Art Students League, offers innumerable hints, instructions, guided comments to help you in painting. Not a formal course. 46 illustrations. Introduction by Helen Sloan. 200pp. 5⅜ x 8½.   23435-5 Pa. $4.00

THE DEPRESSION YEARS AS PHOTOGRAPHED BY ARTHUR ROTH-STEIN, Arthur Rothstein. First collection devoted entirely to the work of outstanding 1930s photographer: famous dust storm photo, ragged children, unemployed, etc. 120 photographs. Captions. 119pp. 9¼ x 10¾.
23590-4 Pa. $5.00

CAMERA WORK: A PICTORIAL GUIDE, Alfred Stieglitz. All 559 illustrations and plates from the most important periodical in the history of art photography, Camera Work (1903-17). Presented four to a page, reduced in size but still clear, in strict chronological order, with complete captions. Three indexes. Glossary. Bibliography. 176pp. 8⅜ x 11¼.
23591-2 Pa. $6.95

ALVIN LANGDON COBURN, PHOTOGRAPHER, Alvin L. Coburn. Revealing autobiography by one of greatest photographers of 20th century gives insider's version of Photo-Secession, plus comments on his own work. 77 photographs by Coburn. Edited by Helmut and Alison Gernsheim. 160pp. 8⅛ x 11.
23685-4 Pa. $6.00

NEW YORK IN THE FORTIES, Andreas Feininger. 162 brilliant photographs by the well-known photographer, formerly with Life magazine, show commuters, shoppers, Times Square at night, Harlem nightclub, Lower East Side, etc. Introduction and full captions by John von Hartz. 181pp. 9¼ x 10¾.
23585-8 Pa. $6.95

GREAT NEWS PHOTOS AND THE STORIES BEHIND THEM, John Faber. Dramatic volume of 140 great news photos, 1855 through 1976, and revealing stories behind them, with both historical and technical information. Hindenburg disaster, shooting of Oswald, nomination of Jimmy Carter, etc. 160pp. 8¼ x 11.
23667-6 Pa. $5.00

THE ART OF THE CINEMATOGRAPHER, Leonard Maltin. Survey of American cinematography history and anecdotal interviews with 5 masters—Arthur Miller, Hal Mohr, Hal Rosson, Lucien Ballard, and Conrad Hall. Very large selection of behind-the-scenes production photos. 105 photographs. Filmographies. Index. Originally Behind the Camera. 144pp. 8¼ x 11.
23686-2 Pa. $5.00

DESIGNS FOR THE THREE-CORNERED HAT (LE TRICORNE), Pablo Picasso. 32 fabulously rare drawings—including 31 color illustrations of costumes and accessories—for 1919 production of famous ballet. Edited by Parmenia Migel, who has written new introduction. 48pp. 9⅜ x 12¼. (Available in U.S. only)
23709-5 Pa. $5.00

NOTES OF A FILM DIRECTOR, Sergei Eisenstein. Greatest Russian filmmaker explains montage, making of Alexander Nevsky, aesthetics; comments on self, associates, great rivals (Chaplin), similar material. 78 illustrations. 240pp. 5⅜ x 8½.
22392-2 Pa. $4.50

THE AMERICAN SENATOR, Anthony Trollope. Little known, long unavailable Trollope novel on a grand scale. Here are humorous comment on American vs. English culture, and stunning portrayal of a heroine/villainess. Superb evocation of Victorian village life. 561pp. 5⅜ x 8½.
23801-6 Pa. $6.00

WAS IT MURDER? James Hilton. The author of *Lost Horizon* and *Goodbye, Mr. Chips* wrote one detective novel (under a pen-name) which was quickly forgotten and virtually lost, even at the height of Hilton's fame. This edition brings it back—a finely crafted public school puzzle resplendent with Hilton's stylish atmosphere. A thoroughly English thriller by the creator of Shangri-la. 252pp. 5⅜ x 8. (Available in U.S. only)
23774-5 Pa. $3.00

CENTRAL PARK: A PHOTOGRAPHIC GUIDE, Victor Laredo and Henry Hope Reed. 121 superb photographs show dramatic views of Central Park: Bethesda Fountain, Cleopatra's Needle, Sheep Meadow, the Blockhouse, plus people engaged in many park activities: ice skating, bike riding, etc. Captions by former Curator of Central Park, Henry Hope Reed, provide historical view, changes, etc. Also photos of N.Y. landmarks on park's periphery. 96pp. 8½ x 11.
23750-8 Pa. $4.50

NANTUCKET IN THE NINETEENTH CENTURY, Clay Lancaster. 180 rare photographs, stereographs, maps, drawings and floor plans recreate unique American island society. Authentic scenes of shipwreck, lighthouses, streets, homes are arranged in geographic sequence to provide walking-tour guide to old Nantucket existing today. Introduction, captions. 160pp. 8⅞ x 11¾.
23747-8 Pa. $6.95

STONE AND MAN: A PHOTOGRAPHIC EXPLORATION, Andreas Feininger. 106 photographs by *Life* photographer Feininger portray man's deep passion for stone through the ages. Stonehenge-like megaliths, fortified towns, sculpted marble and crumbling tenements show textures, beauties, fascination. 128pp. 9¼ x 10¾.
23756-7 Pa. $5.95

CIRCLES, A MATHEMATICAL VIEW, D. Pedoe. Fundamental aspects of college geometry, non-Euclidean geometry, and other branches of mathematics: representing circle by point. Poincare model, isoperimetric property, etc. Stimulating recreational reading. 66 figures. 96pp. 5⅝ x 8¼.
63698-4 Pa. $2.75

THE DISCOVERY OF NEPTUNE, Morton Grosser. Dramatic scientific history of the investigations leading up to the actual discovery of the eighth planet of our solar system. Lucid, well-researched book by well-known historian of science. 172pp. 5⅜ x 8½.
23726-5 Pa. $3.50

THE DEVIL'S DICTIONARY. Ambrose Bierce. Barbed, bitter, brilliant witticisms in the form of a dictionary. Best, most ferocious satire America has produced. 145pp. 5⅜ x 8½.
20487-1 Pa. $2.25

ART FORMS IN NATURE, Ernst Haeckel. Multitude of strangely beautiful natural forms: Radiolaria, Foraminifera, jellyfishes, fungi, turtles, bats, etc. All 100 plates of the 19th-century evolutionist's *Kunstformen der Natur* (1904). 100pp. 9⅜ x 12¼. 22987-4 Pa. $5.00

CHILDREN: A PICTORIAL ARCHIVE FROM NINETEENTH-CENTURY SOURCES, edited by Carol Belanger Grafton. 242 rare, copyright-free wood engravings for artists and designers. Widest such selection available. All illustrations in line. 119pp. 8⅜ x 11¼.
23694-3 Pa. $4.00

WOMEN: A PICTORIAL ARCHIVE FROM NINETEENTH-CENTURY SOURCES, edited by Jim Harter. 391 copyright-free wood engravings for artists and designers selected from rare periodicals. Most extensive such collection available. All illustrations in line. 128pp. 9 x 12.
23703-6 Pa. $4.50

ARABIC ART IN COLOR, Prisse d'Avennes. From the greatest ornamentalists of all time—50 plates in color, rarely seen outside the Near East, rich in suggestion and stimulus. Includes 4 plates on covers. 46pp. 9⅜ x 12¼. 23658-7 Pa. $6.00

AUTHENTIC ALGERIAN CARPET DESIGNS AND MOTIFS, edited by June Beveridge. Algerian carpets are world famous. Dozens of geometrical motifs are charted on grids, color-coded, for weavers, needleworkers, craftsmen, designers. 53 illustrations plus 4 in color. 48pp. 8¼ x 11. (Available in U.S. only) 23650-1 Pa. $1.75

DICTIONARY OF AMERICAN PORTRAITS, edited by Hayward and Blanche Cirker. 4000 important Americans, earliest times to 1905, mostly in clear line. Politicians, writers, soldiers, scientists, inventors, industrialists, Indians, Blacks, women, outlaws, etc. Identificatory information. 756pp. 9¼ x 12¾. 21823-6 Clothbd. $40.00

HOW THE OTHER HALF LIVES, Jacob A. Riis. Journalistic record of filth, degradation, upward drive in New York immigrant slums, shops, around 1900. New edition includes 100 original Riis photos, monuments of early photography. 233pp. 10 x 7⅞. 22012-5 Pa. $7.00

NEW YORK IN THE THIRTIES, Berenice Abbott. Noted photographer's fascinating study of city shows new buildings that have become famous and old sights that have disappeared forever. Insightful commentary. 97 photographs. 97pp. 11⅜ x 10. 22967-X Pa. $5.00

MEN AT WORK, Lewis W. Hine. Famous photographic studies of construction workers, railroad men, factory workers and coal miners. New supplement of 18 photos on Empire State building construction. New introduction by Jonathan L. Doherty. Total of 69 photos. 63pp. 8 x 10¾. 23475-4 Pa. $3.00

TONE POEMS, SERIES II: TILL EULENSPIEGELS LUSTIGE STREICHE, ALSO SPRACH ZARATHUSTRA, AND EIN HELDEN-LEBEN, Richard Strauss. Three important orchestral works, including very popular *Till Eulenspiegel's Marry Pranks*, reproduced in full score from original editions. Study score. 315pp. 9⅜ x 12¼. (Available in U.S. only)
23755-9 Pa. $8.95

TONE POEMS, SERIES I: DON JUAN, TOD UND VERKLARUNG AND DON QUIXOTE, Richard Strauss. Three of the most often performed and recorded works in entire orchestral repertoire, reproduced in full score from original editions. Study score. 286pp. 9⅜ x 12¼. (Available in U.S. only)
23754-0 Pa. $7.50

11 LATE STRING QUARTETS, Franz Joseph Haydn. The form which Haydn defined and "brought to perfection." (*Grove's*). 11 string quartets in complete score, his last and his best. The first in a projected series of the complete Haydn string quartets. Reliable modern Eulenberg edition, otherwise difficult to obtain. 320pp. 8⅜ x 11¼. (Available in U.S. only)
23753-2 Pa. $7.50

FOURTH, FIFTH AND SIXTH SYMPHONIES IN FULL SCORE, Peter Ilyitch Tchaikovsky. Complete orchestral scores of Symphony No. 4 in F Minor, Op. 36; Symphony No. 5 in E Minor, Op. 64; Symphony No. 6 in B Minor, "Pathetique," Op. 74. Bretikopf & Hartel eds. Study score. 480pp. 9⅜ x 12¼.
23861-X Pa. $10.95

THE MARRIAGE OF FIGARO: COMPLETE SCORE, Wolfgang A. Mozart. Finest comic opera ever written. Full score, not to be confused with piano renderings. Peters edition. Study score. 448pp. 9⅜ x 12¼. (Available in U.S. only)
23751-6 Pa. $11.95

"IMAGE" ON THE ART AND EVOLUTION OF THE FILM, edited by Marshall Deutelbaum. Pioneering book brings together for first time 38 groundbreaking articles on early silent films from *Image* and 263 illustrations newly shot from rare prints in the collection of the International Museum of Photography. A landmark work. Index. 256pp. 8¼ x 11.
23777-X Pa. $8.95

AROUND-THE-WORLD COOKY BOOK, Lois Lintner Sumption and Marguerite Lintner Ashbrook. 373 cooky and frosting recipes from 28 countries (America, Austria, China, Russia, Italy, etc.) include Viennese kisses, rice wafers, London strips, lady fingers, hony, sugar spice, maple cookies, etc. Clear instructions. All tested. 38 drawings. 182pp. 5⅜ x 8.
23802-4 Pa. $2.50

THE ART NOUVEAU STYLE, edited by Roberta Waddell. 579 rare photographs, not available elsewhere, of works in jewelry, metalwork, glass, ceramics, textiles, architecture and furniture by 175 artists—Mucha, Seguy, Lalique, Tiffany, Gaudin, Hohlwein, Saarinen, and many others. 288pp. 8⅜ x 11¼.
23515-7 Pa. $6.95

YUCATAN BEFORE AND AFTER THE CONQUEST, Diego de Landa. First English translation of basic book in Maya studies, the only significant account of Yucatan written in the early post-Conquest era. Translated by distinguished Maya scholar William Gates. Appendices, introduction, 4 maps and over 120 illustrations added by translator. 162pp. 5⅜ x 8½.
23622-6 Pa. $3.00

THE MALAY ARCHIPELAGO, Alfred R. Wallace. Spirited travel account by one of founders of modern biology. Touches on zoology, botany, ethnography, geography, and geology. 62 illustrations, maps. 515pp. 5⅜ x 8½.
20187-2 Pa. $6.95

THE DISCOVERY OF THE TOMB OF TUTANKHAMEN, Howard Carter, A. C. Mace. Accompany Carter in the thrill of discovery, as ruined passage suddenly reveals unique, untouched, fabulously rich tomb. Fascinating account, with 106 illustrations. New introduction by J. M. White. Total of 382pp. 5⅜ x 8½. (Available in U.S. only)   23500-9 Pa. $4.00

THE WORLD'S GREATEST SPEECHES, edited by Lewis Copeland and Lawrence W. Lamm. Vast collection of 278 speeches from Greeks up to present. Powerful and effective models; unique look at history. Revised to 1970. Indices. 842pp. 5⅜ x 8½.   20468-5 Pa. $8.95

THE 100 GREATEST ADVERTISEMENTS, Julian Watkins. The priceless ingredient; His master's voice; 99 44/100% pure; over 100 others. How they were written, their impact, etc. Remarkable record. 130 illustrations. 233pp. 7⅞ x 10 3/5.   20540-1 Pa. $5.95

CRUICKSHANK PRINTS FOR HAND COLORING, George Cruickshank. 18 illustrations, one side of a page, on fine-quality paper suitable for watercolors. Caricatures of people in society (c. 1820) full of trenchant wit. Very large format. 32pp. 11 x 16.   23684-6 Pa. $5.00

THIRTY-TWO COLOR POSTCARDS OF TWENTIETH-CENTURY AMERICAN ART, Whitney Museum of American Art. Reproduced in full color in postcard form are 31 art works and one shot of the museum. Calder, Hopper, Rauschenberg, others. Detachable. 16pp. 8¼ x 11.
23629-3 Pa. $3.00

MUSIC OF THE SPHERES: THE MATERIAL UNIVERSE FROM ATOM TO QUASAR SIMPLY EXPLAINED, Guy Murchie. Planets, stars, geology, atoms, radiation, relativity, quantum theory, light, antimatter, similar topics. 319 figures. 664pp. 5⅜ x 8½.
21809-0, 21810-4 Pa., Two-vol. set $11.00

EINSTEIN'S THEORY OF RELATIVITY, Max Born. Finest semi-technical account; covers Einstein, Lorentz, Minkowski, and others, with much detail, much explanation of ideas and math not readily available elsewhere on this level. For student, non-specialist. 376pp. 5⅜ x 8½.
60769-0 Pa. $4.50

UNCLE SILAS, J. Sheridan LeFanu. Victorian Gothic mystery novel, considered by many best of period, even better than Collins or Dickens. Wonderful psychological terror. Introduction by Frederick Shroyer. 436pp. 5⅜ x 8½. 21715-9 Pa. $6.00

JURGEN, James Branch Cabell. The great erotic fantasy of the 1920's that delighted thousands, shocked thousands more. Full final text, Lane edition with 13 plates by Frank Pape. 346pp. 5⅜ x 8½. 23507-6 Pa. $4.50

THE CLAVERINGS, Anthony Trollope. Major novel, chronicling aspects of British Victorian society, personalities. Reprint of Cornhill serialization, 16 plates by M. Edwards; first reprint of full text. Introduction by Norman Donaldson. 412pp. 5⅜ x 8½. 23464-9 Pa. $5.00

KEPT IN THE DARK, Anthony Trollope. Unusual short novel about Victorian morality and abnormal psychology by the great English author. Probably the first American publication. Frontispiece by Sir John Millais. 92pp. 6½ x 9¼. 23609-9 Pa. $2.50

RALPH THE HEIR, Anthony Trollope. Forgotten tale of illegitimacy, inheritance. Master novel of Trollope's later years. Victorian country estates, clubs, Parliament, fox hunting, world of fully realized characters. Reprint of 1871 edition. 12 illustrations by F. A. Faser. 434pp. of text. 5⅜ x 8½. 23642-0 Pa. $5.00

YEKL and THE IMPORTED BRIDEGROOM AND OTHER STORIES OF THE NEW YORK GHETTO, Abraham Cahan. Film *Hester Street* based on *Yekl* (1896). Novel, other stories among first about Jewish immigrants of N.Y.'s East Side. Highly praised by W. D. Howells—Cahan "a new star of realism." New introduction by Bernard G. Richards. 240pp. 5⅜ x 8½. 22427-9 Pa. $3.50

THE HIGH PLACE, James Branch Cabell. Great fantasy writer's enchanting comedy of disenchantment set in 18th-century France. Considered by some critics to be even better than his famous *Jurgen*. 10 illustrations and numerous vignettes by noted fantasy artist Frank C. Pape. 320pp. 5⅜ x 8½. 23670-6 Pa. $4.00

ALICE'S ADVENTURES UNDER GROUND, Lewis Carroll. Facsimile of ms. Carroll gave Alice Liddell in 1864. Different in many ways from final Alice. Handlettered, illustrated by Carroll. Introduction by Martin Gardner. 128pp. 5⅜ x 8½. 21482-6 Pa. $2.50

FAVORITE ANDREW LANG FAIRY TALE BOOKS IN MANY COLORS, Andrew Lang. The four Lang favorites in a boxed set—the complete *Red, Green, Yellow* and *Blue* Fairy Books. 164 stories; 439 illustrations by Lancelot Speed, Henry Ford and G. P. Jacomb Hood. Total of about 1500pp. 5⅜ x 8½. 23407-X Boxed set, Pa. $15.95

AMERICAN ANTIQUE FURNITURE, Edgar G. Miller, Jr. The basic coverage of all American furniture before 1840: chapters per item chronologically cover all types of furniture, with more than 2100 photos. Total of 1106pp. 7⅞ x 10¾. 21599-7, 21600-4 Pa., Two-vol. set $17.90

ILLUSTRATED GUIDE TO SHAKER FURNITURE, Robert Meader. Director, Shaker Museum, Old Chatham, presents up-to-date coverage of all furniture and appurtenances, with much on local styles not available elsewhere. 235 photos. 146pp. 9 x 12. 22819-3 Pa. $6.00

ORIENTAL RUGS, ANTIQUE AND MODERN, Walter A. Hawley. Persia, Turkey, Caucasus, Central Asia, China, other traditions. Best general survey of all aspects: styles and periods, manufacture, uses, symbols and their interpretation, and identification. 96 illustrations, 11 in color. 320pp. 6⅛ x 9¼. 22366-3 Pa. $6.95

CHINESE POTTERY AND PORCELAIN, R. L. Hobson. Detailed descriptions and analyses by former Keeper of the Department of Oriental Antiquities and Ethnography at the British Museum. Covers hundreds of pieces from primitive times to 1915. Still the standard text for most periods. 136 plates, 40 in full color. Total of 750pp. 5⅜ x 8½. 23253-0 Pa. $10.00

THE WARES OF THE MING DYNASTY, R. L. Hobson. Foremost scholar examines and illustrates many varieties of Ming (1368-1644). Famous blue and white, polychrome, lesser-known styles and shapes. 117 illustrations, 9 full color, of outstanding pieces. Total of 263pp. 6⅛ x 9¼. (Available in U.S. only) 23652-8 Pa. $6.00

Prices subject to change without notice.

Available at your book dealer or write for free catalogue to Dept. GI, Dover Publications, Inc., 31 East Second Street, Mineola, N.Y. 11501. Dover publishes more than 175 books each year on science, elementary and advanced mathematics, biology, music, art, literary history, social sciences and other areas.